ROUTLEDGE LIBRARY EDITIONS: WW2

Volume 43

WESTERN GERMANY

WESTERN GERMANY
From Defeat to Rearmament

ALFRED GROSSER

Routledge
Taylor & Francis Group
LONDON AND NEW YORK

First published in 1955 by George Allen & Unwin Ltd.

This edition first published in 2022
by Routledge
2 Park Square, Milton Park, Abingdon, Oxon OX14 4RN

and by Routledge
605 Third Avenue, New York, NY 10158

Routledge is an imprint of the Taylor & Francis Group, an informa business

© 1955 George Allen & Unwin Ltd.

All rights reserved. No part of this book may be reprinted or reproduced or utilised in any form or by any electronic, mechanical, or other means, now known or hereafter invented, including photocopying and recording, or in any information storage or retrieval system, without permission in writing from the publishers.

Trademark notice: Product or corporate names may be trademarks or registered trademarks, and are used only for identification and explanation without intent to infringe.

British Library Cataloguing in Publication Data
A catalogue record for this book is available from the British Library

ISBN: 978-1-03-201217-9 (Set)
ISBN: 978-1-00-319367-8 (Set) (ebk)
ISBN: 978-1-03-207983-7 (Volume 43) (hbk)
ISBN: 978-1-03-207990-5 (Volume 43) (pbk)
ISBN: 978-1-00-321237-9 (Volume 43) (ebk)

DOI: 10.4324/9781003212379

Publisher's Note
The publisher has gone to great lengths to ensure the quality of this reprint but points out that some imperfections in the original copies may be apparent.

Disclaimer
The publisher has made every effort to trace copyright holders and would welcome correspondence from those they have been unable to trace.

WESTERN GERMANY

FROM DEFEAT TO REARMAMENT

Alfred Grosser

TRANSLATED BY
RICHARD REES

George Allen & Unwin Ltd
RUSKIN HOUSE MUSEUM STREET LONDON

FIRST PUBLISHED IN 1955

This book is copyright under the Berne Convention. Apart from any fair dealing for the purposes of private study, research, criticism or review, as permitted under the Copyright Act 1911, no portion may be reproduced by any process without written permission. Enquiry should be made to the publisher
© *George Allen & Unwin Ltd.*, 1955

*

Translated and revised from the French
L'ALLEMAGNE DE L'OCCIDENT
(Gallimard)

Published in the U.S.A. under the title
THE COLOSSUS AGAIN

*Printed in Great Britain
in* 11 *point Baskerville type
by J. W. Arrowsmith Ltd.,
Winterstoke Road, Bristol* 3.

INTRODUCTION

THERE is no lack of books about Germany, and the best of them give a satisfactory account of many of the elements of the contemporary German situation.[1] It is not, therefore, our purpose to offer another historical explanation of present-day Germany. What seems to be needed is a general account of her most recent development and an analysis of her most immediate problems.

Can such a task be performed with any exactitude? A contemporary study of any country is always difficult, because the lack of perspective distorts our understanding and judgment. Much of the available information is fragmentary, much of it inaccessible, and yet concerning any particular issue there is so much information extant that precise conclusions are impossible. But in a study of Germany the main difficulty lies elsewhere, in the fact that international affairs and German affairs are inextricably involved together; Germany's internal affairs having been determined equally by the Germans themselves and by the occupying powers, whose influence was felt in minor as well as major developments. Moreover, the collapse and chaos in 1945 caused a far profounder rupture than, for example, the period of the liberation in France. There was, at least in appearance, a total economic, political, and social breakdown; though the speed of recovery in certain directions is now showing that some of the disruption was only superficial and could be made good through the action of forces which have remained intact and whose permanence we must try to account for. There is in Germany, much more than in any other nation, an unanalysable interdependence between the phenomena to be explained. A psychological situation requires to be interpreted through economic data which are themselves determined by a political situation which is determined, in its turn, by a psychological state. Every attempted explanation seems to become circular.

A really satisfactory study of present-day Germany would therefore be almost impossible, even if a group of specialists were to co-operate. But some attempt needs to be made now, although it must necessarily be incomplete and inexact at many points. Just as a statesman has often to make up his mind upon incomplete evidence because he cannot wait for fuller information, so the general public, whose vote affects the choice of leaders, has to form an opinion about events long before their interconnected causes can be clearly recognised. But it is nevertheless possible, given the chance, to see beyond the superficial facts and so avoid crudely categorical judgments based upon an "opinion" which is no more than prejudice. A news agency reports a duel between German students, or a change of name by the refugees' party, or a serious conflict between the trade unions and the Chancellor; a sub-editor gives a headline to this piece of news, which, more often than not, goes without editorial comment; and the public reads it next morning. The aim of this book is to offer both to the journalist and his reader an outline of the present German situation which will enable them to see such events in their real context, so that the one will present the news and the other will read it in the light of understanding rather than prejudice.

It is a very ambitious project, for the book should be both brief and complete, explanatory and impartial. In the attempt to eliminate superfluous detail we have no doubt sacrificed much that would confirm the picture presented, but the works which supply such confirmation are listed in the bibliographies at the end of each chapter. They are not necessary for an understanding of the text and the reader who is pressed for time can ignore them.

But the more one's material is compressed, the more one tends to abandon description for elucidation; and in a subject like this there can be no such thing as impartial elucidation. It is constantly necessary to invoke ideas which one believes to be true but whose truth is not universally acknowledged, and there is no descriptive style which does not imply a particular way of seeing, which others may contest. All the writer can do, then, is to resist as far as possible his own prejudices and deal openly and honestly with his material, presenting objectively what he knows, not concealing his method of approach, but laying no claim to an unattainable absolute objectivity. Such objectivity, however desirable, would in any case not be the same thing as detachment. One may not write with detachment of injustice and misery, and least of all if one is convinced of one's own, and the reader's, share of responsibility for their existence.

Up to now we have been speaking, somewhat deceptively, of "Germany", but after the first chapter this book will deal almost exclusively with *one* of the two Germanies. By what right? A more complete study, dealing as much with eastern as with western Germany, would certainly be preferable. But the differences between the two are so fundamental as to make them almost two different countries. The book would therefore have to be twice as big, unless the part devoted to western Germany were halved. But this apology is specious, for the truth is that the author feels unable to inform others about eastern Germany because his own information is inadequate. He has had no opportunity to go there, is acquainted with only a very small number of the relevant books and documents, and possesses little precise or verifiable information; whereas the data for western Germany are superabundant. It has been necessary therefore, while acknowledging the enormous omission, to confine this study to the latter area.

What should be the angle of approach? We may start with the simple statement that the essential fact for western Germany is its separation from eastern Germany and that in 1945 the wishes or actions of Germans counted for little beside the will of their conquerors. We are thus led first to examine within the framework of world politics the original causes and the manner of the separation of Germany into two parts, and this will form the subject of our first chapter. It will enevitably raise a number of points to be developed in later chapters, for while the split between the U.S.S.R. and the U.S.A. was growing it profoundly affected many aspects of Germany's internal evolution. We can then return to the 1945 situation to observe the chaos which followed collapse and especially to attempt to clarify the countless and interminable discussions which then raged around the question of Germany's guilt. It is only after making the necessary discriminations and establishing the least contestable facts that a useful analysis of the process of "denazification" and the general policies of the occupying powers can be made.

In contrast with the chaos and misery of 1945 are the political stability and economic expansion of 1954. Our third chapter will discuss western Germany's economic recovery and the currency reform of June, 1948, with what appeared to be its magical first effects. We shall have to expose the strength and weakness of the German economy, its potentialities and its present degree of integration within larger economic units, more particularly the Europe of O.E.E.C. and the Schuman plan. We shall try to discover who directs it, how it is that the old leadership has returned, and above all who are the beneficiaries and who the victims of this speedy rehabilitation. This will be the essential theme of our fourth chapter which deals with the social structure of western Germany. It will not be possible to review all the varied groups which constitute present-day German society, but we shall consider particularly three of them: the refugees and expelled persons, the workers and their unions, and the young, who are in Germany more difficult to define but also more differentiated than in many other countries, especially France. But since it is the young who are Germany's future we must distinguish the various influences to which they are exposed today, and this leads to our study in the fifth chapter of the contemporary intellectual and moral forces in Germany, with special emphasis upon those that operate in depth in such diverse ways as the Churches, the schools, the Press, and the cinema. We shall avoid overestimating, as people are too much inclined to do in France, the influence of literature, philosophy, and the arts.

Only after this does it become possible to discuss Germany's political life. It is true that politics have an effect upon economic development and social structure, and upon the forces we have just been discussing; but it is a fairly simple matter to indicate this effect, whereas political life cannot be understood without a previous knowledge of the other spheres. It is not simply epiphenomenal, it is largely a superstructure; and this is true even for countries like Britain and France with a strong political tradition. It is much truer still for Germany where such a tradition hardly exists. Germany's political life includes not only the functioning of federal régime and parliament and the evolution of parties but also the evolution of public opinion as expressed in the formation of groups and other manifestations. We shall try to avoid hasty generalisation when discussing the various reactions of public opinion towards rearmament and the reuniting of Germany. Our next subject will be a brief examination of a specific international problem: the French attitude towards Germany and Franco-German relations. We shall describe the development of various trends of French opinion since 1945 and the progress made in Franco-German relations, as well as the repercussions upon them of the rearmament problem. Our conclusion will not be complacent, but we think it will be impartial.

We were fully aware in commencing this book of the difficulties and dangers in our path, and we make no claim to have escaped them. We hope nevertheless that the synthesis we have attempted will have some positive value.

I have taken the opportunity given me by this admirable English translation of my work to revise the first six chapters up to April, 1954, and chapter 7 and the concluding chapter to 1 September, 1954.

A.G.

NOTES TO THE INTRODUCTION

[1] In particular Jacques Angel, *L'Allemagne* (Paris, 1945), a political geography; Robert Minder, *Allemagne et Allemands* (Paris, 1948); Edmond Vermeil, *L'Allemagne, Essai d'explication* (Paris, 1945); and *L'Allemagne contemporaine* (2 vols., Paris, 1952-3). A brief but accurate survey is given in André Drijard, *L'Allemagne* (Paris, 1952). See also the notes to chapter seven.

BIBLIOGRAPHICAL NOTES

The notes at the end of each chapter make no claim to be a complete bibliography of so vast a subject. The author's knowledge of languages has restricted him to publications in French, English and German. The anarchic state of publishing in Germany in the years immediately following the war makes research in certain fields difficult. The appended bibliographies list the sources used, as well as the works found most useful or most characteristic on subsidiary questions. To keep them within reasonable limits, periodicals have been omitted. Some of these, however, in the French language, have a lasting value as a source of information about Germany, whether they are official publications such as *Allemagne d'aujourd'hui* and *Réalités allemandes*, published by the office of the French High Commissioner in Germany (amalgamated in 1952), and the *Notes*, *Études documentaires*, and *Chroniques* published by Documentation française, some of them excellent monographs, or whether they are unofficial, such as *Allemagne*, the bi-monthly bulletin of the Comité français d'échanges avec l'Allemagne nouvelle, or *Documents*, a monthly review devoted to German questions, published by the Bureau international de Liaison et de Documentation d'Offenbourg, the fullest of all. I have taken a great deal from all of them.

CONTENTS

INTRODUCTION		*page* 5
I.	*Grand Alliance to Grand Schism*	13
II.	*Trial among the Ruins*	57
III.	*Economic Recovery*	86
IV.	*The Social Background*	117
V.	*The Moral Background*	156
VI.	*Politics since the War*	182
VII.	*French Opinion on Germany*	228
CONCLUSION		241
INDEX		245

CHAPTER I

GRAND ALLIANCE TO GRAND SCHISM[1]

"I CANNOT but associate myself with the words Mr Eden spoke at the time of the signing of the Treaty: 'Never in the history of our two countries has our association been so close. Never have our mutual obligations in relation to the future been more perfect'," said Mr Molotov at the ratification of the Anglo-Russian treaty in June, 1942. A few weeks earlier he had been assured by Senator Connally and Congressman Bloom, in the name of the American Congress, that the enemies of the U.S.S.R. were the enemies of the United States.[2] This was the time when President Roosevelt wrote: "It will be necessary for them (the Germans) to earn their way back into the fellowship of peace-loving and law-abiding nations. And, in their climb up that steep road, we shall certainly see to it that they are not encumbered by having to carry guns. They will be relieved of that burden—we hope, for ever".[3] It was also the time when Roosevelt's unsuccessful rival for the presidency, Wendell Willkie, spoke of "one world" and asserted: "No, we do not need to fear Russia. We need to learn to work with her against our common enemy, Hitler. We need to learn to work with her in the world after the war".[4] Today this one world is cut in two again and each of the former allies feels itself threatened by the other. The line of cleavage runs through the heart of Germany, and one half has signed a treaty which gives it arms again in order to "participate in the defence of the west within the framework of the North Atlantic Treaty", while the other has militarised its police and laid the foundations for a future army. How is it that the Grand Alliance which was to create a peaceful world gave birth instead to what a French commentator has called "the Grand Schism"?[5] Clearly, there is more in this problem than the history of the partition of Germany, which is no more than one of its major elements. But it is essential to know the main outlines of the story before the Germany of today can be understood.

* * *

Certainly the Grand Alliance was not of long standing. The Munich agreement of 1938 between the western democracies and the fascist states excluded, if it was not actually directed against, the U.S.S.R.; but on 23 August, 1939, Hitler's Germany and the U.S.S.R. agreed upon a partition of Poland, for whose defence Britain and France were to go to war.[6] The new friendship between Germany and Russia was soon to be "sealed with blood" and Mr Molotov was to congratulate Hitler on the fall of Warsaw and to declare at the fifth extraordinary session of the supreme soviet: "The warmongers have declared against Germany a sort of "ideological war" which recalls the old wars of religion. . . . Hitler's ideology, like any other, can be agreed with or not; it is a question of political taste. But anyone can understand that ideologies cannot be destroyed by force or put an end to by war. That is why it is senseless and even criminal to wage a war like this for the "annihilation" of Hitlerism under the pretence of fighting for "democracy"."[7] But in June, 1941, the Germans attacked Russia and "forced" upon her, as Stalin declared on 3 July, a war which the Anglo-Saxon countries and Russia would prosecute "with the firm intention of destroying German militarism and Nazism".[8]

Roosevelt and Churchill had little hesitation in giving Russia the maximum help. An Anglo-Russian agreement was signed on 12 July and on the 27 July Harry Hopkins, Roosevelt's confidential assistant, arrived in Moscow to arrange lend-lease for Russia. Not that relations between America and Russia had ever been cordial. The United States was the last of the great nations to recognise the Soviet government, and only did so in 1933 at the beginning of Roosevelt's presidency;[9] but now the President was anxious to build up friendship and confidence not only for the war alliance but also for the peace to come. Lend-lease was granted without interest or conditions of any kind except repayment of the debt within ten years from the sixth post-war year. Between October, 1941, and 31 May, 1945, Russia received 11 milliards of dollars worth of arms and equipment of all kinds. When there was a delay Roosevelt, on 7 May, 1942, ordered priority even over the western fronts for the deliveries to Russia.[10]

Nevertheless the Russians remained suspicious and exploded

into violent accusations on the slightest pretext. A betrayal of the alliance, a separate peace, a return to the "cordon sanitaire" which was applied to Russia after the first world war; they continued to express in and out of season their fear of these things. And can one say today that they were wrong, when it is known that in a memorandum of 1942 Churchill spoke of "erecting barriers after the war against communist barbarism"?[11] But was Churchill wrong in believing that the Russian view would always be the one Molotov expressed in his speech at the end of the Polish campaign: "The capitalist world has had to withdraw a little recently, while the Soviet Union has increased its territory and population"?[12] Our answers will vary according to our idea of world politics. When Churchill in May 1944 asked if the United States would approve spheres of influence in the Balkans, with Roumania in the Russian sphere and Greece in the British, he was following what is usually called the "realist" tradition of power politics; and when Secretary of State Cordell Hull somewhat indignantly refused, he was true to the so-called "idealist" Roosevelt policy which was embodied in the Atlantic Charter of August 1941.

This document, signed by Roosevelt and Churchill, is now neglected everywhere in the world except in Germany, where it is constantly quoted to prove that the allies' policy and behaviour towards the Germans are a betrayal of their principles. For does not the Atlantic Charter state that no territorial changes should follow an allied victory, that all nations should have free access to raw materials, and should be subject to no foreign influence in working out their destiny? And did not the U.S.S.R. affirm, through its representative at the inter-allied conference in London in September, 1941, its approval of the Charter's principles? For Roosevelt, however, the destruction of Germany was necessary before the Charter could be applied; but which Germany? Stalin himself declared in his order of the day for 23 February, 1942, that "it would be absurd to identify Hitler's clique with the German people, the German State. History shows that Hitlers come and go, but the German people, the German State remain";[13] and after the victory of Stalingrad he encouraged the formation of a "Free German Committee" in order to stimulate the resistance to Hitler in Germany.[14]

Roosevelt's own attitude is most clearly expressed in his memorandum of 26 August, 1944, to Secretary Stimson: "The German people as a whole must have it driven home to them that the whole nation has been engaged in a lawless conspiracy against the decencies of modern civilisation."[15] In his youth he had been in Germany, "where he had attended school and had formed an early distaste for German arrogance and provincialism".[16]

It was this attitude that led to the demand for unconditional surrender which was formulated at the meeting between Churchill and Roosevelt at Casablanca in January, 1943. The demand was addressed not to the army but to the German people as a whole, and its meaning, as Hull immediately pointed out to the President, was not altogether clear. Its timing is largely explicable through Roosevelt's wish to avoid any more such reproaches as he had incurred through treating with Darlan and Peyrouton; but he continued to uphold it later on against all opposition. At the end of 1944 General Eisenhower pleaded with him to define the slogan more clearly, lest it should inspire the German army to an even more desperate resistance, but Roosevelt answered that it was not yet time. Stalin had expressed his disapproval at the Teheran conference the year before. He had himself never employed the term "unconditional surrender", except with reference to "the Hitlerite army" in his order of the day for 1 May, 1943. But Roosevelt was firm and the Yalta declaration read as follows: "We have agreed on common policies and plans for enforcing the unconditional surrender terms which we shall impose together on Nazi Germany after German armed resistance has been finally crushed. These terms will not be made known until the final defeat of Germany has been accomplished." We shall see in the next chapter how much harm this formula provoked in Germany.

In addition to planning for victory it was necessary to decide how a defeated Germany should be dealt with. Many projects were advanced by English and Americans, some of them well considered. Germany was to be transformed, but under strict control, and the danger of allowing her to starve was emphasised, as well as the fact that the countries of Europe are economically interdependent.[17] Every plan provided for German disarmament, but how was this to be understood? For Sumner Welles the essential was to dismember the country and above all to destroy the military influence while avoiding a return to the situation after the first world war when "Allied support was given time and again to the old-line military organisations because it was thought that these alone could prevent Germany from going Communist".[18]

But the group responsible for dealing with Germany's economic power was instructed that disarmament must include "the eradication of these weapons of economic warfare", as Roosevelt wrote to Hull in September, 1944, after reading a report on the I. G. Farben. On the same subject he also wrote: "The history of the use of the I. G. Farben Trust by the Nazis reads like a detective story".[19] There was no overt opposition to Roosevelt's attitude but, later on, when the allied military governments in Germany were formed, there came to the fore a number of men of whom Senator Kilgore wrote in a report at the end of 1945: "Nazi industrial organisation is not repugnant to them and they have shown every disposition to make their peace with it". The director of the economic section of the British Military Government was Sir Percy Mills, who had been a member of the Federation of British Industries delegation which signed a 'gentleman's agreement' with the Reichsgruppe Industrie at Düsseldorf in March, 1939. His American colleague, who was later to occupy a much more important position, was William H. Draper, Jr., formerly treasurer of the American bank whose credit fostered the prodigious growth of the Vereinigte Stahlwerke, the largest steel trust in Germany.

During the war years, however, the influence of such men was still imperceptible and American policy went too far the other way when Roosevelt took to his meeting with Churchill at Quebec in September, 1944, four typewritten sheets from his Secretary of the Treasury, Henry Morgenthau.[20] This brief note, which was soon to be known as the Morgenthau Plan, was the result of several meetings at which Harry Hopkins and Secretary for War Henry L. Stimson had opposed Morgenthau's view and gradually won over Cordell Hull to their own.

Morgenthau's plan provided for the cession of East Prussia and Upper Silesia to Poland and of the Saar and the territory between Rhine and Moselle to France; the German States to be federated; forced labour by German personnel outside Germany, by way of reparations; the internationalisation of the Ruhr, enlarged to include Bremen, Kiel and Frankfurt; and last but not least the total dismantling of all industrial and mining equipment so as to transform Germany into a pastoral country!

On 6 September Roosevelt was still hesitating to accept Morgenthau's views. The Quebec conference opened on the eleventh. On the thirteenth Roosevelt sent for Morgenthau, and on the fifteenth Churchill and Roosevelt initialled the typescript, which henceforth carried the endorsement "O.K., F.D.R., W.S.C." What had happened? The President, who was for once not accompanied by Hopkins, no doubt desired to prepare a Carthaginian peace for Germany and failed to see that she would be unable to survive, even in penury, if Morgenthau's ideas were carried out. Churchill was difficult at first, declaring that he did not want to see England after the war "chained to a dead body". But then he relented, for two reasons, it would seem. Morgenthau pointed out to him the economic advantage to Britain of the disappearance of her German rival and, more important, he obtained in exchange for a stroke of the pen, to which he attached no undue weight, an important concession: Roosevelt agreed that the British should occupy the Ruhr after Germany's defeat instead of the Americans, who would take the South German Zone previously allotted to the British. On the sixteenth Eden arrived at Quebec. Having maintained ever since 1941 that it would be folly to reduce Germany to starvation after the war, he protested violently and had a sharp altercation with Churchill.[21] Hull and Stimson were aghast when they heard the news. They remonstrated severely with Roosevelt, and the press, which also had the information, supported them. Hull was in favour of a twenty-five years period of allied control over Germany and of keeping her at a lower standard of life than the countries she had attacked; but he emphasised to Roosevelt the disastrous effect the Morgenthau Plan would have upon world opinion and upon Germany, whose resistance it would only strengthen, and also its impracticability. Through the efforts of Stimson, Hopkins and Hull the President was in the end partly convinced.

The Morgenthau Plan was never in fact an official part of Anglo-American policy in Germany, but neither was it officially repudiated until President Truman's declaration of 3 July, 1945. A great part of its content is embodied in two essential documents, the Potsdam agreements and J.C.S. 1067 of the American Chiefs of Staff Committee, which were the text-book of American policy in Germany up to July, 1947. As no complete agreement was ever reached in Washington between the President, the State Department, the War Department and the Treasury, there was a long period when the American government had no coherent German policy.

But the discord and disagreement at Washington had little repercussion at the meetings of the Big Three, for the good reason that Roosevelt alone spoke for the United States and his will determined the course of the discussions. The first conference, held at Teheran at the end of 1943, was mainly devoted to the conduct of the war. Two decisive factors in Germany's future were considered: dismemberment and the eastern frontiers. On the principle of dismemberment there was little discussion. At Washington in March Eden, Roosevelt and Hopkins had envisaged the isolation of Prussia and the creation of two or three additional States, and Litvinov, the Russian ambassador, had agreed to this in a conversation with Hopkins. At Teheran Stalin "spoke bitterly of the attitude of the German workers in the war against the Soviet Union" and said that "there would always be a strong urge of the Germans to unite and that the whole purpose of any international organisation must be to neutralise this tendency by applying economic and other measures, including, if necessary, force".[22] Churchill proposed the creation of an Austro-Bavarian State. Roosevelt favoured a dismemberment into five regions, which came up again for discussion at Yalta. In the end, no decision was taken.

Nor was the question of Germany's eastern frontier decided, though it was discussed at length, if vaguely. The real subject of debate was Poland's western frontier, which is geographically the same line. Politically, however, the problem lay elsewhere.

If Russia was to regain the frontier proposed by Britain in 1919, the so-called Curzon line, and not her 1939 frontier which was fixed in 1921 after the Russo-Polish war, then it was thought that Poland should be compensated in the west for what she lost in the east.[23] Here again there was agreement in principle. A transfer of populations was envisaged, but the precise line to which Poland should advance was not defined.

A tripartite committee, the European Advisory Commission, was set up in London to continue the work of preparing for the immediate post-war period. It had been decided upon at a preliminary meeting of the three foreign ministers and its principal task was the delimitation of the future zones of occupation. This task engaged it from January to November, 1944. The work was speeded up when the three governments decided to associate France, now liberated, with the commission. The decision was made on 11 November and the protocol on the occupation zones was signed on the fourteenth. It was thought desirable to get the matter settled before the French representative's arrival, because it was not yet known if France would be one of the occupying powers. There had been no dispute concerning the limits of the Soviet zone or the special régime for Berlin, and agreement was reached without much trouble on both points. But Anglo-American discord continued, even after the Quebec meeting. The occupation of the Ruhr having been settled to Britain's advantage, there still remained the question of Bremen, and Hesse, and other districts. The American government, very dissatisfied, was slow to ratify the agreement, and as the Soviet ratification waited upon the American there was a danger of the agreement being still inoperative when hostilities ceased. At last Hopkins, on his passage through London *en route* for Yalta, saw the need for quick action. American ratification was obtained at Malta on 1 February, 1945, and the Russians followed suit on 6 February. The British had already signed in December.

The Yalta conference of the Big Three opened on 4 February and lasted a week.[24] France was not invited, but she occupied a large part in the discussions. Should she be allotted a zone as one of the occupying powers? Should she be a fourth member of the tripartite control commission to be set up in Berlin after

GRAND ALLIANCE TO GRAND SCHISM

the victory, and thus participate in the administration of Germany as a whole? Churchill and Stalin argued the question before a Roosevelt who was at first inclined to Stalin's view but later came round to Churchill's; Stalin insisted that France had let the German army in too easily in 1940 and that her subsequent contribution to victory had been insignificant. Churchill pleaded at great length for French participation, emphasising particularly that Britain could not bear the whole brunt of containing Germany in the west. At last Stalin declared that he would accept Roosevelt's opinion provided the British and Americans gave France a zone carved out of theirs. It was finally agreed, in the words of the communiqué, 'that France should be invited by the Three Powers, if she should so desire, to take over a zone of occupation and participate as a fourth member of the Control Commission'.

The projected dismemberment of Germany was again discussed, but inconclusively. The protocol stated that the United Kingdom, the United States, and the U.S.S.R. would have supreme authority in Germany and in the exercise of that authority they would take such measures as they considered necessary to preserve peace and security, including disarmament, demilitarisation, and the dismemberment of Germany. A committee consisting of Mr Eden as chairman, and Mr Winant and Mr Gusev (the three members of the E.A.C.) was to study the question of dismemberment and would consider the eventual inclusion of a French member. This implied no formal agreement to proceed to a dismemberment of Germany, but showed that the three powers were agreed that it would take place.

There was much discussion of Poland, both its government and its frontiers. The rivalry between the London exiles and Lublin was then at its height. Stalin reiterated his desire for a Poland 'amicably disposed' towards the U.S.S.R. and Churchill his for a Poland with a liberal political régime. The final compromise was largely favourable to the Lublin government, but on the other hand Stalin consented to sign a declaration on liberated Europe in which it was expressly stated that: ". . . the three Governments will jointly assist the people in any European liberated State or former Axis satellite State in Europe . . . to form interim governmental authorities broadly representative of all democratic elements in the population and pledged to the earliest possible establishment through free elections of Governments responsive to the will of the people. . . ."

Once again there was little difficulty in fixing the eastern frontier of the new Polish State; but it was otherwise with the western frontier, which had been the subject of discussions between the London Poles and the American and British governments during the later months of 1944. These discussions gave rise to two confidential letters. The first, dated 2 November, was written by the Foreign Office in the name of the Prime Minister. It accepted the Oder line, including Stettin, but without precisely defining its southern end, and guaranteed British support even though the United States' attitude should be unfavourable. The second, dated 17 November, was signed by Roosevelt. It stated that he would acquiesce in any agreement that had the support of Poland, the U.S.S.R., and Britain. If a transfer of populations appeared feasible he would not oppose it. On 17 December Churchill spoke in the House of Commons about the advantage to Poland of obtaining in the west richer territories than she was abandoning in the east, and added: "The transfer of several millions of people would have to be effected from the east to the west or north and the expulsion of the Germans (because that is what is proposed—the total expulsion of the Germans) from the area to be acquired by Poland in the west and the north. For expulsion is the method which, so far as we have been able to see, will be the most satisfactory and lasting. There will be no mixture of populations to cause endless trouble as in Alsace-Lorraine. . . . Nor do I see why there should not be room in Germany for the German population of East Prussia and of the other territories I have mentioned. After all, six or seven million Germans have been killed already in this frightful war, into which they did not hesitate, for a second time in a generation, to plunge all Europe"; and he repeated at Yalta that "the six or seven million German deaths, with the million more which they will probably incur before surrendering, should make room in Germany for the displaced populations."[25]

Agreement had still to be reached upon the extent of the

territories to be allotted to Poland in the north and west. The Russian proposal ran: "It has been decided that the town of Stettin shall be Polish and shall mark the western frontier of Poland, which shall be continued along the Oder and then along the western Neisse". Churchill opposed this, saying that Poland could never absorb so much. He proposed to make the Oder the limit, but to give Poland Upper Silesia as well. The American counter-proposal concurred with the British.

Much was at stake. The English and American proposals amounted to fixing the frontier along the eastern Neisse, which flows through the town of Neisse and approximately bounds the 9,700 square kilometres of Upper Silesia, with a pre-war population of $1\frac{1}{2}$ millions. The line of the western Neisse, on the other hand, embraces not only Upper Silesia but also the 26,000 square kilometres of Lower Silesia, with Breslau and Liegnitz and a population of $3\frac{1}{2}$ millions, and a considerable part of Brandenburg as well. It was found impossible to reach a compromise, and the communiqué read: "The three Heads of Government consider that the eastern frontier of Poland should follow the Curzon line with digressions from it in some regions of five to eight kilometres in favour of Poland. They recognise that Poland must receive substantial accessions of territory in the North and West. They feel that the opinion of the new Polish Provisional Government of National Unity should be sought and that the final delimitation of the western frontier of Poland should thereafter await the Peace Conference".

However, the Soviet delegation was more interested in reparations than in any of these questions. Already in 1941, when Harriman, the U.S. ambassador, and Lord Beaverbrook were discussing with him the eight points of the Atlantic Charter, Stalin had said "What about getting the Germans to pay for the damage?"[26] Soviet spokesmen continually reverted to this essential war aim—a justifiable one in view of their immense losses of men and material and of their contribution to the common victory. They called the presence of France in the Reparations Commission "an insult and an attempt to humiliate the Soviet Union".[27] The Russian delegation at Yalta made a proposal that after the war "the German national economy should, first, be deprived for two years of the use of all its factories, heavy machinery, machine tools, rolling stock, and foreign investments and, secondly, should make annual reparations payments for ten years in manufactures or raw materials".

Eden pointed out that the Soviet proposals were self-contradictory. It is impossible to confiscate a defeated nation's current production if you have already confiscated the factories and machines by which it produces. From the American side it was emphasised that there must not be a repetition of the previous post-war period, when German reparations had been financed by American loans. Roosevelt said there would be no loan to Germany this time; he wanted to see a self-sufficient Germany, able to keep herself from starvation. Then they talked figures. The U.S.S.R. proposed to fix reparations at 20 milliard dollars, of which ten would go to Russia, eight to America and Britain, and two to the remaining countries. The agreed protocol allowed for three types of reparations in kind; confiscations for a period of two years from Germany's surrender, a proportion of her current annual production for a period to be fixed later, and a supply of forced labour. It also established a tripartite Reparations Commission to which a resolution "under the heading of proposals to be considered" was addressed by the Russians and Americans: "The Reparations Commission at Moscow will base its discussions upon the Soviet Government's proposal that the total reparations indemnity.... shall be fixed at 20 milliard dollars, of which 50 per cent shall go to the U.S.S.R." The British delegation was opposed to the mention of any specific sum. This text was to have important repercussions later on.[28]

The Crimean conference marked the high point of cooperation between the Big Three, especially in the matter of Germany. The Potsdam meeting, five months later, took place in a sensibly different atmosphere. Much had occurred in the interval. Germany's gradual collapse had begun; the German troops in Italy had been routed; and in mid-March telegrams had been exchanged between Stalin and Roosevelt, the former violently accusing the Americans and British of preparing a separate peace and the latter refuting the charge.

On 12 April Roosevelt died. Four days later Russian and

American troops made contact at Torgau. On the thirtieth Hitler killed himself at Berlin, having appointed Admiral Doenitz as his successor. On 1 May Doenitz spoke on the air to the German people: "Our Leader, Adolf Hitler, has fallen. . . . He was quick to recognise the appalling danger of Bolshevism and devoted his life to combatting it. . . . In his personal struggle to stem the Bolshevik flood he was fighting also on behalf of Europe and the whole of civilisation. . . . The Anglo-Americans, therefore, are no longer waging war for their own nations but solely to assist the spread of Bolshevism in Europe".[29]

This interpretation of the war of 1939, a rather free one, to say the least, was the prelude to an offer of capitulation in the west while continuing the war in the east. Eisenhower categorically refused, as the American government had refused similar offers from Himmler a few days earlier. The U.S.S.R. was kept scrupulously informed of these *démarches*. On 7 and 8 May the capitulation was signed at Reims and Berlin, and on the ninth Stalin addressed a message to the German people in the course of which he said: "While celebrating the victory, the Soviet Union has no intention of dismembering or destroying Germany". His representative on the Dismemberment Committee (which only met twice) had stated on 26 March that "the Soviet government understood that the Yalta decision regarding the dismemberment of Germany was not an obligatory plan for partition but a possibility for exercising pressure upon Germany for the purpose of rendering it harmless if other means proved insufficient".[30]

On 25 May Hopkins, although seriously ill, went to Moscow at President Truman's request to discuss with Stalin the Russian grievances against the west: the invitation of Argentina to the U.N. conference at San Francisco, and of France to the Reparations Commission, the U.S. attitude on Poland, the allocation of the German fleet among the victors, and above all the stopping of lend-lease. While recognising that the withdrawal of lend-lease must be a serious embarrassment to Russia, Hopkins explained that it was legally impossible to continue deliveries after the end of hostilities; he smoothed over the other difficulties, obtained Stalin's agreement to the American view concerning a detail of the United Nations' veto procedure, and assured him that he was mistaken in suspecting Churchill of thinking once more of a 'cordon sanitaire' against Russia. But Stalin was not mistaken. At that very time Churchill was expressing his anxieties about the future to the former U.S. ambassador to Russia in such a way that the ambassador said on his return to Washington: "I said that frankly, as I had listened to him inveigh so violently against the threat of Soviet domination and the spread of communism in Europe, and disclose such a lack of confidence in the professions of good faith of Soviet leadership, I had wondered whether he, the Prime Minister, was now willing to declare to the world that he and Britain had made a mistake in not supporting Hitler, for as I understood him, he was now expressing the doctrine which Hitler and Goebbels had been proclaiming and reiterating for the past four years in an effort to break up allied unity and 'divide and conquer'."[31]

On 5 June the Allies made a joint proclamation announcing that they would take over the government of Germany and had allotted the zones of occupation. On 1 July, in deference to the boundaries fixed by the E.A.C., the American troops withdrew from those parts of Saxony and Thuringia in the Soviet zone to which their advance had carried them, while the Anglo-American forces were taking over their allotted sectors of Berlin. The Potsdam conference opened on 6 July.

* * *

The personalities were new. Truman succeeded Roosevelt and in the middle of the conference, when the British election results were known, Churchill was replaced by Attlee, though this did not alter the British position. Stalin alone was unchanged. Besides Germany, there were a number of difficult problems for the Big Three: Iran, the Roumanian oil plants, the international zone of Tangier, the Black Sea straits, and the peace treaties with Germany's former satellites. Germany, however, remained the chief subject of discussion. It was not difficult to define certain essential principles for "the treatment of Germany during the initial period of control": complete disarmament and demilitarisation, suppression or control of all German industries susceptible of being used for war, the German people to be made to feel that "they have suffered a total military defeat and cannot escape responsibility for what they have brought upon themselves, since their own ruthless warfare and the fanatical Nazi resistance have destroyed the German economy and made chaos and suffering inevitable . . . the National Socialist party and its affiliated and supervised organisations to be destroyed, and all Nazi institutions to be dissolved", war criminals to be tried and "holders of public and semi-public office and of responsible posts in important private undertakings" to be purged. These principles were drawn, verbally to a large extent, and as regards their content completely, from J.C.S. 1067., which document was the American commander-in-chief's directive from May onwards, though it was not made public until 17 October.

But to which Germany or Germanies were these principles to be applied? President Truman arrived at Potsdam with a project of dismemberment which particularly envisaged a southern State comprising Austria, Bavaria, Württemberg, Baden, and Hungary, with its capital at Vienna. He also proposed a permanent international four-power control of the Ruhr-Rhine-Saar area.[32] It seems he was unaware of Stalin's proclamation of 9 May or of the change of attitude which it implied. Anyway, the idea of dismembering Germany was dropped; but Russian propaganda was to pretend later that the story began at Potsdam and that the Soviet Union had always resisted "all attempts by the western powers to dismember Germany into three or even five parts".[33]

So there was to be only one Germany; but its boundaries had to be fixed. The four-power proclamation of 5 June mentioned the frontiers of December, 1937; that is to say, the Versailles frontiers with the addition of the Saar, which had been reunited to Germany after the 1935 plebiscite. This had been the American and English basis for negotiations, but they found themselves confronted with a new situation. They learned that the Russians had signed an agreement on 21 April which entrusted to Poland the administration of territory to the east of the line formed by the Oder and the western Neisse. Eden, and after him Bevin, protested vigorously; and Truman was later to write, with an exaggeration which is obvious in view of the

American position at Yalta: "At Potsdam we were faced with an accomplished fact and were by circumstances almost forced to agree to Russian occupation of Eastern Poland, and the occupation of that part of Germany east of the Oder River by Poland. It was a high-handed outrage."[34]

Churchill was prepared to accept the Oder line, but not the western Neisse. He said the moral responsibility for expelling such a large number of Germans was too great, and observed that a million additional Germans would be introduced into the western zones, "bringing their mouths with them"[35]. The Polish leaders were sent for and maintained their claim to the entire territory made over to them by the U.S.S.R. The final agreement about Germany's eastern territories read as follows: "The conference has agreed in principle to the proposal of the Soviet Government concerning the ultimate transfer to the Soviet Union of the city of Königsberg and the area adjacent to it as described above. . . . The President of the United States and the British Prime Minister have declared that they will support the proposal of the conference at the forthcoming peace settlement. . . . The following agreement was reached on the western frontier of Poland. In conformity with the agreement on Poland reached at the Crimea conference, the three heads of Government have sought the opinion of the Polish Provisional Government of National Unity in regard to the accession of territory in the north and west which Poland should receive. . . . The three heads of Government reaffirm their opinion that the final delimitation of the western frontier of Poland should await the peace settlement. The three heads of Government agree that, pending the final determination of Poland's western frontier, the former German territories east of a line . . . along the Oder River to the confluence of the western Neisse River and along the Western Neisse to the Czechoslovak frontier . . . shall be under the administration of the Polish State and for such purposes should not be considered as part of the Soviet zone of occupation in Germany."

This text has been the subject of conflicting interpretations. In the east it was held to allot finally the territory east of the Oder-Neisse line to Poland, and this interpretation was acted upon with increasing confidence. In January, 1949, the Polish parliament passed a law bringing these regions under the Polish ministry of the interior; and in June, 1950, the governments of Poland and the Democratic German Republic signed an agreement making the Oder-Neisse line the definitive frontier. Truman's wireless speech of 9 August, 1945, on his return from Potsdam is quoted in support, particularly his statement that "the territories to be administered by Poland will give her the chance to provide a better life for her people and a better defence of her frontier with Germany"; and it is argued that the word "delimitation" does not concern the general line of a frontier but only the fixing of its details.[36]

The western argument is that the agreement does not give the territory in question to Poland but postpones any final decision until the signing of the peace treaty. This position seems to be impregnable in law. But there has been a growing tendency to claim, in view of the difference between their reference to Königsberg and their references to the other regions, that the signatories at Potsdam made no commitments to Poland at all. This is going too far. Churchill himself has done no more than maintain his Yalta and Potsdam position—that at the peace treaty Poland should be given the Oder and eastern Neisse line[37]—while protesting against the *fait accompli* imposed by Russia and Poland.

The eastern thesis has nevertheless drawn strength from the confusion that has enveloped another important problem, the transfer of population. According to the Potsdam agreement: "The three Governments, having considered the question in all its aspects, recognise that the transfer to Germany of German populations, or elements thereof, remaining in Poland, Czechoslovakia, and Hungary will have to be undertaken. They agree that any transfers that take place should be effected in an orderly and humane manner".

We shall see in the next chapter that the last point was to remain a dead letter. The meaning of the text is clear. It was a question of ridding the three countries of their German minorities. But how was the expression "in Poland" to be interpreted? The Russians and Poles claimed that Poland extended beyond its 1939 frontiers as far as the Oder-Neisse line and that therefore the millions of Germans inhabiting the regions newly administered by Poland, many of whom had already fled before the advance of the Russian troops, must be expelled. Though difficult to justify by the letter of the agreement, this interpretation has something in common with Churchill's earlier statements, and it gained in force from the virtual acquiescence of the west in the expulsions. A decision of 6 December, 1945, by the Control Commission at Berlin accepted the entry into the British and Soviet zones of 3½ million "Polish" Germans at a time when, according to the Polish authorities, there remained only 2·1 millions in the former German territories. So Mr Molotov was able to claim later that the west had implicitly recognised the Oder-Neisse line, since the transfer of population could not be regarded as a mere "temporary expedient".[38]

We have treated this question in some detail because it is of capital importance in more than one respect. In 1938 the German territories east of the Oder-Neisse line comprised 114,000 square kilometres or 24 per cent of the entire area of Germany. Their mainly agricultural population of 9½ millions provided food for 13½ million Germans. In addition, 17 per cent of German coal production in 1938 was from Silesian mines. The influx of some twelve million Germans—"expelled from their homes" (*Heimatvertriebene*) in the western terminology, or "voluntarily displaced" (*Umsiedler*) in the eastern[39]—posed enormous economic and social problems in the reception areas. And, finally, the amputation of one quarter of Germany's territory complicated the reparations problem from Potsdam onwards; the Soviet Union maintaining against the west that the wealth of the remaining three-quarters should provide the total sum—for it was unthinkable to make confiscations from Polish assets!

The section of the Potsdam agreement dealing with this problem was the result of arduous discussion. Two of the three types of reparations proposed at Yalta are unmentioned: confiscation from current production and forced German labour abroad. The out-and-out confiscation, for which no total figure was fixed, would be effected by the Soviet Union, both for herself and for Poland, in the Soviet zone. The other countries were to take their share from the western zones, which were also to hand over to the U.S.S.R., in exchange for coal, foodstuffs, and other specified materials, 15 per cent of all industrial equipment in excess of Germany's peace-time requirements and another 10 per cent of it outright, by way of reparations. The preceding section of the agreement, however, contained a phrase which looked harmless enough but was in fact vital: "Payment of reparations should leave enough resources to enable the German people to subsist without external assistance". Here is the principle maintained by Roosevelt at Yalta. But no-one at Potsdam seems to have asked whether, if this principle was respected, the payment of reparations would ever be possible for a ruined and overpopulated Germany, deprived of her richest agricultural lands.

The contradiction is certainly not resolved by the "economic principles" of the next section of the agreement: the German war potential to be destroyed and "productive capacity not needed for permitted production [whose amount the agreement does not fix] shall be removed in accordance with the reparations plan recommended by the Allied Commission on Reparations and approved by the Governments concerned, or if not removed shall be destroyed". Here there is a serious confusion between two distinct proceedings: the destruction of factories and plant for security reasons, and the removal of plant abroad for reparations. (In future we shall distinguish so far as possible between these two operations by referring to the first as 'dismantling' and the second as 'confiscation'.) This confusion, which was already apparent in the Yalta debates, became inextricable in those of subsequent years; and in the same way the indefiniteness of the word 'excessive' made more difficult the task of reducing "the present excessive concentration of economic power" particularly exemplified in cartels, trusts and other monopolistic arrangements.

The agreement does at least presuppose that the economic principles it sets out will be applied in common by all the signatories. According to article 14: "During the period of occupation Germany shall be treated as a single economic unit. To this end common policies shall be established in regard to . . . (*d*) import and export programmes for Germany as a whole; (*e*) currency and banking, central taxation, and Customs; (*f*) reparations and removal of industrial war potential. . . ."

It is equally laid down in the "Political Principles" of the agreement that "so far as is practicable, there shall be uniformity of treatment of the German population throughout Germany". At the same time, however, "the administration of affairs in Germany should be directed towards the decentralisation of the political structure and the development of local responsibility". Besides the negative purposes of the occupation, demilitarisation and denazification, the Political Principles also indicate a positive aim: "To prepare for the eventual reconstruction of German political life on a democratic basis and for eventual peaceful co-operation in international life by Germany". Besides decentralisation, other methods are recommended to this end: "All democratic political parties with rights of assembly and of public discussion shall be allowed and encouraged throughout Germany", and "Subject to the necessity for maintaining military security, freedom of speech, press, and religion shall be permitted, and religious institutions shall be respected" and "the formation of free trade unions shall be permitted".

The conference closed on 7 August, just when the first atom bomb was exploded. On the eighth the Soviet Union declared war on Japan, three months after Germany's surrender, as prescribed at Yalta. But did she only do so because the bomb would hasten Japan's capitulation, which was in fact signed on 2 September? Relations between the allies were not improved by the Hiroshima explosion, and the United States' Secretary for War suggested that the U.S. ought to have confided the secret of the bomb to Russia in order to avoid discord and preserve confidence.[40] But the suggestion is seen to have little weight in view of the many and profound causes of dissension between the powers after Potsdam.

* * *

On 30 July, 1945, the Control Commission held its first meeting in Berlin, and by 10 August it had settled its method of functioning. There would be the Commission proper, comprising the four commanders-in-chief and a committee composed of their deputies and the directors of specialised departments corresponding to ministries. But what were the Commission's powers to be?[41] Its competence extended over Germany as a whole; but each of the commanders-in-chief exercised supreme authority in his own occupation zone and therefore possessed a sort of dual personality. At Berlin he had one vote out of four in deciding whether to issue a directive to himself at Baden-Baden (or Frankfurt, as the case might be). Since it is more convenient to govern alone than as a quartet the "zone commander" personality generally prevailed over the "Commission member" personality. The zones very soon came to resemble independent countries with frontiers almost impassable for men and materials alike. There was another reason for this sealing off of the zones, equally unrelated to the east-west dissensions. The fact is that the first steps of the Control Commission were not impeded by conflicts between Russians and Americans—and this notwithstanding all the friction over details, and the darkening international horizon, and the revelation to Britain and America of what the U.S.S.R. meant in the Balkans by "friendly disposed" governments. No, what most often held up the Commission's work in the early stages was the use of the veto by the French.

France had not been invited to Potsdam and was therefore not bound by the decisions of the three Powers. But these decisions had to be implemented by the Control Commission, to which France belonged and which could not act without the unanimous consent of its members. The fact that France was henceforth a member of the Council of Foreign Ministers, which was to frame the future peace treaties, did nothing to resolve this fundamental contradiction. However, the French government informed the three Powers on 7 August that it accepted the main lines of the Potsdam agreement, with the reservation that "it could not assent a priori to the apparent intention to revive for a certain period a central German government".[42] French policy, therefore, aimed at a federation of States, as well as the complete detachment of the Saar-Rhine-Ruhr area. This meant opposing all measures of a centralising tendency and especially the creation of political parties for the whole of Germany and the setting up of centralised German administrations. But the Potsdam agreement provided for the setting up of such administrations, in particular for finance, transport, communications, foreign trade, and industry. They were to be in the charge of German Secretaries of State under the direction of the Control Commission. The French veto prevented their coming into existence. It may be that, in the event, the conflict between Anglo-Americans and Russians would have made it impossible for them to function satisfactorily; but it is none the less true that French obstruction hastened the growing schism in Germany.

However, the dual function of the commanders-in-chief, and the French veto, merely aggravated a trouble whose roots lay much deeper. The four occupying powers were at first agreed in carrying out the severe policy prescribed at Potsdam. On 20 November, 1945, the Nuremberg Trial began; on 12 January, 1946, a common procedure for denazification was established for all the zones; and on 26 March was signed the very harsh decision on Germany's permitted production. But these agreed measures could not for long conceal the two points of fundamental divergence between the occupying powers. The first of these points emerged in connection with reparations and Germany's balance of payments, and the second concerned the interpretation of democracy.

The Russians and French had been invaded and looted by Germany, and their main interest as occupying powers was compensation for the damage they had suffered. They proceeded at once to confiscations and the removal of plant; the French in an unorganised way, the Russians systematically and on a vast scale. Troops and officials lived off the country, and the more easily because the two zones were primarily agricultural. The German economy was restored for other purposes than an improvement of the inhabitants' rations. As a French official report put it in 1947: "The German population has been set to work in those spheres, especially primary production, which can best assist the recovery of the French economy".[43] Very different was the situation in the other two zones. The English and Americans brought their rations with them; their zones being industrial and urban, they were obliged to import food into Germany to prevent the populations of those devastated areas from dying of starvation. The British and American occupation cost the occupiers 700 million dollars a year. Naturally they wanted to revive Germany's industrial production, so that she could exchange it for agricultural products, and to lower the economic barriers between the zones. Had it not been agreed at Potsdam that Germany should be treated as a single economic unit? Yet the Russians were giving no account to the Control Commission of the confiscations in their zone, and showed no enthusiasm for a common import and export programme. In May, 1946, General Clay decided that until such a programme had been arranged there should be no further contributions to Russian reparations from the western zones.

Confiscations without regard to the economic needs of the other zones were not the only unilateral action of the Russians against the German economy, nor indeed the most important. They very quickly proceeded to structural innovations, such as agrarian reform and the nationalisation of industry. The fact was that the occupying powers had different conceptions of the nature of national-socialism, and therefore also of the means to prevent its revival. The English, for example, acted on the assumption that nazism was an unfortunate accident, a sort of horrible mask which had been forced upon Germany's features; once the mask was torn off, a democratic Germany would be revealed. For the French, every German had been a potential nazi even before the appearance of Hitler, and indeed from the moment that Germany became a unified nation. She must therefore become a federation again before she could be cured. The American view, less clear-cut, was a combination of the English and the French views.

The Russians, for their part, considered the question of a federation quite secondary. If the Germans have a centralising tendency it must be respected, said Mr Molotov.[44] The important thing was to transform the economic and social structure which had made Hitlerism possible; and this transformation should be seen as the positive side of a programme of which "denazification" was merely the negative side. At the same time, the Germans must be given the hope of a tolerable political future. So even before Potsdam, when all political activity was still banned in the west, there was a rebirth of political parties in the regions occupied by Russian troops. Their conception of "democratisation", however, was only a part of the Russians' general theory of liberty under democracy, and on 24 April, 1946, the socialist party in the Soviet zone disappeared in order to form, under compulsion, in association with the much smaller communist party, a new political group called the "socialist unity party" (S.E.D.). The political régime in the eastern zone became more and more totalitarian.

The divergence of view between the allies in Germany was sufficient in itself to lead to a partition of the country. When the American commander-in-chief, in July, 1946, proposed to his three colleagues that the zones should be economically united, he did his best to meet the difficulties put forward but he knew in advance that only the British commander-in-chief would accept the proposal. The economic union of the British and American zones was ratified at New York on 2 December 1946. It led to the creation of a common import and export agency and was denounced by the Soviet authorities as a unilateral measure in violation of the Potsdam agreement.

There was yet another factor which hastened the split in Germany. The allies were beginning to find themselves at odds all over the world. The meetings of the Council of Foreign Ministers in October, 1945, had achieved nothing; the Italian treaty, Austria, the Balkans, Iran, the Far East, had been nothing but fields of controversy between Anglo-Americans and Russians. So both sides began to look at Germany with new eyes. Perhaps the Germans could be made use of in the quarrels between their conquerors. But in that case a milder and more sympathetic attitude was indicated, so that one could saddle the opposing party with responsibility for the harsh measures of Potsdam and the occupation. It was at the meetings of the Council of Foreign Ministers in Paris in April–May and June–July, 1946, that the new race for Germany's favours began. There were disputes about denazification, about reparations, and about the autarky of the occupation zones. M. Bidault repeated that France could not accept any centralised administration until the questions of the Saar and Rhineland had been settled. Mr Molotov then criticised the policy of decentralisation, the excessive scaling down of industry, and the identification of the German people with Hitlerism. In the end the conference decided practically nothing about Germany.

On 6 September, 1946, Mr Byrnes, the American Secretary of State, made a speech at Stuttgart which completely transformed official American policy in Germany, or at least the manner of its enforcement. He did indeed reaffirm to his German audience the United States' support of a revision of the 1939 frontiers in Poland's favour, leaving to the final peace settlement the decision as to the amount of territory to be ceded. But at the same time he announced the end of the occupation's punitive phase and held out prospects of a less gloomy future. There was one passage in his speech, however, which showed that he well understood the problems involved in a change of policy motivated by other considerations than Germany's own welfare: 'It is not in the interest of the German people or in the interest of world peace that Germany should become a pawn or a partner in a military struggle for power between the East and the West.'

The debate between the allies became so sharp that the Control Commission's work was at a standstill. The only points of agreement were out-of-date decrees, such as law No 46 which abolished the Prussian State. The fourth session of the Council of Foreign Ministers opened in Moscow on 10 March, 1947, in a tense atmosphere. On the twelfth the American President defined in a message to Congress what was to become known as the Truman doctrine: Communism to be held in check through the granting of aid, primarily economic and financial, but also military, to any country which it seemed to threaten.

The conference was a fiasco. There were accusations and counter-accusations about the way in which denazification had, or had not, been effected. Six points concerning German economic unity, proposed by General Marshall, the American Secretary of State, were discussed amid considerable confusion: utilisation of resources in common, an import and export programme, reparations, financial reform, freedom of movement, and centralised German administrations. M. Bidault demanded more coal for France and asked Mr Molotov to support the economic reunion of the Saar with France, which had been begun in December and accepted without enthusiasm by Britain and America. When Mr Molotov failed to respond, M. Bidault ceased his efforts to mediate between Russians and Anglo-Americans. There was further discussion of two proposals for four-power treaties, put forward in 1946 by Byrnes and Molotov respectively, each of whom had found the other's inacceptable. Although the conference was prolonged until 24 April, no important decisions were reached, except for the repatriation before 31 December, 1948, of German prisoners of war. A further meeting was arranged for November, in London, but no-one expected it to yield any results. Nor did it. The mutual reproaches were yet more violent and the discord sharper. M. Bidault was more stubbornly opposed than ever to any centralised administration for Germany unless Mr Molotov would relent on the Saar question.

* * *

The failure of the Moscow conference was the beginning of a new phase of post-war history: the "cold war" and the splitting of the world into two parts.[45] Its consequences were particularly marked in France and Germany. In France it led to the immediate withdrawal of the communists from the government and a deepening of the gulf between communists and non-communists. In Germany it hastened the geographical partition of the country, which was both a cause and an effect of the world schism. When Mr Molotov came to Paris to discuss with his colleagues the 'Marshall Aid' plan proposed in General Marshall's speech of 5 June, 1947, it was a foregone conclusion that no agreement would be reached. Ever since the end of April the east German press had attacked with increasing violence the "imperialist" and "nazi" policies of the American occupation. On 5 October the Cominform made its appearance and asserted in its first manifesto that the sole war aim of America and Britain had been to destroy the economic competition of Japan and Germany—an accusation very similar to the theme of Russian propaganda before June, 1941. The manifesto goes on to say that henceforth there are two world-

GRAND ALLIANCE TO GRAND SCHISM 39

fronts, one imperialist and the other socialist and democratic, and that there can be no Munich with the imperialists. On 25 October General Clay authorised the west German press to campaign against communism, thus lifting a taboo which until then had been maintained in the interest of Allied unity and prestige.

From the Moscow failure dates also the progress of both parts of Germany towards sovereignty—first economic and internal sovereignty and then political and external. The first German economic council was set up in the Anglo-American zones on 25 May, 1947. Clearly there could not be indefinite prolongation of a situation, defined at Potsdam as purely provisional, which gave the victors dictatorial powers; unless, of course, it is held that victory confers complete power in perpetuity.[46]

But the re-acquisition of sovereignty by Germany had been intended to follow the growth of democratic sentiment and achievement. In reality, however, it began immediately the east-west schism developed, and the wider the schism the more the victors on each side of it tried to conciliate "their own" part of Germany by promoting it in the scale of sovereignty. The temptations in the west were two: either to pretend that the democratisation stipulated at Potsdam had already been achieved, or else to reject the Potsdam principles *in toto* and repudiate as an absurdity the idea of a special process of democratisation for Germany. Both these temptations were such as to strengthen the hand of those members of the military governments who were more concerned with the east-west conflict than with any profound structural reform of Germany.[47] On 10 October, 1946, General Clay could still say, in a vigorous note to William H. Draper, the director of his economic department: "I am certain that the revival of democracy in Germany is dependent on our ability to develop an economy which is not controlled by a handful of banks and holding-companies".[48] But by July, 1947, Mr Draper's assistant, whose job was the dissolution of cartels, was handing in his resignation on the ground that the task had become impossible.

As the schism in the world developed, and partly as a result of it, the sense of European union became more pronounced. The first impetus was given by General Marshall's plan, and as the

European idea developed its two-fold character remained clearly marked. It combined a constructive internationalism with fear-ridden anti-communism; the proportion of the two sentiments and their mode of expression varying in different men at different times, according to the world situation. The directives in J.C.S.1779 to the American commander-in-chief were as categorical about denazification and demilitarisation as those of J.C.S.1067, which they replaced on 11 July, 1947; but it was stated in the preamble that "an orderly and prosperous Europe requires the economic contributions of a stable and productive Germany . . .", and on 12 July the representatives in Paris of the sixteen countries receiving American aid declared that "the German economy should be integrated into the economy of Europe in such a way as to contribute to a raising of the general standard of life".

Nothing could be more obviously true, but why did it take the disaster of the Moscow conference to make people aware of it? The following year western Germany became one of the beneficiaries under the law of 3 April, 1948, for American aid to Europe and a member of the Organisation for European Economic Co-operation which was set up on April 16. It is true that she was only represented in the O.E.E.C. by the allied commanders-in-chief, but four years later a German was to be elected as its president. In May, 1948, at the Hague, the European Movement declared itself in favour of a federal Europe. Since the possibility of abandoning national sovereignty is expressed in the constitutions of several European countries, notably in the French constitution of 1946, it was easy to conceive of a Germany without sovereignty being integrated into a Europe to which the other countries would have surrendered their own sovereignties. But it was not to be, and western Germany became a State with its own egocentric mission like the others.

In the east, the first 'German People's Congress' (Deutscher Volkskongress) met on 6 December, 1947; and on 20 December the Soviet governor dismissed the president and vice-president of the Christian Democratic party in his zone. In the western zone on 9 February, 1948, the 'Frankfurt Charter' was issued, creating a sort of German Economic Government with an

GRAND ALLIANCE TO GRAND SCHISM 41

executive and a legislative organ. On 10 March the German Economic Commission of the eastern zone was granted wider powers; and on 19 March General Sokolovski walked out of the Berlin Control Commission in a stormy protest against western policy. It was the end of four-power government, and the crisis which broke out in June was so acute that for a moment it seemed to mean war.

On 4 June were made known the decisions of a conference in London of the representatives of Britain, the United States, France and Benelux. An international authority for the Ruhr was proposed and the western military governors were instructed to arrange, in common with the German regional authorities, for the convocation of a constituent assembly for the whole of western Germany. The western authorities also considered that a healthy German economy depended upon currency reform, and having failed to obtain Russian agreement for a common plan they issued a decree on 18 June for a reform in the western zone. The Soviet military government replied on 23 June with a reform in the eastern zone which was also applied to the whole of greater Berlin, and coal and electricity supplies to the western sectors of the city were suspended. On the twenty-fourth the western commanders decreed that a slightly modified western mark should have currency in their sectors; and on the same day the representatives of the "people's democracies" at Warsaw protested against "the western military alliance", "western encouragement of German revisionism" and "unilateral currency reform", and demanded four-power control of the Ruhr and the creation of a central government. On the twenty-eighth the American authorities decreed an 'air lift' to break the blockade of the western sectors; and on 1 July the four-power Kommandantura ceased to function.

Juridically, the problem of Berlin is complex.[49] A protocol of the London Consultative Committee on Europe drew up the city's quadripartite statute, as well as the boundaries of the occupation sectors, in November, 1944. This statute did not expressly affirm that the sole purpose of Berlin's special status was to provide a neutral site for the Control Commission, but no other reason was clearly stated. The Soviet Union claimed that with the end of four-power government this enclave in the

Soviet zone had no further reason for existence, but the western powers replied that the failure of four-power government was the result of Russian policy and that, in any case, it did not make their withdrawal obligatory. There had equally been no mention in the 1944 agreement of free access from the west to Berlin through the Soviet zone; but President Truman had stipulated for this in a letter to Marshal Stalin of 14 June, 1945, which had received no reply, and silence might be taken for consent. The Soviet government claimed, in any case, that there had never been any blockade but only restrictive measures, which came into operation as early as the end of March, 1948.

What was really happening was not a juridical dispute but a trial of strength. Ever since the municipal elections of 20 October, 1946, when the S.E.D. obtained only 19·8 per cent of the total vote, as against the Socialists' 48·7 per cent, the Christian Democrats' 22·1 per cent, and the Liberals' 9·4 per cent, Berlin had provided a sort of index of the relative strength of east and west. It was only after 30 November, 1948, that a separate municipality was created in the eastern sector and the city was administratively divided. It would seem that the U.S.S.R. believed that the air lift could not last through the winter and that the westerners would abandon the city. But the United States made it a question of prestige. The air lift did succeed, more or less, in keeping the three western sectors of Berlin provisioned, and a counter-blockade of the eastern zone was put into force. In February, 1949, negotiations were commenced for ending the crisis and an agreement was signed on 5 May. It provided for the removal of all restrictions on movement affecting Berlin and the eastern zone, and for a meeting of the Council of Foreign Ministers in Paris on 23 May.

Between the commencement of the Berlin negotiations and the meeting at Paris there had been some important new developments. A series of agreements was signed in Washington at the beginning of April by which the French zone was amalgamated with the Anglo-American and a tripartite Allied High Commission was set up, to replace the three military governments as soon as a German government should be formed. An agreement of 17 January established a Military Security Board to "prevent the rebirth of any military or paramilitary organisation or of the militarist outlook" and to regulate western Germany's basic economic resources; and on 26 April the statute of the International Authority for the Ruhr was signed. But the most important event of this month of April, 1949, was the signature, also at Washington, on the fourth, of the Atlantic Treaty—a defensive military alliance of twelve "western" nations, including the three occupying powers of western Germany. On 8 May the constituent assembly, known as the parliamentary council, at Bonn, which had been created on 4 June of the previous year, adopted after endless debate the "basic law" (Grundgesetz) of the future 'German Federal Republic'. The occupying powers had vetoed the inclusion of west Berlin in the new State. In the eastern zone on 15 May elections were held for the third People's Congress, which adopted on the thirtieth a constitution for the 'Democratic German Republic', not including east Berlin.

In such circumstances the meeting of the Big Four had small chance of success. Mr Vyshinsky said he could not accept any of the tripartite decisions, while M. Schuman, French foreign minister since July, 1948, maintained that any quadripartite organisation must acknowledge what had been done in the last eighteen months. The western powers painted a rosy picture of the material and economic progress in their zones, but Mr Vyshinsky produced statistics of a contrary tendency and drew an even more favourable picture of the eastern zone, which Mr Bevin in turn disputed. No progress was made, but nevertheless the points at issue emerged more clearly than ever before. M. Schuman demonstrated that any real German unity depended upon a common democratic structure, and Mr Vyshinsky that it depended upon the unity of the allies. The question of German economic unity—with its two corollaries, the problems of reparations and of structural reform—was once again ventilated in all its aspects. Agreement was impossible, and the ministers separated on 20 June, having issued a completely uninformative communiqué.

On 16 August the first general elections were held in western Germany and in September the Federal Republic began to function. Herr Theodor Heuss was elected president and appointed Dr Adenauer, the leader of the largest party, as

Chancellor. In October the Democratic Republic in its turn elected a President, Herr Wilhelm Pieck, and Herr Grotewohl became Prime Minister, while the Soviet military government was replaced by a control commission. In the west the Petersberg agreement, embodying the occupation statute signed on 24 November by the Chancellor and the three allied high commissioners, entered into force. Henceforth the existence of two Germanies was an accomplished fact.

* * *

The Federal Republic was still far from possessing all the attributes of sovereignty. Its external relations remained in the hands of the high commissioners until 7 May, 1951.[50] The commissioners controlled disarmament, demilitarisation, reparations, and the liquidation of cartels, and they also kept control of foreign trade and the exchanges and possessed a right of veto upon internal legislation, though this right was never exercised to any great effect.* The Ruhr Authority and the Military Security Board were further limitations upon the sovereignty of Bonn; and finally, and above all, the allies reserved the right to withdraw in case of emergency all the powers conferred by the statute, which was an act of grace and not a negotiated treaty.

It was clear, however, that if a united Europe policy was desirable, western Germany would sooner or later have to be granted as much sovereignty as was possible without a too-flagrant violation of the Potsdam principles. The longer this was delayed, the greater the danger of a permanent revisionism in Germany and the brighter the chances for nationalist propaganda. The Federal Republic was invited on 3 May, 1950, to participate as an associate member, along with the Saar which had become a sort of French protectorate, in the work of the European Consultative Assembly at Strasbourg. On 9 May, M. Schuman put forward the plan, which was to bear his name, for pooling western Europe's coal and steel resources. It seemed that western Germany was rapidly approaching economic integration, including complete equality of rights, when, on 25 June, the outbreak of war in Korea brought into

* See chapter III.

the open a question which the European leaders had hitherto handled very gingerly and only discussed with the greatest caution, namely, German rearmament.

The Atlantic Treaty did not necessarily imply a speeding-up of rearmament by all its signatories. The American Senate's foreign affairs committee accepted unanimously, on 6 June, 1949, a report which stated: "The essential objective (of the Treaty) is increased security, not increased military strength", but since "clearly, the capacity of member States to resist armed attack depends primarily upon their basic economic health" a country's contribution to the common defence could consist either in military equipment, or in increased productive capacity, or in the development of its labour resources.[51] Very soon, however, a new conception began to prevail: all the member nations should rearm. And this conception necessarily involved the rearming of western Germany, for it was inconceivable that the French army should be fighting on the Elbe while the Germans stayed at home, or that the American general staff should deprive itself of the human potential of a country which voted 95 per cent anti-communist, in contrast to France which voted 25 per cent pro-communist. Without the Germans it would be difficult to raise, at the price of years of effort, as many as thirty divisions to oppose the two hundred odd which were supposed to be ready, and threatening, in the east. With Germany it would at least be possible to raise fifty.

But it had always been maintained that there could be no question of rearming Germany. Early in 1948 the international christian-democrat association Nouvelles Équipes Internationales, while calling for the integration of the German economy in an economic plan for Europe as a whole, had insisted that "all possibility of rearmament must be prevented".[52] And again in 1950 we find this passage in a book with a preface by General Eisenhower[53]: "If the Western Allies should now rearm the Germans, they would repudiate a series of agreements extending from Potsdam in 1945 to the Petersberg Protocol of November, 1949. That no such action is contemplated has been announced officially and emphatically in Washington, London and Paris. Responsible statesmen have recognised that, whatever the gains from the military point of view of adding six or eight divisions of German troops to the forces of N.A.T.O., politically German rearmament is full of dynamite". When recommending the Atlantic Treaty to the National Assembly, M. René Mayer did not even mention German rearmament[54]; and M. Robert Schuman repeated on several occasions that it would never happen.

But the Korean war created something like a panic, which gave a preponderant influence in the United States to military leaders whose political acumen was not particularly developed[55]; and at the same time the State Department's official theory (that the United States should resist communism primarily because it was being used as a subtle weapon of Soviet imperialism) was attacked by right-wing Republicans who said the real fight was against the principle of communism and socialism,[56] and were not much concerned about the past history of any German ally who could be useful.

In September, 1950, the three foreign ministers and the Atlantic Treaty council held a meeting in New York.[57] Caught between American pressure on one side and French public opinion on the other, the French delegation put forward the idea of a European army, and this enabled the three powers to issue a communiqué on 19 September which was a masterpiece of diplomatic prose: "The Ministers are fully agreed that the re-creation of a German national army would not serve the best interests of Germany or Europe. They also believe that this is the view of the great majority of the German people. The Ministers have taken note however of sentiments recently expressed in Germany and elsewhere in favour of German participation in an integrated force for the defence of European freedom. The questions raised by the problem of the participation of the German Federal Republic in the common defence of Europe are at present the subject of study and exchange of views."

The communiqué issued on 26 September by the Atlantic Treaty council was much more explicit: "The Council was in agreement that Germany should be enabled to contribute to the build-up of the defence of Western Europe."

So the way was paved for negotiations to set up a European Defence Community combined with the negotiation of contractual agreements for restoring to Germany her equal rights with other European nations. The German negotiators were able to use German reluctance to rearm as a lever to extort more concessions in the contractual agreements. The two treaties were signed at Bonn and Paris on 26 and 27 May.*

The texts of the Bonn agreements and the Paris treaty are indissolubly, and intentionally, interconnected, although the only common signatories to both are the Federal Republic and France; the others being in the one case the United States and Britain and in the other Italy and the Benelux countries. France had stipulated that western Germany should only regain her sovereignty on condition of surrendering military sovereignty in advance to the E.D.C. But the rearming and the reacquisition of sovereignty by western Germany were also matters of concern to the former fourth member of the quadripartite alliance, the U.S.S.R.; and in this connection the two documents can be seen to have been drawn up under the influence of somewhat contradictory preoccupations. The E.D.C. treaty breaks completely with Potsdam, both in letter and spirit; it drops the idea of demilitarisation, and it includes one half of the Germany formerly administered by the four victorious powers of 1945 in a military alliance which excludes one of those powers and is in fact directed against it. The Bonn agreements, on the other hand, although they openly proclaim the entry of the Federal Republic into the Atlantic system, exhibit considerable anxiety on the part of the western powers not to violate the Potsdam treaty. They impose strict limitations upon German sovereignty. Article 2 reserves the right of the three powers to conduct all negotiations in respect to Berlin, to Germany as a whole, and to the framing of the eventual peace treaty; and article 3 obliges the Federal Republic to accept representation in the east by one of the three powers. In article 5 a different preoccupation appears: if there is a threat of serious trouble, the three powers may declare a state of emergency and thus revoke all that has been granted by the treaty. The Americans imagined trouble coming from the extreme left; the French imagined it from the extreme right.

Assuming the agreements come into force, what is Germany's

* See below, chapters VI and VII and CONCLUSION.

position? What does Germany represent and how does the contract bind her? The juridical problem of the Federal Republic's sovereignty is complex enough to baffle the most learned specialist. It includes the part of sovereignty which the republic has recovered, the part it ceded before recovering it, the part of which it consents to be temporarily deprived, and the part of which it refuses to be deprived any longer. . . . But the political reality behind the juridical complexity is the fact of western Germany's uncertain status among the nations. The Chancellor may preside at the council of foreign ministers of the six Schuman plan countries, or be received abroad as the head of a friendly government, as at Washington in April or London in May, 1953, and on such occasions it appears that the Federal Republic has a recognised status in European and world politics. But at the Bermuda conference or a conference of the four powers the same Germany seems to relapse into a passive subject of negotiation, and yet there has been no violation or alteration of the text of any international agreement. The conclusion that follows is obvious in the light of the events that have formed the subject of this chapter: the more strained the relations between east and west, the greater will be western Germany's importance in international affairs.

But if the treaties of 26 and 27 May, 1952, come into force, is western Germany definitely committed to the Atlantic coalition? Undoubtedly, according to the general tenor of the texts; and yet there is always paragraph 3 of article 7 of the contractual agreements, and its importance is crucial although its meaning is not too clear. Admittedly it was drawn up in difficult conditions. The original draft, which, up to 23 May, was accepted by all the prospective signatories, provided that in the event of Germany becoming unified the treaty's clauses should apply to Germany as a whole. That is to say, she would be bound by all the clauses of the agreements. But vice-chancellor Blücher and Herr von Brentano, leader of the christian-democrat parliamentary group, judging that this stipulation would effectively destroy eastern Germany's wish for unification, appealed to Mr Dean Acheson as soon as he arrived at Bonn. Mr Acheson at once directed Mr Philip Jessup to amend the draft, which was done by tacking on to the sentence an addendum to the effect that a reunified Germany need not be a party to the agreements unless she were prepared to assume the obligations contracted by the Federal Republic. When the French protested, the contentious article was further lengthened by the addition that this freedom of action by a reunified Germany was in turn limited by the stipulation that she must not make any arrangements in diminution of the rights of the signatories of the 26 May without their unanimous consent. Neither the importance nor the obscurity of this paragraph were fully appreciated until the Berlin conference of February, 1954.

We will not give here a detailed account of the discussions about the ratification of the Bonn and Paris agreements. As regards Bonn, the decisive votes took place in the American Senate on 1 July and in the House of Commons on 1 August, 1952. In the Federal Republic parliamentary ratification of both treaties was obtained in May, 1953, and the President's signature a little more than a year later. But by the end of April, 1954, France and Italy were still not even approaching ratification. In France, as we shall see again in chapter VII, the reopening of the debate between east and west had an important influence upon the attitude towards rearmament and the sovereignty of the Federal Republic.

This debate had been recommenced a few months before the signing of the treaties, at the high level of the occupying governments,[58] and of the United Nations, which, on 20 December, 1951, decided upon a commission of enquiry into political conditions in Germany, and of the Big Four themselves. The U.S.S.R. refused to admit the principle of a United Nations enquiry (with the result that the commission was unable to enter the Democratic Republic), but addressd a note to the three western governments on 10 March, 1952, suggesting the outline of a German peace treaty and proposing reunification. The proposed treaty, though it asserted that the territory of Germany "was defined by the frontiers established according to the decisions of the Powers at Potsdam", contained a number of items designed to please a great many Germans: No restrictions upon civilian production and, particularly, "equal civil and political rights with all other Germans to be restored to all former members of the German army, including officers and generals, and to all former nazis—except those serving sentences for crimes—to enable them to participate in building a democratic and peaceful Germany". (On 2 October, echoing this note, the people's chamber of the Democratic Republic passed a law of amnesty for former nazis and professional army officers.) But the most important paragraphs were those which stated: "Germany shall be authorised to possess such national forces—army, navy and air force—as are necessary for the defence of the country. She is authorised to produce military material and equipment of a type and quality conforming to the needs of the armed forces allowed her by the peace treaty." As it was also stipulated that Germany should not belong to any coalition directed against any of her opponents in the late war, the proposal amounted to placing Germany in a position of armed neutrality.

Once again the principles of Potsdam were quite ignored. It is unlikely that the Soviet note was a sincere proposal for German reunification. It was simply an attempt to prevent signature of the Bonn and Paris treaties and a prelude to the forthcoming appeal to the Germans of the Democratic Republic to accept rearmament and build up the independent national army suggested in the Soviet's proposed treaty. The reply of the west was scarcely more sincere. Western public opinion had been enthusiastic for the note of 10 March, but grew progressively cooler during the exchange of notes from May to September, 1952; and the more so because the policy of military integration in the west had been countered in the east by a harsher internal policy for the Democratic Republic. The S.E.D. congress of July, 1952, adopted resolutions which would transform eastern Germany into a "popular democracy", with such slogans as "centralisation", "collectivisation", and "maximum industrialisation". The application of these principles led to an exodus on the grand scale, and the arrivals of refugees in west Berlin beat all records during the first two months of 1953.

On 6 March, 1953, Stalin died, and the first international gestures of his successors seemed to indicate a wish to reduce tension. The "harsh" tendency still prevailed in eastern Germany on 28 May when labour norms were raised, but with the arrival of Mr Semionov, the new high commissioner, on 5 June there was a spectacular reversal—a sort of liberalisation of the regime, including particularly the settlement of 11 June with the Protestant church. But on 16 and 17 June there was a rising of the Berlin workers, and similar troubles occurred in many towns of eastern Germany. These were repressed with severity by Soviet troops, and the state of emergency lasted until the thirtieth. The international repercussions of this rising were considerable, and it may or may not have contributed to the fall of Beria, who was arrested on 10 July. What is certain is that the west, even if it so desired, could no longer, after the events of 17 June, discount in advance the organisation of free elections for a unified Germany; and the U.S.S.R., for its part, now knew that such elections would reveal an anti-communist majority, especially in eastern Germany.

This situation did not prevent a renewal of notes between the Powers. After an exchange lasting from August to November a four-power conference was arranged. The three western powers conferred first at Bermuda on 4 December, and on January 25 the four-power conference opened at Berlin. It lasted more than a month, but reached no conclusion on the main item of its agenda, the German problem.

It is vain to ask whether the Eden plan or the Molotov plan was presented in the sincere hope of reaching agreement, or whether one side should be blamed for refusing the other's plan. The truth is that there was no possible plan for unifying Germany which could be acceptable to both east and west. The western powers, in 'their proper insistence upon free elections, were in effect defining unification as a simple extension of the Federal Republic as far as the Oder, and how could the U.S.S.R. submit to such a loss of prestige without some sort of compensation? Unfortunately, there appears to be no suitable compensation available anywhere at the moment. Nevertheless, the Berlin conference established that the four powers were accepting the status quo of a divided Germany with better grace than in the past. The mere resumption of contact was valuable, and especially because the tone of the discussions was much less polemical than in 1949.

It is true, nevertheless, that Mr Molotov cleverly embarrassed

M. Bidault with a question of great importance for the future of both Europe and Germany: Would a unified Germany be bound by any agreements contracted by the Federal Republic? As we have seen, this was the problem arising out of article 7 of the Bonn treaty. If M. Bidault said yes, Mr Molotov could reply: "Then why are we here? There is no basis for negotiation". But if he said no, he would increase the fears of all those in France and Italy and Benelux who were uneasy about economic, and, even more, military alliance with a western Germany which might one day become a unified Germany uncommitted by the alliance. M. Bidault's interpretation of article 7, which had so embarrassingly emerged from obscurity, was contested by M. Van Zeeland in Belgium and by M. Schuman in Paris; but the Americans and Germans seem to have been somewhat uninterested in the whole matter, and for a simple reason. They agreed that a united Germany would have freedom of action, but since they also agreed that reunification would not take place if it was to be a mere synthesis of the two Germanies, but only if it meant the merging of the other Germany in the Federal Republic, they did not anticipate that Germany's freedom of action would constitute any great danger.

This point of view assumes that the only authentic Germany is the Bonn Republic. But on 25 March, 1954, the U.S.S.R. took a step which may considerably enhance the international status of the Democratic Republic. By a simple declaration it gave the Democratic Republic complete sovereignty, thus breaking finally with the Potsdam principles and going much further than the concessions made by the west at Bonn to the Federal Republic. The Grotewohl government is empowered to negotiate directly with the western countries and with western Germany. The problem of Berlin is not referred to in the Russian declaration, and this leaves the city exposed to a new menace, for it will now be possible for the U.S.S.R. to cut it off from the outside world through the action of a third party and so pretend to be innocent in the event of a future blockade. Further, the U.S.S.R. will do all in its power to secure recognition and status for the Democratic Republic on both sides of the iron curtain; and already several western countries are anticipating a dual diplomatic representation in Germany, one at Bonn and the other at Pankow.

Thus the Germany of the Potsdam agreement has finally become two separate countries, and the least one can say is that this situation is not a factor of stability in Europe or the world. It can only be a makeshift, but a makeshift whose continuance one must hope for so long as it can only be put an end to by force. The division of Germany is a symbol of world division, and she can never be reunited—except by the capitulation of one of the two great powers—until the day when the United States and the U.S.S.R. decide to make her the first symbol of reconciliation between the two worlds which today are drifting further and further apart. Until the realisation of this dream, the two Germanies will continue to exist, and it is only one of them which will be the subject of the remainder of this book. In our study of it, however, we shall try never to forget the existence of the other.

NOTES TO CHAPTER I

[1] On the questions treated in this chapter see: Harold Strauss, *The Division and Dismemberment of Germany* (Geneva, 1952), which has a full bibliography of the English language sources; Emil Schaefer, *Von Potsdam bis Bonn* (1950), extremely superficial but with a good chronology; James P. Warburg, *Germany—Bridge or Battleground* (New York, 1947), acute and unprejudiced; James P. Warburg, *Germany, Key to Peace* (Harvard, 1953), his proposals, though interesting, have little chance of being adopted; Basil Davidson, *Germany, what now?* (London, 1950); Drew Middleton, *The Struggle for Germany* (London, 1950); J. B. Duroselle, *Histoire diplomatique de 1919 à nos jours* (Paris, 1953).

Collections of documents: Cornides, *Um den Frieden mit Deutschland* (Oberursel, 1948); J. Hohlfeld (ed.), *Dokumente der deutschen Politik*, vol. 6 (1952); Department of State, *A decade of American Foreign Policy, 1941–1949* (Washington, 1950); *Occupation of Germany, Policy and Progress* (1947); *Germany, 1947–1949, The Story in Documents* (1950); Ministère des Affaires étrangères, *Protocole des Réunions du Conseil des ministres des Affaires étrangères* (Paris, 1946–49); *Documents français relatifs à l'Allemagne 1945–1947* (1947); *Soviet Foreign Policy during the Patriotic War, Documents and Materials* (2 vols., London, n.d.); G. Gorse, *L'U.R.S.S. et le problème allemand à travers la presse soviétique* (n.d.); V. Molotov, *Problems of Foreign Policy: Speeches and Statements 1945–1948* (Moscow, 1949); Boris Meissner, *Russland, die Westmächte, und Deutschland* (Hamburg, 1953), excellent on the documentary side, its interpretations at times debatable. Memoirs: R. E. Sherwood, *Roosevelt and Hopkins* (New York, 1948); Winston S. Churchill, *The Second World War* (6 vols. London, 1948–53); and the memoirs of James F. Byrnes, Lucius D. Clay, Cordell

Hull, Admiral Leahy, Edward G. Stettinius, Henry L. Stimson, Dwight D. Eisenhower, Walter Bedell Smith, Harry C. Butcher, and James P. Forrestal.

² Robert E. Sherwood, op. cit., pp. 568, 585.

³ Quoted in H. Morgenthau, *Germany is our Problem* (New York, 1945), appendix.

⁴ W. L. Willkie, *One World* (New York, 1943), p. 87.

⁵ Raymond Aron, *Le grand schisme* (Paris, 1948).

⁶ On the Soviet-German agreement see A. Rossi, *Deux ans d'Alliance germano-soviétique* (Paris, 1949); *Die Beziehungen zwischen Deutschland und der Sowjetunion 1939–1941* (Tübingen, 1949), and issued in English translation by the Department of State under the title *Nazi-Soviet Relations*.

⁷ *Cahiers du Bolchevisme*, 1940, p. 49, quoted in A. Rossi, *Les Cahiers du Bolchevisme pendant la campagne 1939–1940* (Paris, 1952).

⁸ *Communiqué of the Crimea Conference*, Cmd. 6598.

⁹ See V. M. Dean, *The United States and Russia* (Harvard, 1948).

¹⁰ J. R. Deane, *The Strange Alliance* (New York, 1947). An essential book on Russo-American relations during the war. On the technique of negotiations between the two countries see Dennett and Johnson, eds., *Negotiating with the Russians* (New York, 1951).

¹¹ Quoted in Pierre Billotte, *Le temps du choix* (Paris, 1950), p. 25.

¹² Rossi, *Les Cahiers du Bolchevisme*, p. 53.

¹³ G. Gorse, op. cit., p. 9.

¹⁴ On this committee see Einsiedel, *The Shadow of Stalingrad* (London, 1953).

¹⁵ Quoted in Cordell Hull's memoirs, p. 1603.

¹⁶ Statement to General Clay, quoted in his memoirs, p. 5.

¹⁷ Royal Institute of International Affairs, *The Problem of Germany* (London, 1943); Moulton and Marlo, *The Control of Germany and Japan* (Washington, 1944); Walter Lippmann, *U.S. Foreign Policy* (New York, 1943), and *U.S. War Aims* (Boston, 1945), is concerned primarily with the European and the world balance of power, and with the necessity to prevent Germany's playing the role of arbiter between East and West.

¹⁸ Sumner Welles, *The Time for Decision* (New York, 1944), p. 340.

¹⁹ Quoted in J. S. Martin, *All Honorable Men* (Boston, 1950), p. 14. This book is essential for an understanding of German industry, its operation during the war, and its renaissance after the war.

²⁰ Reproduced in H. Morgenthau, op. cit.

²¹ This account is based primarily on the memoirs of Cordell Hull, pp. 1603–22, Henry L. Stimson, op. cit., pp. 560–83, and R. E. Sherwood, op. cit., pp. 818–32.

²² R. E. Sherwood, op. cit., pp. 781, 798.

²³ There is as far as I know no satisfactory study of the question of the Oder-Neisse line. The Polish White Book, *Poland, Germany and European Peace* (London, 1948) contains the essential texts favouring the eastern agreement. The book by Friedrich Hoffmann, *Die Oder-Neisse Linie* (Frankfurt, 1949), which takes the opposite line, is very inadequate. The symposium by d'Harcourt, de Martonne, and others, *Frontière polono-allemande* (Paris, 1946), is mainly historical. It is unlikely that it would be as favourable to Poland if it were now re-issued.

²⁴ The fullest account of the conference is given by Stettinius.

²⁵ Stettinius, op. cit., p. 176.

²⁶ R. E. Sherwood, op. cit., p. 388.

²⁷ James F. Byrnes, op. cit., p. 61, and Sherwood, op. cit., p. 984.

²⁸ On the period immediately before the surrender see W. Lüdde-Neurath, *Regierung Dönitz: die letzten Tage des dritten Reiches* (Göttingen, 1951); Count Folke

Bernadotte, *The Curtain falls* (New York, 1945); General K. Koller, *Der letzte Monat* (Mannheim, 1949); H. R. Trevor-Roper, *The Last Days of Hitler* (London, 1947); Maxime Mourin, *Les tentatives de paix dans la deuxième guerre mondiale* (Paris, 1949); G. Blond, *L'Agonie de l'Allemagne 1944–1948* (Paris, 1952).

[29] The text is given in full in W. Lüdde-Neurath, op. cit., p. 226.

[30] Quoted in Harold Strauss, op. cit.

[31] Quoted in Admiral Leahy's memoirs, p. 442.

[32] Ibid., p. 455.

[33] *Weissbuch über die amerikanisch-englische Interventionspolitik und das Wiedererstehen des deutschen Imperialismus* (Leipzig, 1951), p. 18. Despite its title, this is more a collection of assertions than of documents.

[34] Letter from Secretary of State Byrnes of 5 January, 1946, quoted by W. Hillmann, *Mr President* (New York, 1952), p. 22.

[35] There are no precise records of the discussions. The best accounts are given by Byrnes and Admiral Leahy.

[36] This definition is based on a decision of the Hague court on the Czech-Polish frontier (6 December, 1923) which, in my opinion, deals with a case so different in character that it cannot serve as a valid argument in favour of the eastern contention.

[37] Cf. vol. 5 of Churchill's memoirs, pp. 350 *et seq.*

[38] Speech of 16 September, 1946. The Poles' note at first contemplated a transfer on this scale only with hesitation. See Polish Ministry for preparatory work concerning the peace conference, *The German minority in Poland and the problem of transfer of population* (London, n.d. [1945]).

[39] Cf. *Weissbuch über die amerikanisch-englische Interventionspolitik*, pp. 56–9.

[40] Henry L. Stimson, op. cit., p. 744.

[41] On the general and legal aspects of the inter-allied occupation régime see Michel Virally, *L'Administration internationale de l'Allemagne* (Paris, 1948); W. Friedmann, *Allied Military Government in Germany* (London, 1947); Henri Menahem, *Problèmes économiques allemands et droit international* (Paris, 1950); and E. H. Litchfield and associates, *Governing Post-War Germany* (Ithaca, 1953), particularly chapters 2 and 6. This is a symposium, and many of the contributions by former high officials of the American occupation are outstanding.

[42] *Documents français relatifs à l'Allemagne*, p. 7.

[43] Cahiers Français d'Information, no. 77, *La Zone française d'Occupation en Allemagne* (February, 1947), p. 25.

[44] *Réunions du Conseil des Ministres des Affaires étrangères*, vol. 3, p. 151. See also *Statement made by Dr. Clementis before the Foreign Affairs Committee of the Constituent National Assembly, on 2 December 1947* (Prague, 1947), p. 7. On the economic measures taken in the Russian zone see Haut Commissariat de la République Française en Allemagne, *Étude d'ensemble sur la situation économique et financière de la zone soviétique d'occupation en Allemagne de 1945 à 1950* (Berlin, 1950).

[45] The famous article by *X* (George F. Kennan), 'The Sources of Soviet Conduct' was published in the July 1947 issue of *Foreign Affairs*. It was sharply criticised by Walter Lippmann in *The Cold War* (New York, 1947). See also George F. Kennan. *American Diplomacy 1900–1950* (Chicago, 1951).

[46] This was done by Albert Wyler in *La paix avec l'Allemagne et le droit international* (Paris, 1951).

[47] For the first argument, see Arnold Wolfers, *West Germany, Protectorate or Ally?* (Yale, 1950); for the second see for example the virulent book by Freda Utley, *The High Cost of Vengeance* (Chicago, 1949).

⁴⁸ Quoted in J. S. Martin, op. cit., p. 202.

⁴⁹ See U.S. Department of State, *The Berlin Crisis* (Washington, 1948); U.S.S.R. Ministry for Foreign Affairs, *The Soviet Union and the Berlin Question* (Moscow, 1948); *Doppelte Geldreform in Berlin: Gesetztexte und Erläuterungen* (Berlin, 1948); and *Berliner Schicksal 1945–1952. Amtliche Berichte und Dokumente* (Berlin, 1952), fairly one-sided but very useful.

⁵⁰ See G. von Schmoller, *Die Befugnisse der Besatzungsmächte in der Bundesrepublik Deutschland* (Oberursel, 1950); and G. Jaenicke, *Der Abbau der Kontrollratgesetzgebung* (Cologne, 1952).

⁵¹ The full text is in Department of State, *A Decade of American Foreign Policy*.

⁵² Nouvelles Équipes Internationales, *Le Problème allemand* (1948), p. 11.

⁵³ H. S. Ellis, *The Economics of Freedom: The Progress and Future of Aid to Europe* (New York, 1950), p. 231.

⁵⁴ The text of this report, annotated, is given in René Mayer, *Le Pacte de l'Atlantique: Paix ou Guerre?* (Paris, 1949).

⁵⁵ General Bradley's *A Soldier's Story of the Allied Campaigns* (London, 1951), is convincing on this point.

⁵⁶ The two theories are formulated in Robert A. Taft, *A Foreign Policy for Americans* (New York, 1951).

⁵⁷ The attitude of the French delegation is described in Paul Reynaud, *S'unir ou périr* (Paris, 1951), pp. 182–7.

⁵⁸ See *Aktenstücke zur Beurteilung des Grotewohl-Briefes* (Bonn, 1951).

CHAPTER II

TRIAL AMONG THE RUINS[1]

IT was the first time since 1814 that Germany had known war within her own frontiers—and what a war! The towns were in ruins. Of Frankfurt's 177,000 houses only 44,000 still stood; in Nuremberg scarcely one house in ten was undamaged; 53 per cent of the buildings of Hamburg had been turned into 43 million cubic metres of rubble. Not one of the great cities had escaped the pitiless bombing of which the Luftwaffe had set the pattern in its raid on Coventry. Years later children were still waking in the night with screams of terror from nightmares which recalled the horror of earlier nights when hundreds of thousands of German civilians perished. The fighting on land and Hitler's scorched earth policy had increased the devastation, and not only viaducts and bridges but even the footbridges over village streams had been destroyed. Apart from the peasants in central Germany, few Germans still lived in their homes. Millions of townspeople had fled from the bombings into the country; millions more had fled west before the advance of the Russian troops, and there had been the beginnings of a movement the other way at the first appearance of troops in the west. The population seemed to consist only of women and children and old men, and even boys of fifteen had been given rifles. 1,650,000 men had been killed in action, 2,000,000 were prisoners, and 1,600,000 were missing. Food supplies and transport had completely broken down; there were no posts or newspapers; administration had collapsed, and chaos was unchallenged.

Into this chaos more millions of Germans were to be thrown, expelled from the countries of central and eastern Europe and from the German territories east of the Oder-Neisse line. These expulsions began before the Potsdam conference and were at their height in the winter of 1945–46. The conditions in which they were carried out were appalling.[2] Their justice or injustice is not here in question, though it is a point for discussion whether or not a multi-national State like Czechoslovakia had the right to expel the Sudeten German minority who had lived there for centuries, but whose mere existence—and also the behaviour of some of them—had brought Czechoslovakia to slavery and ruin. But whatever the rights of the case, millions of human beings were forced to leave their homes at twenty-four hours' notice for an unknown destination with no more than fifty pounds of baggage, were thrown into concentration camps, to whose conditions Mr R. R. Stokes, M.P., bore appalled witness in a letter to the *Manchester Guardian* in October, 1945, were transported in herds and forced to make long marches in cold and hunger. Their sufferings can certainly be explained, but nothing can justify them.

They were the consequence of Hitler's "total war", in which the invaded peoples had suffered atrociously until his régime collapsed in total defeat. France, Belgium, and to an even greater extent Poland, the Ukraine and Yugoslavia, had endured massacre, looting, deportations, and systematic devastation. Of the seven or eight million men, women and children thrown into the concentration camps of Dachau, Auschwitz, Buchenwald, and Ravensbruck, only a few emaciated survivors were rescued by the allied troops. Atrocities like these may well have called for vengeance; but the victors did not want revenge, they presumed instead to judge and punish. They put the whole German people on trial, to determine its share of guilt. We shall try to show first what form such a trial should have taken, and next what it actually became. But in speaking of the attitude of the judges and the reaction of the accused we must never forget by what a weight of suffering both parties were oppressed. From the start it made fairness and calmness almost impossible; it guaranteed in advance that there could be no common language between accusers and accused.[3]

We shall not go far into past history, or discuss at any length the categorical judgment which makes Germany responsible for every war and in particular justifies the Versailles treaty as a summary handcuffing of "the outlaw known as Germany".[4] We will simply give by way of contrast an extract from a report drawn up in 1951 by a joint committee of the best-qualified French and German historians: "There is no documentary evidence to justify us in attributing a premeditated will to war in 1914 to any European government or people. Lack of confidence was extreme and government circles were obsessed with the idea that war was inevitable; each suspected the other of aggressive designs; the risk of war was accepted by all, and the only safeguard seemed to lie in systems of alliance and the piling up of arms. Certain milieux of the German general staff considered Germany's chances of success to be greater in 1914 than they would be in the years following; but it cannot be shown that the German government's policy was influenced by this consideration. The great majority of both Germans and French were against war; but in Germany, especially in military circles, there was a greater disposition to accept it if it came. This disposition was the result of the place held by the army in German society...."[5]

What above all concerns us is the phenomenon of Hitlerism, and its atrocities. How far can the German people be said to have accepted them, willed them, and even committed them? First it is necessary to break the vicious circle which stultifies, without our knowing it, most discussions of the subject; to explain the rise of Hitler by an age-long tendency to barbarism in the Germans and to prove the tendency by pointing to the rise of Hitler. It is also quite common to reproach the Germans for having accepted dictatorship and participated in barbarities, while acquitting the Italians without trial for having welcomed Mussolini and the Austrians for having supplied proportionately as many storm-troopers and concentration camp officials as their neighbours. We must guard against studying German behaviour in the light of a racial prejudice similar to the one which we condemn in them.

When Hitler came to power on 30 January, 1933, could he claim the support of Germany as a whole? At the presidential election in the spring of 1932 he had received 11·3 million votes out of 37·7 million at the first ballot and 13·4 out of 36·5 at the second, and Hindenburg was re-elected. In November 1932, at the last general election uncontrolled by Hitler, the national socialist party lost 1·8 million votes, and even in the election of 5 March, 1933, it only got 44 per cent of the total vote. The law of 24 March, 1933, giving the Chancellor extraordinary powers, was only able to be passed by the inert consent of other parliamentary groups.

But that 44 per cent of the electorate should have supported Hitler is already prodigious. How could so many men and women have been so carried away? There is no simple answer. Some came to Hitler because they had no work, and he promised it; some because they hoped he would free Germany from the humiliating consequences of Versailles; some because they despised the feeble Weimar Republic and wanted a "strong" régime; and others, especially women, were rapt into a sort of hysterical frenzy by Hitler's oratory. Then there were others who relied on him to combat Bolshevism, or to relieve them from Jewish business competition. And the list is still far from complete.

One thing, however, is certain. Hitler would never have come to power, and could never have established himself, without the support of right-wing industrialists and a part of the army. Their responsibility is not less because they thought they would make use of him, and not be used by him. The intensity of the nazi propaganda in the March election was not solely due to the fact that Hitler was Chancellor; it was largely the result of a meeting of great industrialists at Goering's house on 20 February, at which Gustav Krupp collected lavish subscriptions. Did they really believe that once Hitler was in power he would "calm down"? Did the deputies of other parties, whose votes had enabled him to dispense with parliamentary control, really believe that he would be got rid of without trouble after disappointing the public by a display of incompetence? No comprehensive judgment is possible, any more than it is possible to say how many of those who voted nazi were bad men, under the influence of an already established tradition of power-worship, aggressive nationalism, and anti-semitism, and how many were average Germans who simply wanted some change which would lift their country out of the misery and despair into which it had been plunged by the defeat of 1918, inflation, and the economic crisis. But, it will be said, had they not read *Mein Kampf* and seen for themselves the brutal and lying methods of the party's shock brigades and propagandists? Here again, no comprehensive answer can be given, especially on the first point. Many Germans, to their discredit, voted for Hitler without having read *Mein Kampf*; and others had read it but took the more violent passages for the frothings of an agitator who would behave differently when he became head of the State; and there were others who approved of the passages.

Once in power, Hitler quickly established an absolute dictatorship and set about realising his programme: work and bread, and a strong Germany freed from the shackles of Versailles. Rearmament soon became open and official instead of clandestine, and then came the remilitarisation of the Rhineland, the annexation of Austria, the annihilation of Czechoslovakia, and the invasion of Poland. At home, persecution went hand in hand with the systematic inflaming of the young to fanaticism. As the régime's character unfolded the reactions of the German people were of every kind. For each of its aspects and for its essence there were some to approve and applaud and others to tolerate, submit, criticise, or oppose. But at least everybody knew that it was inhuman. Even if it were possible to ignore the treatment, in prison and concentration camp, of those whom the régime wished to eliminate, it was impossible to avoid seeing the synagogues in flames and the Jews humiliated and tortured in the streets during the November days of 1938 when the period of wholesale massacres began. Then where was the opposition or resistance to the régime?[6]

Much of it was liquidated in 1933. Most of the socialist and communist and religious leaders were arrested or forced to flee, and many of the intellectuals emigrated. But internal opposition still survived, as is proved by the scale of the repressive measures.[7] Between 1933 and 1939 the regular tribunals condemned 225,000 men and women to approximately 600,000 years of imprisonment for political offences. At least 86 spectacular trials were held of members of left political parties, and by 1939 about a million Germans had spent longer or shorter terms in concentration camps on political charges. A Gestapo report of 10 April, 1939, gives the number of political prisoners in "protective custody" on that day as 162,734 plus 27,369 accused and 12,432 convicted of political offences.[8] When speaking of the concentration camps it is mere justice to recall that it was for the punishment of Germans that they were originally created. There were 20,000 internees at Sachsenhausen in November, 1938, of whom five thousand died before the spring; and those at Buchenwald also were almost exclusively German up to 1943, one quarter of them Jewish and the remainder "Aryan".

But under the police régime perfected by Heinrich Himmler an effective opposition was almost impossible to organise. Every German could feel sure that he was spied upon and kept under threatening observation. A careless word or suspect gesture, to say nothing of secret or open meetings, could expose him to instant denunciation by a policeman or a hired *Spitzel* (informer) or by a nazi fanatic—who might be his own son. Children were taught to put love of the Fuehrer, the incarnation of the Fatherland, before filial love and to note carefully and report any unorthodox word of parent or teacher. For fear of unknown dangers, many Germans were resigned to keeping their thoughts to themselves.

However, the great majority of the population would not have been active opponents, even under less strict surveillance. Democracy was never firmly rooted in Germany, where political liberty had either been freely bestowed from above or, as in 1919, imposed after defeat. And now a situation had arisen which required the Germans to exercise the democratic right not only of judging and voting against the government, but of disobeying it. But the average German, in school and office, in church and factory, had always been taught the same lesson and had learnt it well, the lesson of respect for *Obrigkeit*, for one's superior, for the Authority to whom obedience was due. We shall have to refer to this again in connection with social relations and the attitude of the Churches;* it accounts for the fact that many Germans were able to participate with a good conscience in acts of which they disapproved. The sole responsibility, they felt, was the leader's; and if Authority saw fit to arrest one's neighbour, then surely he must be in some sense guilty. So, in the end, why not do the best one can for oneself? The judge will not get promotion unless he joins the party, so he joins; the industrialist is not asked to join but only to

* See chapters IV and V.

pay, so he pays; the teacher is required to say that the *Lorelei* is not a poem by Heinrich Heine but a popular ballad, so he says it. And after all, is the régime such a bad one? The workers are no longer unemployed, and they enjoy good holidays thanks to the Strength through Joy organisation; the factory owner sees his machines working to capacity; the banker gets unconditional support from the State for financing industry; and everyone is aware of the extraordinary revival of Germany's prestige in "world opinion".

From 1933 to 1939 the German exiles tried in vain to make people see the real nature of the régime, and the opposition in Germany looked in vain for help from abroad. Here and there among the working class and the intellectuals in other countries were a few who understood and wanted to act, but they could make no impression on those of their compatriots who saw Hitler as a great man and the saviour of his country. The former United States ambassador to Germany, James W. Gerard, could write in his review of *The Brown Book of the Hitler Terror:* "No man who attains to great prominence escapes the suspicion of some form of immorality"![9] The revival of Germany's power seemed to provoke envy and fear rather than hostility to nazism; and the 1936 Olympic Games were represented by nazi propaganda as a sort of homage paid by the whole world to the strength and brilliance of the new Germany. Inertia and lack of foresight, mixed with a sort of tacit complicity, prevented any reaction to Hitler's successive strokes of violence, and each of them by its success further consolidated the régime.

When the war came it was accepted in Germany with resignation and no enthusiasm, and for the underground opposition it created a new moral atmosphere; for although defeat would certainly mean the collapse of the régime, it would be a defeat for Germany as a whole and not merely for the nazi party. In the invaded countries nazism could be resisted on ideological and patriotic grounds alike, but in Germany it partook of treason. Now, every German had been exposed to the right-wing propaganda, taken over by Goebbels, which attributed the defeat of 1918 to a "stab in the back" given by revolutionaries to an undefeated army, and every German soldier had been trained to put honour, which for practical purposes meant discipline, above all else. The law of 20 August, 1934, prescribed an oath of absolute obedience to the Fuehrer, ending with the words: "I pledge this oath with my life". This led to many tragic crises of conscience for officers and soldiers alike, as is shown by the extraordinary success after the war of Carl Zuckmayer's play *The Devil's General*. In this piece an air force officer sabotages the planes in his charge, thus bringing death to his closest comrades and defeat to his country—but also to an odious régime, as harmful to Germany herself as to the rest of the world. Did he do right? There were many who thought that victory should come first, and only after it the struggle against the nazis; and certainly it cannot have been easy to decide that Germany's defeat would be to her own advantage. By their demand for unconditional surrender the allies made the task of the opposition inside Germany almost impossible, for they compelled the Germans to choose between Hitler and national ruin.

This demand, formulated at Casablanca, was not a casual expedient but part of a consistent attitude. When the German opposition warned the allies in 1940 of the imminent invasion of the Netherlands, the allies ignored this information coming from a group whose existence they denied; and in 1942 when an American journalist tried to see Roosevelt on his return from Germany—where he had had a long talk with Jakob Kaiser, one of the leaders of the underground movement—Roosevelt refused to see him on account of the "most embarrassing" nature of his mission; and Churchill, although he knew in outline what the attempt of 20 July, 1944, really was, described it in the House of Commons as a settlement of accounts between nazis.[10]

The years 1940 and 1941 were the nadir of the opposition. All accounts agree that it was impossible for the resisters to make any headway during that period of unexampled triumphs. But after the defeat at Stalingrad the atmosphere changed, and from then on the resistance comprised two very different and yet inextricably mingled elements. The first consisted of those who wanted to destroy Hitler in order to put an end to nazi barbarism, and was exemplified in the admirable Hans and Sophie Scholl who were executed at Munich in the spring of 1943, after the pretence of a trial, with four students who were their comrades. At the trial the president observed that the times were happily past when people could go about proclaiming their so-called political faith—and as there had been a number of police reports since 1941 referring to small "asocial" or "oppositionist" groups, we may conclude that heterodox faith was alive in an appreciable number of the young. Of the same type were men like the unfanatical Goerdeler, former mayor of Leipzig, and the trade union leaders Wilhelm Leuschner and Jakob Kaiser, and the "Antifa" (antifascist) groups in Bremen, Lübeck, and a number of the Ruhr towns.

The other element consisted of those who equally wished to rid Germany of Hitler, but only because he was leading the country to disaster. Their conscience was untroubled by the destruction of Rotterdam or Warsaw; it was the ruin of German cities that shocked them, and it was Hitler's errors of strategy and not the nazi régime that inspired their revolt. Recruits were mainly found in the higher reaches of the army and in certain government circles. As soon as the defeats began, opposition groups made contact with the general staff, for without the army's help the overthrow of the régime was inconceivable. A few very exceptional generals, such as the aged Marshal von Witzleben, had long been resisters of the first type. The fanaticism of others, like Jodl, seemed impregnable. But some, like Manstein or Rommel, had wished to "depose" Hitler ever since 1943, for the reason that he was losing the war. It was only later, in the early summer of 1944, that Rommel heard for the first time in his life "the voice of political conscience".[11] He joined the conspiracy of 20 July and paid with his life, while another general, Guderian, especially favoured by Hitler, who had given him a huge domain in Poland, had the consummate hypocrisy to write afterwards: "Personally, I abjure assassination in any form. It is unequivocally forbidden by our Christian religion"![12]

The attempt of 20 July, 1944, rightly became a symbol—unlike that of 13 March, 1943, which was the work of a single group—because representatives of the entire opposition, from the old Prussian nobility to the trade unions, took part in preparing it. The repression which followed was savage: 7,000 arrests, 4,980 shot, hanged, or executed by torture. This conspiracy proved both the extent of the resistance in Germany and its weakness. Even if Count Stauffenberg's bomb had killed Hitler at his headquarters, it is by no means certain that the conspirators would have got control, such was their irresolution and lack of energy in Berlin during the few hours when it was thought that Hitler was dead. What is certain, however, is that if the assassination had succeeded the war would have been shorter and Germany would have been spared most of her destruction. On the other hand it is hard to know what, in such a case, the attitude of the victors to the German people would have been.

* * *

After the war it was the aim of the victors to punish guilty Germans, to eradicate nazism, and to destroy all the seeds from which it could ever spring up again in Germany. The task would have been very difficult, even if they had started with a clear definition of guilt and of the nature of national socialism. In the event the difficulties proved insuperable because of the mistakes they made at the beginning. They approached the task in three ways—the trial of war criminals, "denazification", and an overall policy for the occupation forces—but none of them led to the hoped-for results.

On 13 January, 1942, the representatives of nine German-occupied countries in London signed a declaration denouncing 'the reign of terror' of the occupation, with its mass expulsions, massacres, and execution of hostages, and declaring as a 'principal war aim' the punishment by judicial process of all who ordered, perpetrated, or took part in these crimes.[13] The great powers decided to go further. They carried out the plan for judging war criminals by special tribunal, either in Germany or in the countries where their crimes had been committed; but they also set up an international military tribunal to deal with the major criminals, whether individuals or groups, and with crimes which were far outside the definitions laid down by the Hague Convention of 1907.

This tribunal sat at Nuremberg from 20 November, 1945,

until 1 October, 1946. The principal individuals to come before it were the major surviving leaders of nazi Germany. The accused groups with which it dealt were the Reich government, the general staff, the S.A. the S.S., the S.D. (security service), the Gestapo, and the corps of nazi political directors. In the charter of the tribunal it is laid down that: "In cases where a group or organisation is declared criminal by the Tribunal, the competent national authority of any signatory shall have the right to bring individuals to trial for membership therein before national, military or occupation courts."[14] The crimes for which they could be convicted were of three orders: first, crimes against peace, defined according to the 1928 Briand-Kellog Pact, which outlawed war; second, war crimes, which included "murder, ill-treatment or deportation to slave labour or for any other purpose of civilian population of or in occupied territory, murder or ill-treatment of prisoners of war or persons on the seas, killing of hostages, plunder of public or private property, wanton destruction of cities, towns or villages, or devastation not justified by military necessity"; and finally "crimes against humanity, namely, murder, extermination, enslavement, deportation, and other inhumane acts committed against any civilian population, before or during the war, or persecutions on political, racial or religious grounds in execution of or in connection with any crime within the jurisdiction of the Tribunal, whether or not in violation of the domestic law of the country where perpetrated".

At the end of the long trial, which we cannot here describe in detail, the following judgments were pronounced: twelve of the accused were condemned to death, one of them *in absentia*, three were condemned to life imprisonment, and four to sentences between ten and twenty years. Three were acquitted, with the Soviet judge dissenting. The accused groups were for the most part found criminal, except the general staff and the Reich cabinet, and in these cases also the Soviet judge dissented. In studying the principles and conclusions of the tribunal we must limit ourselves to those aspects which most directly influenced the problem of defining collective guilt.

According to article 8 of the statute: "The fact that the defendant acted pursuant to order of his government or of a superior shall not free him from responsibility, but may be considered in mitigation of punishment if the Tribunal determines that justice so requires". The purpose of this article is clear. It was to prevent the accused from sheltering behind the orders of a superior. In a totalitarian régime this would mean that in the end the dictator himself would be the only guilty party. But the article implies that the accused, particularly if he was a soldier, ought to have been prepared to risk his life every time he received an order which he judged to be immoral. A French witness for the prosecution related at the trial that he, as a doctor, was made to select which of the sick should be transferred to a place where, to his knowledge, they were going to be liquidated, and the following exchange took place between the witness and the defence:[15]

"Why did you not say: 'I know what you are going to do, and I refuse to obey this order'?"

"Because it would have meant my death."

"Yes—and what would it have meant for any German who refused to obey a similar order?"

In every country in the world the refusal to obey an order while bearing arms has always been punishable by death; and the defence counsel for members of armed forces recalled this fact at every one of the numerous trials which took place after 1945.

On the other hand, if discipline had been allowed as an excuse it would have been impossible to speak of the collective guilt of organisations like the Waffen-S.S. and the Gestapo. The verdict condemned collectively all those who had become or remained members of these organisations knowing that they were responsible for criminal acts as defined by article 6 of the statute. But did a young man who was drafted to a section of the S.S. or the Gestapo (Secret State Police) necessarily know that these bodies committed crimes? And, once enrolled, could he get out without giving the reason and so risking death or concentration camp? The Nuremberg procedure, however, did not declare a man guilty for belonging to a criminal group; it only declared him liable to trial, and his effective participation in some specific crime had to be proved before he could be condemned. In one country only, France, was a law passed which rejected the fundamental legal principles of individual responsibility, and of placing the burden of proof upon the prosecution and not the defence. The French law of 15 September, 1948, laid down that "when a crime . . . is imputable to the collective action of a detachment or group forming part of an organisation condemned as criminal by the International Military Tribunal . . . all the individuals belonging to this detachment or group may be considered co-authors of the crime unless they can prove that they were forcibly enrolled and that they did not participate in the crime".[16] It was only the trial, in 1953, of German and Alsatian S.S. who had taken part in the massacre of Oradour that decided the French parliament to annul these provisions.

While the excuse of obedience to orders was advanced for the lower ranks, the excuse of ignorance was continually appealed to in the defence of the leaders, especially diplomats and military men. One atrocity would be explained as the independent act of a local authority, another as having been committed by police orders which by-passed the normal hierarchical channels. Each accusation and each trial thus presented special problems, and it cannot be claimed that all of them found equitable solutions. The problem of ignorance in any case vastly exceeds the scope of the trials. It concerned not merely those who appeared before the military tribunals but the whole population of Germany. It was asserted among the victors that the German people could not have failed to know what crimes were being perpetrated in the concentration camps and the occupied countries. The majority of Germans replied that they had known nothing at all. The two assertions, which were debated for years in the Press, in books, and in conversation, are both of them exaggerated. Many Germans really did have no idea of the crimes that were being committed in Germany's name; but others saw the forced labourers from the camps of torture being driven to work, or the machine-gunning or burning of some occupied village. Here again hasty generalisation should have been avoided. But the victors generalised in two contradictory ways. On the one hand they said to the Germans: "You are responsible for crimes of which you cannot have been ignorant", and on the other hand they launched a full-scale campaign of information, if not propaganda, to prove to these same Germans that the crimes in question had really been committed. It should have been unnecessary to turn such a blaze of limelight upon the Nuremberg trial, if the German people already knew all about the horrors to be revealed! This inconsistency considerably affected the attitude of Germans towards the revelation of nazi atrocities. There were many—as is shown by the large circulation of Kogon's book on the concentration camps—who wanted to know what atrocities had been committed; but many others, resenting the accusation of complicity hurled at them by the victors, preferred to rebut it either by treating the revelations as propaganda, or by a counter-attack, accusing their accusers of similar misdeeds, or else by firmly deciding to remain ignorant.[17]

It should have been realised that the Germans had just learned, through disaster, how false Hitler's propaganda had been, and that this made them very suspicious of any new propaganda. A differently conducted information campaign, with Germans playing a larger part in it, would have done more to allay their suspicions. But the manner in which the trials, particularly Nuremberg, were organised and presented could give the impression of a judgment founded on victory rather than justice.[18] There was a widespread reaction in Germany to the effect that: "We lost the war, so they say we are guilty. If Germany had won, the Russians would have been put on trial for the massacre of Polish officers at Katyn. See how cautiously they handled that affair at Nuremberg." As time went on the fact that a Russian judge and prosecutor had participated at the trial became more and more significant, for the western powers were soon accusing their ally of crimes similar to those that had been condemned at Nuremberg. Then came the Korean war, and the east imputed atrocities to American soldiers; and before that there had been the French debate on the conduct of the war in Indo-China. And in every case the accused governments claimed that they were the victims of lying propaganda. On which the Germans commented: "You are on the horns of a dilemma. Either you have committed, or permitted, crimes and in that case you have no right to set yourselves up with a good conscience as innocent dispensers of justice; or else you are victims of propaganda, which you ask us to disbelieve, and in that case you have no right to reproach us for having taken as propaganda the radio talks from London on German atrocities, or even your revelations of them after the war." In 1945 the allies decided against setting up a tribunal of neutrals to judge the big nazi criminals; but the passage of time has made it clear that this was a very grave error.

Nevertheless it would be wrong to make the allies solely responsible for the attitude of those Germans who did not want to know what Hitlerism had really been. Often it was due to fear, because once they knew the truth they would have to admit to themselves that they had always suspected it but refused to take it seriously, since that would have meant either taking a dangerous stand or else becoming an accomplice through one's silence. The fear of knowing was the symptom of guilt for a sin of omission. An appreciable number of Germans recognised and did not hesitate to confess openly that they had been guilty of weakness or cowardice and so bore a share of responsibility for crimes committed by others. They tried to lead as many as possible of their compatriots to a similar examination of conscience, which called for great humility and ability to forget one's own sufferings. Few words recur so often in German writing of that period as *Besinnung*—self-recollection. But this sense of responsibility could not be expressed in law or weighed by a judge; and this is what the occupying powers failed to remember when they undertook the process of "denazification".

The process was regulated by the sum total of a series of sometimes inconsistent orders. It alternated between severity and leniency,[19] and it was entered upon without any satisfactory previous definition of the principles which should guide it. The intention was, quite rightly, to deal only with individual cases, and the idea of collective guilt is nowhere mentioned.* But what cases should be dealt with? The first choice to be made was whether to purge all offenders or only the most important.

* It is important to distinguish between collective guilt and collective *responsibility*. The latter describes a fact and carries no moral condemnation. The collectivity of German citizens is in a sense civilly responsible towards other peoples for wrongs inflicted by the German state.

The former alternative was chosen because it appeared the more drastic, with the result that thirteen million dossiers had to be examined in the American zone alone. There was the double risk of foundering in a sea of paper or else of trying to save the situation by a switch to the collective accusations which were supposed to have been rejected. The next choice concerned the kind of offences to be tried, and here the principle established in the American zone, and afterwards extended to the others, was disastrously oversimplified. The primary test of guilt was to be membership of nazi organisations. The innumerable questions of the *Fragebogen* which the Germans had to fill in were essentially concerned with membership of the party itself or of its many political, paramilitary, sporting and cultural affiliations. But, as we have seen, membership of the party was not an infallible proof of nazism, and on the other hand many of those who had helped the régime had never belonged to the party.

There was a joke which soon became popular all over Germany: "What are the three meanings of the initials P.G. of which the third explains the other two? *Prisonnier de Guerre* (prisoner of war), *Partei-Genosse* (Party member), and *Pech gehabt* (had no luck)". It was especially among officials, whether administrative, legal or educational, that party membership had been made obligatory, or at least necessary if one wished to avoid ruin. So how was a purge to be combined with the carrying on of administration? Already in July, 1945, General Clay was writing in a report to General Eisenhower; "All too often, it seems that the only men with the qualifications . . . are the career civil servants . . . a great proportion of whom were more than nominal participants (by our definition) in the activities of the Nazi Party."[20] At first, too, the factor of age was forgotten. Yet could a boy who had never known any school but Hitler's be held guilty for becoming an active party member? In the end, there was an amnesty for those born after 1919, that is to say, for those who were less than fourteen when Hitler came to power. This was certainly not an error on the side of leniency!

The offences charged were not such as to incline the accused to plead guilty, and often it was much less a question of convincing him he had committed some specific offence than of saying to him: "Since you held such or such a position you must have known of the crimes being committed by others; since you profited from the régime, you are its accomplice". The accused were listed in five categories. In the highest were the important offenders and in the lowest the *Mitläufer* or followers and hangers-on. To be removed from a higher category to a lower was a favour which came to be known among the Germans as "receiving promotion". The system was such that the really guilty men, the ones who had knowingly assisted Hitler to make the régime what it became, had every chance of getting off lightly, for the following two reasons: First, their cases became indistinguishable among the mass of all the others; and second, they benefited from a psychological reaction which the allies ought to have foreseen: the fact that the threat of punishment hung over the heads of millions and millions of Germans prevented the mass of the population from siding with the victors against those Germans who had brought ruin upon them. There arose, on the contrary, a sort of solidarity against the allies among all the accused Germans, no matter what their degree of guilt.

In order not to give the impression of a justice based upon victory instead of law, and in order to reduce the mountains of dossiers, the occupying powers decided to entrust the purge more and more to the Germans themselves, though still keeping a general control. But where were judges to be found whom the people would recognise as fair? Against the returned antifascist exiles it was objected that they could not know what the German situation under Himmler had been, with all its constraints and inevitable compromises; and members of the internal opposition were considered to be often unable to prove their active resistance and to be as much compromised as many of the accused. And all of them were regarded as merely puppets of the allies. In the circumstances it is not surprising that satisfactory justice was not always administered. But worse than that, there was injustice, pure and simple. The thoroughness of the purge varied according to the usefulness of the accused to the occupying powers. In the early days of Hitler certain Jews could be seen wearing armbands with the initials

W.W.J.—*wirtschaftlich wertvoller Jude* (economically useful Jew); and under the occupation there was a class which might be called 'economically useful nazis', though this time without armbands. A rigorous purge of teachers was essential for the country's spiritual future—but what about the 'managers' of the German economy, who had played such an important role in Hitler's accession to power, had flattered and been cossetted by the régime, and had done everything to help it in preparing and then in prolonging the war? Under the pretext that their assistance had been technical and not political, and on the ground, often well justified, that their abilities were required for coping with the economic chaos, all but the most prominent of them were left alone, including many who were certainly much guiltier than the little town clerk and elementary schoolmaster who were purged and thrown into destitution.

There was another problem, and an essential one, that had been overlooked. If there was to be 'denazification' on the grand scale, what was to be done with those who were purged? It is possible when dealing with a limited number of people to condemn some of them to be no more than street cleaners or office boys and to forbid certain professions or occupations to others, but not when one is dealing with hundreds of thousands. When this was perceived, two kinds of palliative were resorted to: amnesties and temporary suspensions of function. The latter involved the implication that a 'nazi' official could be transformed into a 'democrat' by the simple expedient of being given leave without pay for two or three years. It seems more likely that he would merely resume his work filled with rancour and bitterness; and there is no doubt that this is what in fact happened. It was the most deplorable of the effects of a method of 'denazification' that was at once too severe and too lenient, too broad and too restricted. Its result has been to create in Germany a peculiar social class consisting of the 'denazified'. Embittered, and in a position to believe that they have been punished for their opinions, they have often become averse to politics of any kind, from fear of being denounced once again to future tribunals. Of all the after-effects of a bungled 'denazification' this one was the most lasting.[21]

* * *

If the occupation régime had shown the German people what conception of justice and democracy the victors had to set against Hitler's arbitrary fiats, if there had been a coherent policy of material and psychological reconstruction alongside the repressive measures and the purges, the mismanagement of the denazification would have had less serious results. But unfortunately it was not so.[22] By the mere exercise of absolute sovereignty, the victors did not appear to be particularly democratic, and the fact that they began by showing a total and systematic mistrust of all Germans without exception was not encouraging to those who looked to them as liberators. But it must be remembered that J.C.S.1067 laid down that "Germany will not be occupied for the purpose of liberation but as a defeated enemy nation", and accordingly no "fraternisation" was at first allowed, and the underground opposition groups which emerged to greet the victors in confidence and hope were forbidden to indulge in any political activity. When the commanders-in-chief set to work in their zones they were faced with a double task: to bring order from chaos, and to take long-term measures for democratisation. To start with the working assumption that the two tasks were separable meant necessarily to neglect the second for the first. In criticising the occupation, however, it should always be borne in mind that the task before the allied authorities was immense: the rebuilding of a German administration to carry out the allies' orders, the restoration of communications, re-opening of factories, and provisioning of the population. In addition it was necessary to arrange, in the American zone alone, for the return to their countries of two million persons "displaced" by the Germans, and for the repatriation of the greater part of three million American soldiers from various parts of Europe, while finding place for $4\frac{1}{2}$ million refugees and expelled persons from the east. There can be no question that the achievement of the military governments was prodigious.

For their immediate and long-term objectives the commanders-in-chief required a considerable administrative personnel in addition to the occupation troops. The composition and recruitment of this personnel played an essential role in the functioning of the occupation. The general trend was progressively to replace military by 'assimilated' personnel—the latter being civilians in uniform holding temporary rank. But in practice there were considerable differences between the three zones. The British administrators were often of very high technical ability, and as it was their government's policy to carry out direct administration, even in local affairs, they were very numerous—approximately twenty-two thousand in 1946. They administered Germany as they would have administered a crown colony, with the same calm activity and contempt for the "natives". Both officials and soldiers behaved with a distant correctness and lived so far as possible apart from the German population, although the non-fraternisation order was revoked at the end of 1945. From 1946, however, the quality of the British personnel deteriorated perceptibly. As the occupation continued, the better elements wanted to return home, where they could get permanent work, and they were often replaced by men who had been unable to find well-paid jobs in England. The political tendency of the British occupation was in general conservative, in spite of there being a Labour government in London.

The American administrators numbered only about five thousand at the end of 1946, although their zone was a little larger and nearly as populous as the British.* With very few exceptions, they lacked really first-class men, although on the whole administrative discipline was high. In local affairs they exercised control but did not directly administer. The chief positions were held by technicians from the administration, the army, and the universities; but after 1946 they were gradually replaced by industrialists and business men. All of them alike wished to continue to enjoy "the American way of life" and failed to understand what an effect the luxury which seemed to them normal must have upon famished Germans. Nor did the American troops imitate the discretion of their British comrades. The euphoria of victory and the hurry of repatriation led to an incredible relaxation of discipline. Early in 1946 General MacNarney drew attention in an order of the day to the principal misdemeanours in the army he com-

* 107,500 sq. kilometres as against 97,700, and 17·1 million inhabitants as against 22·3 million, according to the census of 1946.

manded: intensive black-marketeering, absence without leave, dangerous driving, drunkenness, venereal disease, slovenly appearance.[23] From 1946, discipline improved but the black market continued to flourish. The temptation to get a Leica camera in exchange for cigarettes was too great.

The lifting of the ban on fraternisation made it possible to go more safely and openly with German girls and one result of this, apart from the increase of illegitimate births, had a certain political importance. Never having lived under an occupation and knowing almost no history, the soldiers rebelled against their government's harsh occupation policy. How could the welcoming family of Lisbeth or Hanna have anything in common with the nazi criminals? Thus they adopted in another form the same attitude as military chiefs like General Patton, and the businessmen administrators. Patton was removed from his command in Bavaria because he was utterly opposed to denazification on the ground that there was no more difference between nazi and anti-nazi Germans than between republican and democratic Americans;[24] and the businessmen administrators would not admit that *Bankdirektor* Müller had ever been anything but a decent and completely non-political business man. The total of these reactions, which were spontaneous rather than considered, and acted upon rather than formulated, had a profound effect upon the day-to-day application of American policy.

The French zone, with 42,800 sq. kilometres and 5,900,000 inhabitants, was by far the smallest of the three, but it had the largest number of occupation personnel. The reason for this was not that the French administrators were proportionately more numerous than the British, but the proximity of France. The personnel of the other zones also had the right to bring their families, but in the French zone the definition of 'family' was so loose as to include grandmothers-in-law and grand-nephews. Prone to make confiscations on their own account, accessible to the temptations of the black market, arrogant and exacting towards the Germans, and meanly asserting the prestige of a victory to which most of them had contributed nothing at all, these lazy and parasitic 'occupiers' were the scandal of the French occupation in Germany. Nor was the working personnel irreproachable. It had been recruited haphazardly and at the same time as the first purges in France. Thus a good many of the officials were former 'collaborators' who were escaping from embarrassments at home. Such men were not too well qualified to undertake "denazification" in collaboration with colleagues who had been members of the resistance.

If discipline among the troops was better than in the American zone, it was very poor among the central, regional and local chiefs. The commander-in-chief at Baden-Baden behaved like a pro-consul and was not over-attentive to instructions from Paris; and the provincial delegates at Coblenz, Freiburg and Tübingen were in no hurry to obey orders from Baden-Baden. On lower levels it was the same. Everyone was revelling in the act of government and in the enjoyment of an almost absolute authority. So as worthily to represent the French Republic in a country believed to respect only force and to admire munificence, a large part of the occupation's budget was spent on luxury. Car parks, large-scale entertaining, brilliant fêtes, shooting parties, special trains and boats—such was the example set by the higher grades and imitated so far as possible by the local kinglets. This provocative façade obscured from the majority of Germans an important element of the French occupation—a number of officials who not only took their work seriously but were also, without doubt, the only ones in all the three military governments with a profound grasp of Germany's psychological problems. That they achieved good work in spite of the general atmosphere of the French occupation is enough to prove their value and their determination.

The outward appearance of the occupation, therefore, hardly gave the impression of virtuous conquerors come to raise the morality of defeated delinquents. Yet this was the dominant theme of the whole programme of "re-education." All Germans, and especially the young, had been exposed to an evil influence and were therefore in a certain sense badly educated, and must be re-educated so as to become good democrats. And since it was agreed that at home in the United States, Britain and France there was true democracy, all that was needed was to establish in Germany, whether by persuasion or force, the American, British or French systems of general and political education. It followed that German youth was exposed to three remarkably different influences.[25] In the American zone, for example, education was based on the principle that healthy democracy springs from the political development of the individual, independent of any framework of political or religious theory. So clubs and youth parliaments and non-political interdenominational groups were encouraged at the expense of any organised movements with a clear ideological tendency. On the same principle, the American military government would not allow political newspapers but only granted licences to organs of general information, whose editorial staff was obliged to include representatives of various political tendencies. As the American authorities possessed considerable resources they were able not only to establish *Amerikahäuser* (America Houses) but also to finance all kinds of centres and institutes for German youth; but it was not until 1950 that these financial benefits reached their culmination when the McCloy fund financed a large number of students' hostels, children's villages, and other social welfare institutions. The powers in the other two zones, however, judging that the American system promoted a sort of vague and invertebrate idealism, went the other way and encouraged the clear and open expression of the most diverse tendencies; and it is legitimate to mention here—since the English and Americans admitted it later—that the most fruitful method of approach to the younger generation of Germans was conceived in the French zone.

The French cultural effort in Germany took many forms: from the remarkable schools for teachers to the creation of the university of Mainz, from the drafting of text-books (sometimes disastrously bad) to the introduction of the baccalauréat. Being much wider in scope than the work of the other occupying powers, it had more successes and also more failures. But the really original French action was carried out against the general tendency of the administration and against the isolation of the zone, which was a sort of political dogma of the French occupation. A trade union or political leader was not allowed to leave the zone to meet a colleague in the American or British zones, and the people of Mainz and Freiburg never saw a French newspaper, although those of Düsseldorf and Munich could buy the *Daily Mail* or the *New York Times* at any news stall.

A few occupation officials perceived the inconsistency of this policy and had the courage to act accordingly. They saw the unreason of blaming young Germans for being nationalist while at the same time forbidding them any contact with the world outside Germany; they were wise enough to renounce the pharisaism of "re-education", admitting that not everything in Germany was bad and that everything that was happening in France was not perfect. They added that German youth must be free to learn and to meet the youth of other countries, and were perceptive enough to recognise that many of the young leaders of the Hitler Youth had been more remarkable for their personal qualities than for fanaticism, and that it was absurd to treat them as pariahs for the rest of their lives. Already in 1945, though cautiously at first, international meetings were arranged, and a movement was thus started which was to spread continually and be imitated in the other zones. We shall return to it later.*

Unfortunately it happened too late, when a great part of the population had become bitter and hostile to the occupying forces, who seemed too unaware of the fact that the people whom they were asking to admire their high principles were themselves hungry and wretched, and who failed to see that among the masses about whom they generalised there were millions of individuals each of whom had lived through a personal tragedy.[26] At the end of 1946 there were in Hamburg 100,000 sufferers from oedemas due to undernourishment, and at Cologne only 12 per cent of the children were of normal weight. According to the United Nations' experts the daily requirement of calories for health and normal work is 2,650, but the official ration in Germany was 1,500 and the real ration often much below 1,000. Whole families were crowded in underground bunkers without water or light. Clothes and medicine were unprocurable, and money had lost all value. The result was a profound demoralisation, for what point was

* See chapter vii.

there in working if a few cigarettes would buy as much food as a tram-driver's monthly wage? And why go hungry when you could get packets of chocolate or coffee beyond price simply for obliging an American soldier? The subways of stations were filled with boys proposing bargains of every sort; and if there are today ten times more prostitutes in Cologne than before the war, it is because the extreme misery of the years 1945-47 gave rise to habits which are not so easily unlearnt.

Influential people abroad saw the need to do something about Germany's deplorable state.[27] A number of private individuals, in rich America and impoverished England, had been sending food parcels to individuals in Germany ever since the end of hostilities; and many charitable and, in particular, religious organisations combined in a movement whose proportions are partly explained by the Germanic origin of a large number of Americans. It was the campaigns of Victor Gollancz in England and Herbert Hoover in America, however, that attracted the most attention. Gollancz behaved with great discretion and never allowed his indignation at the miseries of Germany and the mistakes of the allies to blind him to the past and present suffering of other countries; but the former president of the United States went much further and almost represented Germany as the innocent martyred victim of ruthless conquerors. Many an American family felt morally obliged to help a German family without realising, very often, that there were also families in Caen or Belgrade to whom a food parcel would not have come amiss.

German gratitude was on the whole somewhat restrained, and foreign help was accepted as though it were a very inadequate atonement for undeserved suffering. Unbiassed observers could not avoid the impression of a concerted playing-up of Germany's miseries, in order to induce a relaxation of the harsh occupation policy and also to discourage confiscations of production or plant. The figures in the Hoover report which showed that famine would have been much worse without the official Anglo-American aid were hardly quoted at all in Germany, and from Gollancz's book the photographs of emaciated German children were much more often reproduced

F

than the descriptions of Hitler's concentration camps. Listening to the complaints from almost every German they met, foreign visitors were invariably struck with their extraordinary self-centredness. People in Germany were quite unconcerned at hearing about the meagre rations in occupied France, and were even unaware that the French were still rationed. When they were told, the information was received with smiles of incredulity.

To sum up in a word the most tragic aspect of those dismal times, it was incomprehension. Visitors to Germany did not comprehend the misery of the Germans, and the Germans could not or would not comprehend the horrible acts of which their misery was the sequel. There were many Germans who allowed no credit for foreign aid or for the efforts of the occupying powers to set the German economy to rights, but had eyes only for the "Morgenthau plan" aspect of the occupation policy; accordingly, they saw their country's prodigious economic recovery as taking place in spite of the victorious powers, and their pride in it was a mixture of arrogance and defiance.

NOTES TO CHAPTER II

[1] The most easily accessible statistical sources for chapters two to six are: Mehnert-Schulte, *Deutschland-Jahrbuch* (Essen, 1949) and the later edition (1953) with some important sections of a general character; and *Statistisches Jahrbuch für die Bundesrepublik Deutschland* (Stuttgart, 1952) which is to appear annually in future. *Sozialtaschenbuch* 1952. *Deutsche Sozialstatistik für die Praxis* (Frankfurt, 1952), published by the Institut zur Förderung öffentlicher Angelegenheiten is also very useful. Guidance on official statistical material is given in *Bibliographie der amtlichen westdeutschen Statistik 1945-1951* (Munich, 1952).

Few accounts of Germany in defeat were published in 1945 and 1946; they became more frequent after 1947. For the first period, see Edgar Morin, *L'an zéro de l'Allemagne* (1946), well informed and highly critical; S. K. Padover, *Psychologist in Germany* (London, 1946), extremely useful for his remarks on the state of mind in Germany in 1944-45; P. Knauth, *Germany in defeat* (New York, 1946); W. L. Shirer, *End of a Berlin Diary* (London, 1947), analysing the origins of the conflict between the Morgenthau and Hoover proposals; S. Spender, *European Witness* (London, 1946). For the second period, see Esprit, *Les Allemands parlent de l'Allemagne* (June, 1947, special number), the best collection of essays by Germans; R. J. Havighurst, *Report on Germany* (Rockefeller Foundation, duplicated, 1947); Fédération de l'Éducation nationale, *Allemagne 1947* (Paris, 1947). Edgar Morin's *Allemagne, notre souci* (Paris, 1947), and G. Soria's *L'Allemagne a-t-elle perdu la guerre?* show a marked bias against the western zones. Gustav Stolper's *German realities* (New York, 1948), is frenziedly anti-communist. Victor Gollancz, *In darkest*

Germany (London, 1947), may be compared with Pollock and Meisel, *Germany under occupation* (Ann Arbor, 1947), containing the Hoover report, which draws pro-German conclusions from the same terrible reality, and with Jean Guignebert, *A l'écoute de l'Allemagne* (Paris, 1947), where the same facts give rise to anti-German observations.

[2] See *Dokumente zur Austreibung der Sudetendeutschen* (Munich, 1951); J. Kaps, ed., *Die Tragödie Schlesiens 1945–1946* (1953); Bundesministerium für Vertriebene, *Dokumentation der Vertreibung der Deutschen aus Ost-Mitteleuropa* (1953); F. Bednar, *The transfer of Germans from Czechoslovakia from the ideological and ecclesiastical standpoint* (Prague, 1948), an apologia by a leading Czech Protestant for expulsion which reveals in guarded terms the frightful conditions in which the expulsions occurred; Father E. J. Reichenberger) *Ostdeutsche Passion* (Düsseldorf, 1948), vehement and extreme in tone; Kirchliche Hilfstelle Muenchen, *The Martyrdom of Silesian Priests* (Munich, 1950); Goettinger Arbeitskreis, *Dokumente der Menschlichkeit aus der Zeit der Massenaustreibungen* (Kitzingen, 1950), a collection of eye witness accounts of acts of humanity performed by men of all nations during the great exodus, which involuntarily give a shattering picture of what happened.

[3] The vast bibliography on this question may be divided into three categories (apart from those listed in notes 18 and 22). There are first of all the implacable accusers like Emil Ludwig, *The Moral Conquest of Germany* (New York, 1945); Lord Vansittart, *Black Record* (London, 1941); and F. W. Foerster, *Europe and the German question* (London, 1941). Secondly, there are the writers who view the question in a broader philosophical and historical perspective, such as Friedrich Meinecke, *Die deutsche Katastrophe* (3rd ed., Wiesbaden 1947); Gerhard Ritter, *Europa und die deutsche Frage* (Munich, 1948); W. Röpke, *Die deutsche Frage* (Zurich, 1945), an important book; Reinhold Schneider, *L'homme devant le jugement de l'histoire;* Max Picard, *Hitler in uns selbst* (Zurich, 1946); and E. Niekisch, *Das Reich der niederen Dämonen* (Hamburg, 1953), a book which has aroused passionate discussion in Germany.

Finally, there are the analysts, well-informed, objective, and humane, such as Karl Jaspers, *Die Schuldfrage* (Heidelberg, 1946), and *Die Antwort an Sigrid Undset* (Constance, 1947); Ernst von Schenk, *Europa vor der deutschen Frage* (Berne, 1946), which shows a deep understanding of the problem; Max Pribilla, *Deutschland nach dem Zusammenbruch* (Hamburg, 1947); Karl Barth, *Zur Genesung des deutschen Wesens* (Stuttgart, 1947); Martin Niemöller, *De la culpabilité allemande*; Ernst Wiechert, *Rede an die deutsche Jugend* (Berlin, 1947); H. Zbinden, *De l'avenir de l'Allemagne* (Paris, 1947); and, most important, Robert d'Harcourt, *Comment traiter l'Allemagne?* (Paris, 1946), and *Les Allemands d'aujourd'hui* (Paris, 1948).

[4] F. W. Foerster, op. cit., p. 414.

[5] The full text is given in *Les Entretiens Franco-Allemands*, a special number of the bulletin issued by the Société des Professeurs d'Histoire et de Géographie de l'Enseignement public (March, 1952).

[6] The basic work on the opposition is G. Weisenborn (ed.) *Der lautlose Aufstand: Bericht über die Widerstandsbewegung des deutschen Volkes 1933–1945* (Hamburg, 1953). See also Inge Scholl, *Die weisse Rose* (Frankfurt, 1952), a moving book; H. Rothfels, *The German Opposition to Hitler* (Illinois, 1948), essential in spite of its tendency to overestimate the scope of the opposition; the first chapter in the symposium edited by G. A. Almond, *The Struggle for Democracy in Germany* (University of North Carolina, 1949): R. Pechel, *Deutscher Widerstand* (Erlebach, 1947); M. Mourin, *Les complots contre Hitler* (Paris, 1948); and Allan W. Dulles, *Germany's Underground* (New York, 1947). Of the accounts written by those who took part the best are

Ulrich von Hassell, *The von Hassell Diaries* (London, 1948); H. B. Gisevius, *To the Bitter End* (London, 1948); F. von Schlabrendorff, *Revolt against Hitler* (London, 1948). Some good portraits of the principal actors are to be found in Graf Lutz Schwerin von Krosigk, *Es geschah in Deutschland* (Tübingen, 1951). The best account of the attempt of 20 July is given in Eberhard Zeller, *Geist der Freiheit: Der 20 Juli 1944* (Munich, 1952).

For the resistance of the churches see the notes to chapter v.

[7] See, for example, Great Britain, Foreign Office, *Papers concerning the treatment of German nationals in Germany 1938-1939* (London, 1939). An outstanding German book on the concentration camps is Eugen Kogon's *Der S.S. Staat* (*The Theory and Practice of Hell*, London, 1950).

[8] The figures are given in G. Weisenborn, op. cit.

[9] Quoted by H. Rothfels, op. cit., p. 17.

[10] Ibid., pp. 140 and 152.

[11] Desmond Young, *Rommel* (London, 1950). See also Lutz Koch, *Erwin Rommel* (Stuttgart, 1950). The same tendency is expressed, with greater insolence, in W. Lüdde-Neurath, op. cit., and more clumsily in General Karl Koller, op. cit. For a general historical account of the German general staff see W. Goerlitz, *Der deutsche Generalstab* (Frankfurt, 1950). On the attitude of the army see also A. Heusinger, *Befehl im Widerstreit* (Tübingen, 1950), and J. W. Wheeler-Bennett, *The Nemesis of Power* (New York, 1954).

[12] H. Guderian, *Erinnerungen eines Soldaten* (Heidelberg, 1951), p. 314.

[13] The text is given in Inter-Allied Information Committee, *Punishment for War Crimes* (London, 1942). The bibliography of the Nuremberg trial is very large. One of the first books to appear was Marcel Merle, *Le procès de Nuremberg et le châtiment des criminels de guerre* (Paris, 1945). Good introductions to the subject are Donnedieu de Vabres, *Le procès de Nuremberg* (thesis, duplicated, 1947); Telford Taylor, *The Nuremberg Trials* (New York, 1949); Heinze and Schilling, *Die Rechtssprechung der Nürnberger Militärtribunale* (Bonn, 1952). The proceedings were published in International Military Tribunal, *Trial of the Major War Criminals* (42 volumes, 1947-49). For the defence see Carl Haensel, *Das Gericht vertagt sich* (Hamburg, 1950); Laternser, *Verteidigung deutscher Soldaten: Plädoyers vor alliierten Gerichten* (Hamburg, n.d.).

[14] This and the following quotations are taken from D. de Vabres, op. cit.

[15] *Le Procès de Nuremberg: L'accusation française* (1946-47), pp. 137, 190.

[16] See Raymond de la Pradelle, *L'affaire d'Ascq* (Paris, 1949).

[17] See Eugen Kogon, op. cit. Symptomatic of the wish to know the facts is the great success of the book by Max Fechner, *Wie konnte es geschehen?* (Berlin, 1946).

[18] No German could be more virulent in counter-charge than the book by a Frenchman, which has been banned, M. Bardèche, *Nuremberg, ou la terre promise* (Paris, 1948).

[19] See, for example, J. Sigmann, *Qu'est-ce qu'un nazi?* (no place or date); Hass-Simon, *Die Denazifierung, Gesetz und Verfahren* (Heidelberg, 1946).

[20] Lucius D. Clay, op. cit., p. 67.

[21] To grasp the nature and extent of this phenomenon see Ernst von Salomon, *Der Fragebogen* (Hamburg, 1951), which in a year and a half sold more than 160,000 copies.

[22] For the organisation and functioning of the occupation see the publications of the Department of State already cited, Lucius D. Clay, *Decision in Germany*, M. Virally, op. cit., W. Friedmann, op. cit., H. Menahem, op. cit., and Alexander Lane, *Verfassung und Verwaltung der vier Besatzungszonen Deutschlands* (Mainz, 1948);

M. Martin, *La législation française en Allemagne* (Baden-Baden, 1947); H. Holborn, *American Military Government* (Washington, 1947); H. Zink, *American Military Government in Germany* (New York, 1947); E. Plischke, *The Allied High Commission for Germany* (Bad Godesberg, 1953); E. H. Litchfield, op. cit. Severe criticism of the principles of the occupation is to be found in R. Nadolny, *Völkerrecht und deutscher Frieden* (Hamburg, 1949), and the charge of nazism against the occupiers in Yves Farge, *La guerre d'Hitler continue* (Paris, 1948), which is frequently inaccurate and extreme, and the charge of anti-German savagery in Freda Utley, op. cit., and Father E. J. Reichenberger, *Europa in Trümmern* (Graz, 1950).

[23] The text is given in Warburg, *Germany, Bridge or Battleground*, p. 83.

[24] Quoted in J. S. Martin, op. cit., p. 169.

[25] See for example Centre d'études de politique étrangère, *L'éducation de l'Allemagne occupée* (Paris, 1949), and for the American attitude, Department of State, *Young Germany, Apprentice to Democracy* (Washington, 1951).

[26] On this point see in particular V. Gheorghiu, *La Vingt-cinquième heure* (Paris, 1949); the two novels by Hans Werner Richter, *Die Geschlagenen* (Munich, 1949), and *Sie fielen aus Gottes Hand* (Munich, 1951); and Karl Vogel, *M–AA 509* (Memmingen, 1951), a fairly objective account by a 'trusty' of an American internment camp for Nazis; and G. H. Mostar, *Im Namen des Gesetzes* (Hamburg, 1950), on the surface a banal account of a trial before a German tribunal, but in fact a human and varied picture of German post-war chaos.

[27] Compare Victor Gollancz, op. cit., and Pollock and Meisel, op. cit. On private American aid see E. McSweeney, *Amerikanische Wohlfahrtshilfe für Deutschland, 1945–1950* (Freiburg, 1950).

CHAPTER III

ECONOMIC RECOVERY[1]

IN September, 1946, there were ten thousand hospital patients in the Düsseldorf area suffering from deficiencies due to hunger. In June, 1952, the president of the Rhineland-Westphalia Diet announced that the seats of the chamber at Düsseldorf were to be replaced by larger ones. Having been installed six years earlier, they were no longer broad enough for the bulk of the average deputy of 1952. In 1946 the index of industrial production was 33 (1936 = 100), and eight years later it was nearly 190. So here we have both symbol and proof of Germany's prodigious recovery and swift return to prosperity. We should need, however, to know one more figure before being able to conclude that success has been complete, namely, how many of the ten thousand starvation cases of 1946 are still in want. Certainly, the figure will be high. At the time when the production index reached 160 the Stuttgart education inspector made a survey which showed that out of the 45,900 children attending his schools there were 4,073 who had no bed of their own. So we must beware of supposing that the economic recovery and strength of Germany necessarily imply the prosperity of all its inhabitants.*

After the defeat German industry was at a standstill, but not destroyed.[2] So little was produced and the visible destruction in Germany was so striking, that the potential of production might have seemed to be decisively reduced. But this was not the case. Although the towns were wiped out, the destruction of plant was only 10 per cent for metallurgy, 10–15 per cent for the chemical industry, 15–20 per cent for engineering, and 20 per cent for textiles. There were a number of reasons for this comparative immunity: the efficient camouflaging of factories and the German system of dispersal, the allies' concentration on the bombing of towns "to sap the morale of the population", which left the factories relatively intact,

* The figures in this chapter have been brought where possible to the end of 1954.

and finally the "selective" bombings which spared certain factories in which non-German companies had an interest. The immense I.G. Farben head office, which remained intact at Frankfurt while three-quarters of the town was destroyed, stands as the symbol of a war which was not quite total, for certain people.[8] Such productive capacity as did survive the war was considerably diminished by the policy of the victors. The level of production was fixed by the quadripartite plan of 26 March, 1946, at about 50 per cent of 1938, the best prewar year. Among the products completely banned were petrol, synthetic rubber and radioactive material; steel might not exceed $7\frac{1}{2}$ million tons a year—less than the 1938 production of the Vereinigte Stahlwerke alone; the basic chemical industry was reduced to less than 40 per cent of its 1936 production, and the pharmaceutical industry to 80 per cent. Furniture, glass and bicycles were almost the only articles whose manufacture was uncontrolled; but there was to be the maximum possible production of coal.

This policy was intended to destroy the economic basis of German military power and thus make available some "surplus" material for distribution as reparations to the victors. At the same time it sought to decentralise Germany's industry and liquidate the system of trusts and cartels through which six banks and seventy combines had been able to control two-thirds of German industry and six combines to own, in 1938, 98 per cent of the foundries and 95 per cent of the steel output of the Ruhr. The limitation of production, confiscations, and the transformation of industry were in theory three separate objectives, but in practice they were intermixed and soon appeared as three inextricably combined methods towards a single end—the permanent weakening of the German economy.

When in due course this tendency was reversed and it became the official policy to reestablish the economy, there were those who thought—or pretended to think—that a return to the former level of production must necessarily be accompanied by the reintroduction of certain features of the former industrial organisation. During the two years from 1945–47 the debate continued in the American military government between those who wished to make a distinction and those who confused the issue in order to persuade American and German opinion that any discrimination against the former masters of the German economy was simply another aspect of the "Morgenthau plan" policy. Yet when the British authorities arrested Hugo Stinnes and thirty-nine other members of the mining cartel on 6 September, 1945, and took over the control of the Krupp factories on 16 November, they did not appear to damage Germany's capacity for industrial production in any way. On the other hand, by 1949, article 18 of the Ruhr International Authority agreement appeared to be out of date and to discriminate against Germany when it made the Military Security Board responsible for preventing persons convicted or liable to be convicted "of having encouraged the aggressive designs of the national socialist party" from holding managerial or proprietary interests in the coal, coke or steel industries of the Ruhr or in the professional and commercial organisations of those industries.

Such confusion would never have been possible, had the allies not begun by completely misunderstanding Germany's economic situation. The secretary of the international reparations agency declared in March, 1947: "The over-industrialisation of Germany for military purposes has created conditions in which, despite destruction and the exceptional wear and tear of war, there remains an industrial potential which in any case ... is vastly superior to the requirements of a peace-time economy." After the publication of the first Anglo-American plan to raise the economic level of Bizonia, the same agency reported: "The effect of the new plan will be to retain sufficient capacity in the Bizonal Area to approximate the level of industry prevailing in Germany in 1936, a year that was not characterised by either boom or depressed conditions."[4] In other words, Germany's peace-time needs in 1947 should not be greater than in 1936; and this might have been so if there had been no ruined towns, no loss of territory east of the Oder, no partition of the country, no refugees, no occupation costs, and no social charges resulting from the war. Certainly the Germany of 1938 was over-industrialised, but could one reasonably say the same of western Germany after the war?

The present area of the Federal Republic is 245,000 sq. kilometres* and in 1939 it contained a population of 39·3 millions. The 1946 census showed a population of 43·7 millions, in spite of military and civilian war casualties; by the 1950 census, after the return of prisoners and a new influx of refugees from the east, there were 47·7 millions, and today the figure is approaching 50 millions. The density of population thus increased from 160·4 inhabitants per sq. km. in 1939 to 178·1 in 1946 and 194·4 in 1950. Such figures do not necessarily mean poverty. For Great Britain, Holland and Belgium respectively they are 206, 275, and 282.[5] But a country so densely populated, unless it is to live off charity, must be able to feed its people, either by itself producing the food it needs or else by importing it in exchange for raw materials or manufactured goods.

Pre-war Germany, in spite of possessing rich agricultural lands in the east, was obliged to import 20 per cent of her food; but the deficit for the three western zones, when separated from the regions east of the Oder-Neisse line and then, almost immediately afterwards, from the Soviet occupation zone, was more than 50 per cent. Intensive agriculture had long been practised all over Germany, but increased efforts were now made in the three zones and by 1952 the yield of wheat in tons per acre was 1·2 for the Federal Republic as against approximately 1 ton for Britain, 0·7 for France, and 0·4 for the United States. For potatoes the corresponding figures were approximately $8\frac{1}{2}$, $7\frac{1}{2}$, 5, and 6 tons respectively, and for barley 0·94, 0·82, 0·4, and 0·35. But in 1953, in spite of intensive production, western Germany's food deficit was still 4 per cent in meat, 26 per cent in sugar and eggs, 28 per cent in flour, and 55 per cent in fats; and this although individual consumption remained relatively low.[6]

It was therefore indispensable that industry should produce not only for reconstruction needs but also, and above all, to make possible the import of food; and since the imports were required to feed a considerably increased population, it is misleading to compare total production with that of 1936. The average index figure for 1950 was 109·5, but when allowance is

* In 1937 Germany's area was 470,000 sq. kilometres, with a population of 69·3 millions.

made for the increase of population since 1936 it only amounts to 86. A country cannot export unless other countries will import, and we shall study in this chapter Germany's problem of finding outlets for her exportable goods—bearing always in mind that she had no alternative between dying of starvation and living on the charity of the United States, unless she could revive and develop her own industry. If the allies had all of them admitted that the situation left Germany no other choice, the Germans would have been less critical of their treatment of the German economy, even when that treatment was in other respects inconsistent and vacillating.

We will examine in turn the application of each of the three principles already mentioned—confiscation, limitation of output, and transformation of industry. The costs of the occupation and the various types of reparations come under the heading of confiscation; the former representing a very heavy financial and economic burden upon Germany's resources.[7] From 1946 to 1950, in the three western zones combined, the annual percentage of total taxation reserved to pay for the occupation was 42 per cent (in 1946), 38, 33, 26, and 28 per cent (in 1950). If we take the figures for the French zone separately, from 1946 to 1949, they are as high as 86, 49, 41, and 38 per cent. The 1950 figure represents 96 marks* per head for the total population, or 210 marks per head (the monthly salary of a clerical worker) for the active working part of it. The money was spent in a variety of ways, and too often it went in luxuries for the occupation personnel and their families. Thus, for the period July, 1949 to June, 1950 alone, 14,258 electric refrigerators were purchased for the Americans and British.

That the nations victimised by Hitler had a right to reparations is incontestable, and they exerted it in various ways. The German merchant marine had been divided among the Big Three at Potsdam, and they re-allocated a part of their shares to other countries. The transatlantic liner *Europa* was given to France and re-named *Liberté*. German industrial patents were annulled, and it was claimed later in Germany that the free

* One mark = approx. 1s. 8d. or 24 cents.

use of German patented processes was equivalent to a reparations payment of several milliard marks to the users. Prisoners were kept at work abroad long after the war. There were 470,000 of them in France at the end of 1945 in factories, building and agriculture, and when they were liberated between April, 1947, and April, 1948, 116,000 of them elected to remain in France as free workers. Between 1946 and 1948 9½ million cubic metres of timber were sent from the French zone to France as partial compensation for the 30 million cubic metres taken from French forests during the German occupation, and the Saar, with its mines and metals, was incorporated into the French economy. But it was intended to obtain the bulk of reparations from the dismantling of industrial plant.[8]

What should have been done was to decide quickly which factories or parts of factories were to be confiscated and to organise in careful detail their removal to and reassembly in the confiscating country. But in fact it was done slowly and by fits and starts, and the confusion was made worse by a blurring of the distinction between dismantling for removal and pure and simple destruction. After 1947, and still more after 1949, the occupying powers changed their policy, first permitting and then encouraging Germany's economic revival. As a result there were continual hesitations and reversed decisions, and the list of factories for dismantling became a sort of *peau de chagrin*, diminishing from 1,800 in March, 1946, to 858 in August, 1947, and 697 in February, 1949, in which year most of the actual dismantling was done. Of all the removals of metallurgical equipment after 1945, 93 per cent was carried out in 1949.

But the results of dismantling were often a disappointment, for the material lost much of its value when disassembled and, moreover, one part of a factory would go to Belgium and another to France, while a third was left to rust in Germany. And after 1948 a new and unsatisfactory development was liable to occur: the no-longer new material received by the confiscating countries was liable to be replaced in Germany by ultramodern machinery from the United States. In all, about a milliard dollars' worth of plant was removed, but with delays and hesitations and to a growing chorus of German protest.

The removals of plant were creating unemployment; at Duisburg-Hamborn the livelihood of more than 100,000 people depended entirely upon the Thyssen steel-works, which remained on the list for dismantling until 1949. Clearly, said the Germans, this policy condemned Germany to remain in misery. It could be argued in reply that the other European countries had the right to priority in reconstruction, and this principle was asserted in many allied pronouncements from 1945 to 1949; but the dismantling was effected in such a way, and with so many apparently arbitrary decisions, that the argument was deprived of much of its force.

In theory the purpose of destroying industrial installations was to make the future production of war material impossible; but a number of factories listed for destruction could have been converted for peaceful purposes, and a great many of those that were not condemned were by no means unsuitable for conversion to war production. The fact is that it is no longer possible today to classify a factory as producing exclusively for peace or for war, and it was natural that the Germans should get the impression that the real motive for dismantling was fear of German competition. In the end it became clear that the occupation authorities were being subjected to two kinds of pressure: a factory producing watches, for example, would be suppressed because a British firm wanted to eliminate a rival, and another, producing poison gas, would escape because it belonged to a company in which an American trust was interested.

France in particular seemed to be insisting upon the limitation of German production, especially of steel, much less in order to prevent Germany from getting priority in reconstruction or to make more coal from the Ruhr available for export than because she was opposed to the slightest recovery of any sort of economic power by her formidable neighbour. The variations of the permitted maximum for steel production make a long story, which lasted until the simultaneous announcement on 25 July, 1952, of the termination of the Ruhr authority and the lifting of all restrictions upon the German metallurgical industries.

In regard to the reorganisation of German industry also the

motives of the occupying powers may well have appeared ambiguous. The wish to weaken was sometimes mixed, especially in the French, with the purpose of "denazifying", and the fear of any too-effective reform with the ideal of "democratising". But agrarian reform appeared necessary as a result of the enlarged population and the high proportion of peasants among the refugees from the east; and it had taken place in the Soviet zone immediately after the end of the war, being almost completed by the end of 1945. Seven and a half million acres were expropriated without compensation, and 5 million of them were redistributed to small-holders, including 650,000 refugees.

In western Germany, however, reform was on a very small scale. The essential reason for this was the dearth of great properties in the western zones. Whereas 47 per cent of the estates in the Russian zone exceeded the 250 acres which were the legal maximum, the corresponding figures for the British and American zones were 10 per cent and 3 per cent. However, it would have been possible to provide land for a much larger number of new proprietors if stricter regulations had been framed and if their implementation had not been hampered, especially in Bavaria, by the hostility of the landed nobility and also of the executive officials. In the American zone, in August, 1946, a sort of sliding scale was established for reducing estates, from 10 per cent to 50 per cent being confiscated from estates of more than 250 and less than 1,250 acres, and from 50 per cent to 90 per cent from those exceeding 1,250 acres. By May, 1950, only 170,000 acres had been listed and 50,000 redistributed, of which little more than 24,000 went to refugees. In Schleswig-Holstein a British order of September, 1947, limited the size of estates to 375 acres, and the socialist majority in the Diet further reduced the limit to 275 with the result that 11,400 new holdings could be created. Finally, in the French zone, when it was established that the military government's order of October, 1947, would be applied in all to a total of less than about 35,000 acres, the reform quickly became a dead letter.

We cannot here describe in detail the development of the allies' policy of 'deconcentration'.[9] The British set up control groups for coal and steel and effected a preliminary decartellisation; the Anglo-American law no. 75 entrusted German experts with the task of reorganisation; and the tripartite law no. 27, of 16 May, 1950, paved the way for the settlement finally accepted by the Federal government. Anglo-American differences, French vetoes, and open or covert German obstruction acted and reacted upon each other in complicated ways, and the participants changed their ground continually as the European and world political situation evolved.

In the end there was to be a triple deconcentration. The nine great combines (Vereinigte Stahlwerke, Krupp, Mannesmann, Klockner, Hoesch, Otto Wolff, Gutehoffnungshütte, Reichswerke, and Flick) were dissolved and replaced by twenty-six metallurgical undertakings and twenty-eight coal- and coke-producing companies. For example, the Vereinigte Stahlwerke was replaced by thirteen metallurgical companies, nine mining companies, one holding company and one commercial company. Whereas before the war the Vereinigte Stahlwerke alone, as we have said, produced 8·5 million tons a year, or 40 per cent of Germany's total steel production, the largest of the new metallurgical companies, the Dortmund-Horder-Hütten-Union, produced only 2·2 million tons, or 15 per cent of the total. Deconcentration on the vertical plane is best illustrated by a single figure: in 1938 metallurgical interests controlled 56 per cent of coal production, but they were now to control only 26·5 per cent. According to German technicians and economists this is an excessive and rationally indefensible deconcentration, seriously disadvantageous to the Ruhr in the international field.

Finally, on the commercial side, the central coal-selling agency was dissolved on 31 May, 1953, to be replaced by six agencies in the Ruhr. There were already at the time four others in the rest of the country. A federal coal office, representing consumers, producers, mine-workers, and the ministries concerned, is responsible both to the Federal government and to the Schuman plan authority. There remains the case of 'George'. GEORG, the Essener Gemeinschaftsorganisation Ruhrkohle, is in fact a selling agency for Ruhr coal, and the Luxemburg high court is due to pronounce on its case before March, 1955. In the meantime George continues to fight his dragon, which is the Charbonnages de France. According to the Germans, if he collapses fifty German coal companies will be left to fight for themselves, which will involve at least the closing of thirty-five pits at present producing at a loss in the Bochum-Dortmund area.

As a result of all these measures, was the German economy profoundly altered from what it had been before the war? In considering this question we must distinguish between ownership and management. In the field of management there was both alteration and restoration.* A German Federal law confirmed the British authorities' introduction of co-determination in the coal and steel industries, but nevertheless, from 1945 until today, we have seen the gradual re-installation of all the former "managing" personnel—not only metallurgical technicians but also bankers like Hermann Abs and Robert Pferdmenges, about whom we shall have more to say. The same thing has happened in the chemical industry. The same influential men are once again in charge of I.G. Farben. Fritz Gajowski, the great explosives specialist, has regained his old position as manager of Dynamit A.G. at Troisdorf; Professor Hoerlein is on the managerial board of Farbenfabrik-Bayer A.G. at Leverkusen; and Otto Ambros, who, as director of I.G. Farben was in charge of chemical products at Auschwitz, the infamous German concentration and extermination camp, is "adviser" for the development of the former I.G. Farben factories in south Germany.[10]

As regards the ownership of mines and factories no definite decision has yet been taken. The Rhineland-Westphalia Diet voted for nationalisation, but the British military government imposed its veto on the ground that such a decision could only be taken by a future central parliament. In Hesse, however, the government was able to carry out some nationalisation, under article 41 of the constitution of the *Land*, without incurring the American veto. But it cannot be said that the measures have been effectively carried through, because although the owners have been expropriated ever since 1 December, 1946, it was still in doubt six years later, owing to the inadequacy of the law, who was to assume the vacant

* See chapter IV.

ownership. The result is that the 'socialised' industries today belong to nobody, not even to the state. For the Ruhr mines and steelworks decree no. 77, confirmed by law no. 17, leaves the decision to a freely elected representative German government, and for the time being they remain in sequestration. But it is easy to foresee, in the light of the Krupp affair, the sort of solution towards which events are moving.

On 31 July, 1948, Alfred Krupp von Bohlen und Halbach, son and heir of the Krupp who financed Hitler, was sentenced as a war criminal to twelve years' imprisonment and the loss of all his property, by an American war tribunal. The regularity of the trial was open to question, and the American high commissioner first suspended the tribunal's decision in regard to Krupp's fortune and then remitted the greater part of the prison sentence. Krupp made a triumphal re-entry into his good town of Essen and discussed his own future with the German and allied experts concerned with deconcentration. The settlement finally reached in August, 1952, allowed Krupp to remain in possession of all his property but he renounced his steel and mining interests—realising probably about 300 milliard marks (say £25 million or $75 million) by the sale of his shares. On the other hand he retained possession of a heavy engineering works and also various interests in a number of commercial and engineering companies; and he will easily reach an understanding with the new owner of the Hamm wire-works and the Düsseldorf rolling-mills, for the new owner is his sister. The Krupp combine no longer exists, but Alfred Krupp is once again a power. His return to the family home, the Villa Hügel, is profoundly symbolic, for this house was the headquarters after the war of the trustees commission, administrators during the sequestration of the Ruhr metal industries. When he gives a reception Krupp will often honour his guests, including perhaps an allied high commissioner, by introducing them to his old grandmother, Bertha, who gave her name to the biggest Krupp guns of 1914. Nor is the Krupp case an isolated one. The French metal industry, with financial backing from the French government, is negotiating directly with the Flick family for the purchase of one of the most important of the Ruhr coal mines. The French taxpayer's money goes into the pocket of the Flicks. . . . It is easy to understand Krupp's answer to a journalist in the interview he gave to *European Newsweek* (reprinted in *Industrie Kurier*, 7 January, 1954). To the question "Do you consider you were unjustly treated by the occupying powers after the war?" he replied: "War and its aftermath inevitably bring suffering of all kinds. What happened to many industrialists in Germany and other countries which lost the war is now a thing of the past".

The majority of Germans disapproved of nearly all the measures adopted by the occupying powers. The currency reform of June, 1948, alone escaped criticism, if not of its details at least of its principle; and it is even forgotten now in Germany that it was imposed by the allies in face of the hesitations of German experts, including Professor Erhard. It was the indispensable preliminary for Germany's economic revival[11] and the visible proof of its success appeared like a miracle. Overnight, the shop windows became full, factories reopened or speeded up, and the poverty of a whole country seemed suddenly transformed into a relative prosperity. The index figure for industrial production, which was 51 in June, reached 61 in July and 79 in December.

It became apparent that western Germany's poverty was not so extreme as had been thought and that farms, factories, and stores had been carefully saving up stocks of provisions, raw materials, and goods until the day when there should be a sound currency. A chemist who on 17 June "regretted to have to inform" a mother of a family that the medicine she required for her sick child was unprocurable, found himself on 20 June miraculously able to provide it—although there had been no deliveries to his shop in the interval. Far from paying any penalty, the peasants, industrialists and merchants who had made illegal secret hoards were greatly favoured by the method of application of the reform.

The very complicated process was based in theory upon two principles, but only one of them was in fact applied. There was a drastic deflation without any spreading of the losses involved. Owners of real property had a great advantage over people with money savings. The general rate of exchange was 1 for 10, or 10 new DM. (Deutsche-mark) for 100 RM. (the old Reichsmark). But cash holdings and credit balances were almost the only assets to which this rate was applied. Those with reserves in specie and bank deposits were even more harshly treated, getting only about 6·5 DM. for 100 RM.; and as for private investors in the public funds, they got nothing at all. Meanwhile official prices and salaries were unaltered, being simply made payable in DM. instead of RM.; but since real prices had hitherto been those of the black market, the workers and salaried employees were among the gainers from the deflation. The real victims, therefore, were people with savings, and many of them fell into utter destitution. In the confused debate which raged for four years around the problem of equalising burdens (*Lastenausgleich*) the disasters inflicted by currency reform (*Währungsschaden*) were treated as comparable to those of the war and the occupation.

The return of abundance permitted liberalisation of foreign exchange control and then, in November, 1948, the unfreezing of wages and the revival of collective bargaining, while the end of the black market and the creation of a new destitute class increased the number of unemployed. Ration cards were soon abolished, which marked the end of the rationing policy and the triumph of Professor Erhard, who had been in charge of economic affairs in the bizonal economic council since March, 1948. This burly, sanguine, headstrong man of fifty, full of optimism and self-confidence, was the initiator of a newly-named economic policy—Soziale Marktwirtschaft, to which the nearest English approximation is "social market-economy". A specialist in industrial economics, he was rejected by the nazis for refusing to join the party, but his technical qualifications procured him the Bavarian ministry of industry and commerce in October, 1945, and he held the post until November, 1946. He was president of the bizonal consultative commission on finance and credit in 1947 and then became director of the economic council at Frankfurt. He joined the C.D.U. (Christian Democratic Union) before the general election of August, 1949, in which his Soziale Marktwirtschaft was the principal issue. The majority which became the government consisted of his supporters, and the opposition, of his opponents. He was

ECONOMIC RECOVERY 99

appointed Federal minister of economics on 20 September, 1949, and at the next general election four years later the coalition victory was as much, if not more, a tribute to Erhard as to the Chancellor himself.

His policy derives from the neo-liberalism of the German-Swiss economist Wilhelm Röpke, and accordingly, when the Federal government sought an authoritative foreign opinion for support against criticisms it appealed to Professor Röpke and was gratified to obtain the neo-liberal's endorsement of its neo-liberalism.[12] The term Soziale Marktwirtschaft is intended to express a two-fold purpose; first, to avoid 'planning' and allow free play to the natural mechanisms of the market; but, second, to control the conditions in which the markets have free play, so as to ensure an all-round and 'social' development of the economy and not, as hitherto, a development solely in the direction of private profit for individuals.

This policy was threatened at the beginning of 1951, when Professor Erhard's optimistic *laisser-faire* theories seemed to be contradicted by the rise in prices due to the Korean war, the world-wide difficulties in the procurement of raw materials, and the effect of the war scare upon consumption. The Chancellor lost confidence in Professor Erhard's policy and inclined to the views of his finance minister, Dr Fritz Schaeffer, who advocated drastic fiscal measures and something like a policy of austerity. The Christian Democrat and Liberal parliamentary groups, however, supported Erhard and, although there was a sharp controversy over some proposed taxation, it died down when the economic situation improved. The victory lay with the minister of national economy and his principle of meeting the crisis by an increase of 'social product' rather than by a decrease of purchasing power.

But a second offensive has been in progress since the end of 1953 in the matter of industrial agreements. Professor Erhard's position is uncompromising: liberalism must be complete, which means that prices must be freely arrived at through free competition. No fixed minimum prices and no ceiling prices either. On 19 November, 1953, addressing a meeting of organised supporters of his policy, Erhard declared that he would do his best to make the forthcoming anti-cartel legislation as strict as possible. On 4 December, Herr Fritz Berg, president of the German association of manufacturers, complained in a speech at Hagen that in a depression free competition does not necessarily favour the most useful undertakings because many of them are in danger of succumbing before the weight of capital, or lack of scruple, of other companies. He went on to advocate, in a certain measure, the principle of cartels, in which he has the support not only of Dr Schaeffer but also, surprisingly, of the trade unions and the Socialist party. It is hard to see how Professor Erhard can resist such a coalition, but in the meantime he continues to rely upon the traditional liberal resources, namely, credit, tax manipulation, and the encouragement of investment.

The German banks have always conceived it to be their first duty to assist economic development by a bold credit policy instead of increasing their own capital without risk through a high bank rate and making loans to prosperous firms only.* With Professor Erhard's encouragement this policy has achieved remarkable results. On 29 March, 1952, the three great German banks were 'deconcentrated', each of them being replaced by three new banks—the Deutsche Bank by the Norddeutsche Bank, the Rheinisch-Westfälische Bank and the Süddeutsche Bank; the Dresdener Bank by the Hamburger Kredit Bank, the Rhein-Ruhr Bank and the Rhein-Main Bank; and the Commerz Bank by the Commerz und Diskonto Bank, the Bankverein Westdeutschland and the Commerz und Kreditbank. The old shares were exchanged for new between mid-December, 1953, and mid-March, 1954, and the nine new banks have already a volume of business equal to that of the three old banks before the war. With dividends of 8 and $8\frac{1}{2}$ per cent, their shares head the list in Germany.

Besides bank credits there were also credits from abroad, most of which, as we shall see, became in the end free gifts. But credit alone could produce only a partial recovery.

* It should be noted that a bold, and even rash, credit policy is traditional in Germany. Such a policy does create real wealth, but at the risk of a money crisis. This is one of the reasons why Germany is always more affected than other countries by international crises, and also why she recovers more quickly. The extraordinary recovery now in progress is to some extent an example of this, and so also was the crisis of 1932 and the accession to power of Hitler.

The mainspring of the system was the principle of self-financing. To facilitate this the percentage of profits for distribution as dividends was limited to 6 per cent and a generous allowance for amortisation was made in the profit and loss account, thus making it possible to raise prices without showing an increased profit. Above all, big profits and large incomes were leniently taxed, and on 4 April, 1950, a "minor fiscal reform" was proposed which would make important concessions in their favour. This was met with a veto from the high commissioners on 20 April, the Americans being particularly indignant at a reduction of taxes at the very moment when the Federal Republic was asking them for more aid. But in face of the German ministers' explanations and of violent press criticisms of the high commission's interference in the Federal Republic's internal affairs (an interference authorised by the occupation statute) the allies withdrew their objection on 29 April and the reform entered into operation almost intact.

In every wage discussion between employers and workers the principle of self-financing has played and continues to play a very important role. In an engineering strike in August, 1951, for example, the unions asserted that the investment policy, and in particular, the system of financing from reserves, had raised the industry's profits by 50 milliard DM., of which 30 milliard ought to have been distributed as wages and also, through keeping down the price of the product, to the general public. The employers contested the figure, saying it was in fact only 10 milliards, but their main argument was that the money in question had been used to create 1,100,000 new jobs and had thus reduced poverty and unemployment more effectively than a rise in wages or a small price reduction would have done.

Professor Erhard's policy was not framed with the intention of benefiting all industries equally. Basic industries enjoyed priority over industries producing consumer goods, and it was even contended that, in principle, a part of the latter's profits should be invested for the benefit of the former. For two years the consumer industries were to pay $3\frac{1}{2}$ per cent of their profits into the Industrie-Kreditbank, which was created for this purpose with a management board of twelve members—six representatives of the employers, three of the workers, and three of the administration—whose function it was to allocate the investment in the basic industries of the milliard marks which were expected to be raised by this method. As many as 311,297 undertakings were made liable to contribute, but the results were disappointing. The undertakings in question resisted the law, claiming that the production index of the basic industries was much higher than that of the consumer goods industries and, further, that it was contrary to liberal principles to compel certain undertakings to give credits to others. Both the economic justification and the juridical validity of the law were attacked, and in the end the consumer industries appear to have gone a long way towards establishing their point. In 1952 their production index was 21·5 points below that of the basic industries, but by 1953 they had advanced by 16·3 per cent as against an advance of only 8·4 per cent by the basic industries, thus reducing the gap between them to 11 points. But in 1954 once again the development of the basic industries was by far the most important. In October they reached an index of 220, while consumer industries had not reached 180. Priority for basic industries will long continue to be an essential part of the investment policy, as is shown by the allocation of credits provided for in the re-equipment plan of the Notgemeinschaft für reparationsgeschädigte Industrie (Association to assist industries hit by reparations). The industries handling raw materials are to receive 74 per cent of the total—the reconstruction budget for Thyssenhütte alone amounting to 350,000,000 DM.

The justification for setting up this Notgemeinschaft, says the national federation of industry, is that "re-equipment is the most economical method of creating new permanent jobs",[13] which is an essential aim of Soziale Marktwirtschaft. Supporters of this policy always present statistics of unemployment alongside statistics of those at work. In the area now covered by the Federal Republic there were 12,200,000 people at work in 1938, and in 1948 this figure was higher by 800,000. In spite of seasonal variations due to the relative scarcity of jobs between the end of autumn and the beginning of spring, the situation has improved every year—the number of employed in 1951,

1952, 1953, and 1954 respectively reaching (in millions) 14·7, 15·2, 15·8, and 16·5 on 30 June each year.

The figure for unemployment, on the other hand, which was 400,000 at the time of the currency reform, soared to extravagant heights: 800,000 in September, 1948, 1,200,000 in March and 1,600,000 in September, 1949, and 1,800,000 in March, 1950, but after that it remained more or less stable for about two years. In February, 1951, it still stood at 1,800,000. The improvement during the summer months was more marked in 1952 and 1953, so that in August, 1953, on the eve of the election, there were less than a million unemployed. But the winter of 1953–54 produced the peak figure, in February, of 2,042,000 (as against the February, 1953, peak of 1,822,000). It is true that with the warmer and drier weather of March, which particularly favoured an increase in building, the figure dropped again to 1,427,000, but this was still 2·5 per cent above the March, 1953, figure.

In any case, it is still an enormous figure, and the more so considering that a large proportion of the unemployed are heads of families. Professor Erhard's opponents claim that a full employment policy would reduce it considerably; but his supporters reply that a certain level of unemployment is always necessary, to exert pressure upon the labour market. They add that unemployment in Germany is the symptom of a structural defect in industry, caused particularly by the unsatisfactory distribution of manpower. At the end of May, 1953, for example, the unemployment rate was 3·2 per cent in Württemberg-Baden and 3·5 per cent in North Rhineland and Westphalia, as against 11·1 per cent in Lower Saxony, 13·4 per cent in Hamburg, and 15·7 per cent in Schleswig-Holstein. But would not a "planned economy" make it possible to remedy the maldistribution? This is one of the fundamental questions posed by the refugee problem.*

In the general picture of brilliant economic recovery, however, unemployment is only a small blot.[14] The mark, which was worth only one-eighth of a U.S. cent in the black market in 1947, is now worth 24 cents at the official rate and 25 per cent more in the free market. Production in many essential

* See chapter IV.

sectors is still soaring. The 4,000 automobiles a month of June, 1948, had become 33,000 by the autumn of 1950 and 58,170 by March, 1953, reaching a total of 518,190 automobiles in 1954, as against 5,559,000 in the United States, 769,165 in Great Britain, and 444,262 in France; and in shipbuilding, which was still forbidden to her in 1949, Germany has now regained third place among the nations, after Britain and the United States, with 503,508 tons completed by 1952. At the beginning of 1953 the North Sea and Baltic yards had received orders for two million tons, of which 1,200,000 are on foreign contracts. Although there had been long discussions about authorising an annual steel output of 11 million tons, the Federal Republic actually produced 15·4 million tons in 1953 and 17·4 million in 1954. There was a parallel peak in the number of employed, for the manpower figure in the steel and iron industries was slightly less in 1953, although there had been a rapid yearly increase until then; and we shall find the same phenomenon in the coal industry. But the fact remains that industrial reconstruction is in excellent train, and this makes possible an even more rapid progress in housing than in the past.

Until the spring of 1950 the building industry had been employed chiefly on factory sites and offices—to say nothing of hotels, bars, cinemas, and luxury shops. But already in 1949 there was a rapid increase of new or repaired houses: the 15,000 of the first quarter increasing to 21,000, 30,000, and 54,000 in the second, third and fourth quarters respectively. Then came the law of 24 April, 1950, which provided for the construction of 1,800,000 houses in six years, at the rate of 300,000 a year; but in fact 360,000 were built in 1950, 430,000 in 1951, 440,000 in 1952, and 550,000 in 1953 and 1954. For the building of houses to be let at less than one DM. per sq. metre, with a total area between 32 and 65 sq. metres, the law allowed credit at a reduced rate, or interest free, and also subsidies from the central government, the *Land*, or the municipality; and the construction of houses of less than 80 sq. metres with a rent of less than 1½ DM. per sq. metre was tax free.

Although the scale of the rebuilding operations seems enormous, it is still insufficient when one remembers that even at the end of 1950 the shortage of houses was estimated at 4·8 millions. Believing that a still further effort was possible, the new minister of reconstruction—the young Liberal Preusker—drew up a plan for extending the programme by three years. But the banker Pferdmenges, who has the Chancellor's ear, replied with a violent attack upon 'social' building. In a speech on 6 December, 1953, he called for an end to building subsidies and the restoration to the capital market of the three milliard DM. of which it would be deprived by the excessively low rents and by the subsidies. His argument is based upon figures which no-one disputes, namely, that rents are only 13 per cent higher than in 1938 while building costs have increased by about 120 per cent. It may be noted, however, that private capital seems to have adjusted quite comfortably to the new conditions, since the general building increase in 1953 of 19 per cent included a 25 per cent increase of private building. But Dr Pferdmenges' argument raises the whole question of how the word social should be interpreted in the expression Soziale Marktwirtschaft.

What is at issue is the distribution of the national income. In an "open letter" to taxpayers in June, 1952, the Federal finance minister explained that every 100 DM. spent by the Bund, that is, by the central administration, included 40 DM. for occupation charges and 39 DM. for social charges.[15] "The Federal government", he added, "is not responsible for the fact that Hitler launched a total war and led the German people to total disaster." That is true enough—but it seems to assume that the population as a whole is bearing the weight of the disaster and that the benefits from any improvement in the economic situation are being equally shared; and this is by no means the case.

An examination of the way in which the national income is distributed shows that Soziale Marktwirtschaft is not leading Germany towards its official objective of a generally shared prosperity. The incomes of non-wage-earners, particularly industrialists and merchants, increased by 65 per cent while wages were rising only very slightly. The trade unions' economic institute drew up a table showing the distribution of incomes for the month of May, 1950, according to which 63·95 per cent of the population had a monthly income of less than 250 DM. and received only 35·59 per cent of the total national income, while 2·3 per cent had a monthly income of over 1,000 DM. and received 16·49 per cent of the total income. In the next chapter we shall examine in detail the inequalities which these figures reflect. It may be true that the position of the wage-earners has improved since 1952, but nevertheless, as we shall see, the lot of the 'economically weak' is still far from enviable. The distribution of the Federal budget has somewhat altered since 1952, and in his big budget speeches of 28 January, 1953, and 22 January, 1954, Herr Schaeffer gives only the total figure for social charges: 7·6 milliards for 1952–53 and 8·75 milliards for 1954–55, as against 5·2 milliards for 1950–51. The truth is that, since the budget as a whole has increased on a far greater scale and reached 27·1 milliards in 1954–55, the proportion allocated for social charges continually diminishes—from 39 per cent in 1951 to 32·3 per cent in 1954.* Pensions to war victims have remained ridiculously low and indemnities to victims of nazism are insignificant. There is, therefore, a dark corner of social injustice in the brilliant picture of German recovery.

Nor is the picture without some serious economic flaws, notably the railways and coal. At the end of 1953 the *Bundesbahn* had an operational deficit of 600 million DM., which would not be too serious if the Federal railway system were being made over and modernised. But the railways have been the Cinderella of Soziale Marktwirtschaft, because there was no inducement to invest. The present situation is that the *Bundesbahn* is far from having repaired the four milliard DM. worth of war damage and its service, apart from a few luxury trains, is one of the slowest and most unpunctual in Europe. This is largely because the state has not protected it against competition from road transport, most of which is in private hands, with the result that in 1953 there were 22,700

* It should be remembered that the federal budget is only a part of the total national budget, for the *Länder* have wide financial autonomy and retain 62 per cent of the taxes they raise. This is especially relevant when considering the cost of the occupation (or, if Germany rearms, of military expenditure), which the German Press prefers to treat as a proportion of the federal budget, as though it were the only one.

motor coaches on the roads, as against 9,600 in 1936, and 529,200 lorries, as against 157,600.

Equally unsatisfactory is the state of coal production. In western Germany (excluding the Saar) in 1950, 1951, 1952, and 1953 the production, in millions of tons, was 110, 111, 130 and 127 respectively; and this is certainly a considerable improvement upon the 35 million tons of 1945. But it is still some way from the 137 million tons of 1938 and 1943. The total number of miners is higher than before the war, but the average output per man has fallen off considerably. In 1953, with about 1 ton 6 cwt. per man per day, it was 17 per cent less than in 1952. The figure for 1938 was about 1 ton 14 cwt. One of the essential reasons for this is the scarcity of miners of the right age (only 26 per cent between 31 and 45 years, as against 42 per cent in 1946 and 52 per cent in 1938) and another is the small attraction of mining for the unemployed. Of the 537,900 underground workers enrolled between 1946 and 1953, 406,900 have left again. The truth is that the authorities more or less neglected the coal industry, and it was not until 1951 that the government drew up a plan for modernising the mines and providing houses for miners.

What is the explanation of this lack of interest at a time when shortage of coal was retarding the development of the German economy? It is that the international authority for the Ruhr compelled Germany to export much more coal than she wished and at a price which she considered derisory. On 10 August, 1951, vice-Chancellor Blücher resigned from the international authority in protest; and today, although the authority no longer exists, Germany is still not mistress of her own coal resources. There is a High Authority of the European Coal and Steel Community and its price decisions have caused great discontent in Germany. They amounted to abolishing or lowering the subsidies in Germany for domestic coal and transport by rail or water, which meant a price rise for German consumers, and they also fixed the maximum selling price abroad at a figure below the prevailing rate. As regards the coal production policy of the Coal and Steel Community, it is hard to form an opinion at a time when it appears to be completely inconsistent. All the plans seem to presuppose increased production—the Ruhr to reach 150 million tons per annum, which would require an investment of 3·7 milliard DM.— and yet there was a recession in 1953 with surplus coal piling up at the pit-heads. In the six coal and steel pool countries there were 10·5 million tons in February, 1954, and in Germany at the end of March there were 4·4 million tons of unpurchased coal and coke, while 30,000 miners were idle one day a week and a large number had to be released.

But coal is only one aspect of the fundamental German and European economic problem, namely, the problem of Germany's foreign trade.

With the institution of the Coal and Steel Community western Germany regained equality of rights in the economic sphere.[16] It so happened that Chancellor Adenauer presided at the council's first meeting at Luxemburg in September, 1952, and there were some who saw in this a sign of Germany's future economic predominance on the continent. The fact is that for Germany the return of economic equality and the return of economic power were simultaneous; but this was not what the other countries had foreseen in 1947 and 1948. When General Marshall, in his famous Harvard speech of 5 June, 1947, said that countries which schemed against the economic revival of other countries could not expect American aid, it was hardly perceived in Europe that these words could very well be applied to the "punitive" policy directed against Germany. When the three western powers sanctioned an increase of Germany's industrial activity, at their conference in London in August, 1947, they declared that: "The three delegations agreed that the measures about to be taken should not result in priority being given to the rehabilitation of Germany over that of the democratic countries of Europe. They consider it necessary that German resources should contribute to the general rehabilitation of Europe." Germany was still regarded as an object to be used and not as a partner; but at the next meeting the attitude had definitely changed and the three powers and the Benelux countries declared on 6 March, 1948, that: "for the political and economic well-being of the countries of western Europe and of a democratic Germany there must be a close association of their economic life." On 16 April the constituent countries of the Organisation for European Economic Cooperation proclaimed the wish to do their utmost to increase productivity, both individually and collectively, and to make the most efficient use of the resources at their disposal.

So German equality was recognised in principle, although the three zones were still represented by the commanders-in-chief; but the extent to which the commanders-in-chief felt themselves the champions of Germany's economic revival is shown by the fact that in September, 1948, Generals Clay and Robertson obtained 414 million dollars of Marshall aid for the three zones instead of the 364 millions originally allocated. But equality was not to become an established fact for another four years, and the majority of Germans believe today that it was by no means granted by other countries but that Germany had to grasp it in their despite. The Socialist objection to the Schuman plan was essentially that the policy of other European countries, and especially France, was still dominated by the desire to obstruct Germany's development by any and every means, and that the Schuman plan was one of them. This does not make international negotiations any easier.

The economic association of several nations demands a fair distribution of burdens, and Germany's associates are burdened with a military expenditure from which she is at present free. Germany, on the other hand, has to pay the costs of the occupation; but she will be relieved of these with the restoration of sovereignty and the decision to rearm, and they will be replaced by a financial contribution whose amount has been the subject of sharp controversy. The Atlantic Council finally fixed it, on 25 April, 1953, at 950 million DM. per month for the transitional period from 1 November, 1953 to 30 June, 1954. But since E.D.C. has not come into force and the occupation charges are only 600 million per month, the financial year 1953–54* has yielded the Federal Republic a saving of 1,750 million DM. on the budget estimates. The 1954–55 budget provides for an expenditure of approximately 9 milliard DM., but the exact sum cannot be fixed until two other points have been settled: first, the question of German rearmament must be decided in principle, and, second, the

* The German financial year commences on 1 April.

amount of the financial charges arising from the new negotiations for the period commencing 1 July, 1954, must be known. There are two essential questions for which the solutions found have been purely provisional, because the German negotiators will always return to them: the refugees, and Berlin. The rehabilitation of the refugees is a heavy expense for the Federal Republic,[17] and the provisioning and economic support of the former capital costs about two milliard marks a year. But is Germany alone responsible for the expulsion of populations from the east, and is she alone interested in keeping west Berlin "western"? The Bonn government considers that assistance to the refugees and to Berlin should be counted as an integral part of Germany's contribution to the common effort, but this view is by no means universally accepted.

In addition to these Germany has other financial obligations which are certainly hers alone—her external debts. After long and difficult negotiations between Germany and Israel, the moral aspect of which we shall refer to later,* an agreement was signed at Luxemburg in September, 1952, between Chancellor Adenauer and the Israel foreign minister. The Federal Republic undertook to provide goods to the value of 3·45 milliard DM. free of charge in annual instalments of 200 or 300 millions' worth. For the first year Germany requested, in accordance with the agreement though not with her own economic situation, to be allowed to send only 245 millions' worth, which was finally allocated as 175 millions' worth of goods (including 83 million in metallurgical products and 30 million in foodstuffs) and 75 million paid in England against petrol delivered to Israel. A month earlier, on 8 August, a compromise had been arrived at by the London conference on Germany's pre-war and post-1945 debts. The post-1945 debts were to be met by an annual payment of 300 million DM. for thirty years, commencing 1 April, 1953; Britain reducing her claim from 562·8 to 420 million dollars and France hers from 15·7 to 11·8 million dollars. The United States, to whom two milliard dollars were owing, renounced her claim.

The German debt to America was two-fold: Marshall aid and the special credits under G.A.R.I.O.A. (Government and

* See chapter VI.

relief in occupied areas). It was not originally intended that Germany should benefit from Marshall aid on the same footing as other countries; everything she received was to be a loan. But in fact she shared on the same terms as the others, receiving four-fifths as a gift and one-fifth as a loan, and up to 8 July, 1952, she had received about 1·4 milliard dollars. The G.A.R.I.O.A. funds also were distributed as loans, amounting to about two milliard dollars, and it was in effect this debt that the United States agreed to cancel. Germany certainly cannot complain that she was overlooked in the distribution of American manna!

But the American government, as we have said, has for some time been feeling this assistance a burden and wishes that Germany would balance her accounts better. Can imports be cut? So long as the occupying powers controlled Germany's foreign trade they tried to prevent the import of luxuries and in general to keep all imports down to a reasonable quantity. In 1949 the figure was the same as for 1936, and at that moment the new Federal government became responsible for foreign trade and was able to put its liberal policy into effect.

By October the index figure for imports reached 113, rising to 165 in November and 172 in December, when the figure for exports was only 68. Some of the imports were certainly not essential. For example, Germany imported nearly 21 lb. of citrus fruit, bananas and similar fruit, per head of population in 1950, as against 19 lb. in 1936. But on the other hand the large-scale purchases of raw materials gave Germany reserves which enabled her to weather better than her neighbours the world rise in prices after the outbreak of the Korean war. To the criticism that its policy is not austere the Federal government can reply that the import of luxury articles is more spectacular than really harmful in its effects on the country's balance sheet. "De luxe" imports may even be necessary to rectify Germany's accounts with certain countries. When, for example, the tax on coffee was reduced by parliament in mid-July, 1953, from 10 DM. to 3 DM. per kilo, this was not a mere vote-catching device but a way of increasing Brazilian imports when Brazil had become one of Germany's largest creditors. It is exports that are the real problem.

On 13 May, 1949, the European affairs committee of the International Chamber of Commerce stated in a report that all measures designed to increase Germany's trade with eastern Europe would help to solve the problem of Germany's foreign trade and of general European recovery.[18] On 7 February, 1950, deliveries of Ruhr steel to countries beyond the 'iron curtain' ceased. The agricultural countries of eastern Europe had long provided the natural outlet for German manufactures, and still today they could use what the Ruhr produces, while the Federal Republic could feed its population with the food they provided in exchange. But the splitting of the world in two has upset this economic balance. In 1952 only 1·4 per cent of the Federal Republic's imports and only 1·2 per cent of its exports were from and to eastern Europe. Even between western and eastern Germany trade has become insignificant, and although secret exchanges continue their extent should not be exaggerated. The Federal Republic has now no alternative except to seek outlets in the west. (Though there is another possible solution. Instead of producing for export, Germany could support herself by manufacturing arms, which the United States would pay for. But we have not—or we have not yet—reached that point.)

To export to the west means to enter into competition with British, French, and even American industry;[19] and Germany's commercial and industrial system is such as often to give her the victory in this unceasing competition. Today, 50 per cent of the automobiles imported by Holland and Sweden are German, and German tenders for supplying factory installations and locomotives have been accepted by Egypt and Peru. In 1948 Germany accounted for 1·8 per cent of total world exports; in 1950 this had become 3·5 per cent and in 1954 nearly 5 per cent. Britain, already uneasy at the re-emergence of Japanese competition, is beginning to feel anxious; and France, wondering what would happen if customs barriers were abolished all over Europe, feels her industry threatened.

The situation is particularly well illustrated in the motor industry. In 1953 the four leading exporters were Britain with 302,233 cars, the United States with 154,459, Germany with 137,883, and France with 81,339. But in 1954 German exports exceeded those of the United States, Germany having managed to export 47 per cent of her output. (It should be noted that between 1950 and 1954 exports from Great Britain fell from 69 to 47 per cent of output, French exports from 32 to 21·8 per cent, while in the Federal Republic they rose from 27 to 47 per cent, and in the United States the increase was only from 4 to 6 per cent.)

What is the real relation between Germany's exports and imports? The Federal Republic's exports to the Far East increased by 250 per cent between 1950 and 1953, but what is even more significant is that exports form an ever-growing proportion of the Republic's total production and its balance of trade is becoming more and more one-sided. Although in 1947 only 37·4 per cent of imports were paid for by exports, the percentage became 44·9 in 1948, 50·4 (with a record deficit of 1·1 milliard dollars) in 1949, 99·2 in 1951 and 104·2 in 1952; and in 1953 exports exceeded imports by 1814 million DM. as against 684 million DM. for the preceding year. The movement continued throughout the following year and at the end of 1954 Federal reserves of gold and foreign exchange amounted to 11 milliard DM. as against 2 milliard at the beginning of 1952.

But it is within the European Payments Union that this imbalance is most clearly seen, for in April, 1954, Germany was creditor for one milliard dollars, or twice her agreed quota. Between 1950 and 1953 she had in effect doubled her exports to the E.P.U. countries, while increasing her imports by only one-third. What are the remedies for this situation? So far as it is of Germany's making, her partners propose three. They all agree in demanding that she should pay off her external debts more quickly, and Britain in addition lays emphasis on the fact that Germany has no military expenditure. If the British government urges speedy German rearmament, its concern is more economic than military. The French, on the other hand, point out that Germany's excess of exports is partly achieved by keeping down internal consumption. In Germany the private consumer enjoys only 55 per cent of the national income, as against 65 per cent in France and 67·5 per cent in Britain.

H

What is certain is that the problem of outlets for export has involved the European countries in an economic cold war. After a meeting between leaders of the French national council of employers and the German national federation of industry at Düsseldorf on 8 and 9 November, 1951, a Franco-German industrial committee was set up, and there was a second meeting in Paris from 13–15 March, 1952. The French delegation adumbrated "close co-operation with German industry in the provision of capital and material for the development of French overseas territories"[20]—a proposal similar to President Truman's point four, which suggests the creation of new outlets through assistance to underdeveloped countries. But such a programme seems a remote ideal, especially in a period of rearmament.

For the present, competition continues, and steel presents a special problem. Will Germany reassemble dismantled rolling-mills? The French are quick to point out that the French mills in 1953 could handle a great deal more steel than their own. In the first quarter of 1952 only 6·8 million tons were produced in France and the Saar, and on 4 July the president of the metallurgical chamber declared that the maintenance of the Franco-Saar union was a vital necessity for France and that the union must modernise its equipment so as to reach an annual production of 20 million tons. At the same time Germany was planning a modernisation which would considerably increase the capacity of her largest steel works, allowing the August-Thyssen-Hütte to produce 900,000 tons a year, the former Hermann Goering works at Watenstedt 500,000, and the Krupp works 100,000. This led to a sharp quarrel in the O.E.E.C. and France demanded that consideration of the eight German modernisation projects be postponed to a later session. But the French motion was lost and six of the eight projects were unanimously accepted, the two most important (August-Thyssen and Reichswerke) being opposed by France and Britain. This quarrel was simply a visible sign of the urgency of the export problem and of the struggle industrial for power among the European nations.

Since then the situation has not improved. So long as the problem of export outlets remains unsolved, national rivalries will remain acute within the Coal and Steel Community; and, let us not forget, the possible solutions are few—intensive rearmament, with all the consequences it involves, trade with the east, including China, and investment in underdeveloped countries. But if things go on as they are, the competition between European countries will disintegrate, both psychologically and politically, a unity which is at present scarcely more than an aspiration, and will revive old complexes of superiority and dormant fears.

NOTES TO CHAPTER III

[1] The basic work on this question is André Piettre, *L'Economie allemande contemporaine 1945–1952* (Paris, 1952); informative and penetrating, with comprehensive statistical and bibliographical references. The special number of *Documents* entitled *Problèmes de l'Industrie d'Allemagne occidentale* (1954) is very useful. On the German economy before 1945 see Charles Bettelheim, *L'Économie allemande sous le nazisme* (Paris, 1946); and L. E. Davin, *Les finances de 1939 à 1945*; *L'Allemagne* (Paris, 1950). For the economy of the Ruhr see W. Helmrich, *Das Ruhrgebiet* (Munster, 1949), and the section on the Ruhr in Weydert, Levassort, and Lebee, *Études économiques allemandes* (Paris, 1951), and the section on Germany's economic situation in G. A. Almond, *The Struggle for Democracy in Germany*, written by the former chief of the Western European economic branch of the Department of State research division.

[2] Excellent studies of the German economy in 1947 and 1948 have been published by the Deutsches Institut für Wirtschaftsforschung, *Die deutsche Wirtschaft zwei Jahre nach dem Zusammenbruch* (Berlin, 1947), and *Wirtschaftsprobleme der Besatzungszonen* (Berlin, 1948).

[3] For American and British connections with German industry see James S. Martin, op. cit., and Deutsches Wirtschaftsinstitut, *Ausländische Beteiligungen an Westdeutschen Unternehmen* (Berlin, 1951).

[4] Epigraph and p. 12 of Section II of the 1947 report of the Secretary of the Inter-Allied Reparations Agency for 1947 (Brussels, 1948). The difficulties and dangers of the question can be seen from a comparison of the studies made by the Centre d'Études de politique étrangère, *Contrôle de l'Allemagne*, and *Le rôle de l'Allemagne dans l'économie européenne* (Paris, 1949).

[5] Criticism of the *Lebensraum* theory and an analysis of the post-war situation is to be found in Hans Fuelster, *Volk ohne Raum* (Hamburg, 1947). See also R. Nimptsch, *Uebervölkerung, Bevölkerungsausgleich und Arbeitsmarkt* (Cologne, 1952).

[6] André Piettre, op, cit., p. 25. On post-war agricultural policy see A. W. Schuttauf, *Grundfragen der Agrarpolitik* (Munich, 1952), and W. Niklas (Federal Minister for Agriculture), *Sorgen um das tägliche Brot* (Hamburg, 1951), which also gives the texts of the laws and statistical data.

[7] See Institut für Besatzungsfragen, *Sechs Jahre Besatzungslasten* (Tübingen, 1951), slightly tendentious in the presentation and interpretation of statistics, but full and scholarly.

[8] The most concise and closely reasoned German criticism of dismantling is to

be found in W. Hasenack, *Betriebsdemontagen als Reparationen* (Essen, 1948). For decartellisation see H. Hennig, *Entflechtung und Neuordnung der westdeutschen Montanindustrie* (Berne, 1952); Herckenroder, Schäffer, and Zapp, *Die Nachfolger der Ruhrkonzerne* (Düsseldorf, 1953); and H. Steiner, *Grossenordnung und Horizontale Verflechtung in der Eisen- und Stahlindustrie* (Kiel, 1952). For the history of the combines see K. Pritzkoleit, *Männer, Mächte, Monopole* (Düsseldorf, 1953), written for the general reader; lively and well informed, though not very profound; and G. Baumann, *Eine Handvolle Konzernherren* (Berlin [East], 1954), violent and partisan.

[9] A clear account of this development is given in André Piettre, op. cit., which, however, ignores the currents below the surface described in James S. Martin, op. cit.

[10] J. E. Dubois, *The Devil's Chemists* (Boston, 1952).

[11] See André Piettre, op. cit., and P. Frank, *Die Neuordnung des deutschen Geldwesens* (1949).

[12] W. Röpke, *Ist die deutsche Wirtschaftspolitik richtig?* (Stuttgart, 1950). A brief examination of this policy is given in F. Boehm, *Die Aufgaben der freien Marktwirtschaft* (Munich, 1951), and E. Preiser, *Die soziale Problematik der Marktwirtschaft* (Munich, 1951). Professor Erhard's book, *Germany's Comeback in the World Market* (London, 1954) is devoted almost entirely to the question of exports.

[13] See pp. 109-10 of Bundesverband der deutschen Industrie, *Jahresbericht* (Cologne, 1952), very useful for German industrial structure and policy. The report for the following year is no less interesting.

[14] See for example the three government reports published by the Presse und Informationsamt der Bundesregierung, *Deutschland im Wiederaufbau* (Bonn, 1951, 1952, and 1953), and *Sechs Jahr danach: vom Chaos zum Staat* (Wiesbaden 1951). On the same theme see Hans Scholz, *Drei Jahre Bundesrepublik Deutschland* (Munich, 1952), and Bundesministerium für den Marshallplan, *Bericht über die Durchführung des Marshallplan* (1953). The annual reports of the Bank Deutscherländer are fuller.

[15] For the distribution of receipts and expenditure on the central, regional and local levels see G. Wacke, *Das Finanzwesen der Bundesrepublik* (Tübingen, 1950).

[16] A convenient bilingual edition of the text of the treaty establishing the Coal and Steel Community was published in U. Sahm, *Der Schuman-Plan* (Frankfurt, 1951).

[17] See Bundesministerium der Finanzen, *Flüchtlingslasten und Verteidigungsbeitrag* (Bonn, 1951); F. Edding, *Die Flüchtlinge als Belastung und Antrieb der westdeutschen Wirtschaft* (Kiel, 1952); and T. Oberländer, *Das Werk der Vertriebenen* (Munich, (1951). The notes to the following chapter giver a fuller bibliography of the refugee question.

[18] L. F. Otto, *L'Allemagne et le Commerce européen* (Paris, 1949). On former German export outlets see E. Zaleski, *Les courants commerciaux de l'Europe danubienne* (1952).

[19] For American aid see Brownes and Opie, *American Foreign Assistance* (Washington, 1953). For German debts, Auswärtiges Amt, *Deutsche Auslandsschulden* (Hameln, 1951). On intra-European payments see W. Diebold, *Trade and Payments in Western Europe 1947-1951* (New York, 1952).

[20] *Jahresbericht* of the Bundesverband der deutschen Industrie, op. cit., p. 14.

CHAPTER IV

THE SOCIAL BACKGROUND

WOULD western Germany's economic revival have been equally rapid under some other policy than Professor Erhard's? It is impossible to answer with certainty, but what is incontestable is that no policy could have succeeded without the intensive labour of the whole population. The office employee who built his own house after hours or lent his neighbour a hand, the cold and hungry worker who cleared up the débris of the ruined workshop, the researcher who swept the plaster off the laboratory floor and performed his first experiment before the windows were in or the roof repaired—these were the real architects of Germany's revival. Perhaps there is only one safe generalisation: "The Germans have worked hard"—to which might possibly be added: "The lot of the Germans has improved". In 1948 there were 449 new diagnoses of tuberculosis per 100,000 of population; by 1949 this had fallen to 326 and by 1950 to 265.[1] But the improvement has been very unequally shared.

As we saw when studying the question of war guilt, it is important not to generalise. It is even more important to realise how impossible it is to answer such meaningless and, alas, such frequent questions as, How do "the Germans" live? and, What do "the Germans" think? To ask such questions is to forget that every human life is unique. It was in 1948 that the German recovery really started, and yet the same year saw the record number of 87,000 divorces—a proof of the family upheavals caused by the end of the war and its aftermath.

But generalisations not only prevent us from seeing the trees, they also blind us to the wood as a whole. Germany today has two million more inhabitants than at the 1950 census, and one might expect that such an increase would lead to large-scale emigration to less-populated countries. A Federal emigration office was instituted on 8 May, 1952, and already in 1951 there had been 85,000 German overseas emigrants, of whom 40,000 went to the United States and 32,000 to Canada. The flow has since been kept up at the rate of about 80,000 emigrants a year. But these departures are more harmful than healthy for Germany.

The aggregate figure for population increase between 1939 and 1950 is misleading. It needs to be interpreted in the light of the fact that the able-bodied workers have increased by only 10 per cent while the dependent population has increased by 33 per cent. The war-wounded number 1,500,000, of whom one-half have a 50 per cent disability or worse, and there are nearly a million widows. The balance of age groups has been so badly upset by the fall in births between 1915 and 1919 and the war casualties between 1939 and 1945 that there are today only 380,000 Germans living who were born in 1917, as against 770,000 born in 1907 and 815,000 born in 1937; and between the ages of thirty and forty there are 133 women for every hundred men. Now, obviously, it is the young and enterprising, the skilled men, who have the energy and courage to start life again in a new country, and who are welcomed there. The disproportion between the active and the dependent population is made all the greater by their going. Emigration would only be useful for Germany if each emigrant took with him three others who are incapable of work; and even then only if the receiving country would accept the same ratio of skilled to manual workers as obtains in Germany. These are the true facts about emigration, and they are especially relevant when discussing the refugee problem.

The word 'refugee' is a misdescription,[2] but is nevertheless used in Germany, for want of a better, to cover two distinct categories of residents in the Federal Republic, the *Heimatvertriebene* and the *Zugewanderte*. The former are persons evacuated or expelled from the German territories east of the Oder-Neisse line or from central and eastern European countries. On 1 October, 1951, they numbered eight million, or nearly 17 per cent of the total population of western Germany. On the same date there were 1,700,000 *Zugewanderte* (3·6 per cent of the total population). These were people who had escaped either before or after the end of the war from the Soviet zone or from Berlin. It should be noted that more than a third of them came originally from east Germany or from abroad and were evacuated or expelled into the Soviet zone, from which they fled again to the west. Psychologically and politically these *Ostzonenflüchtlinge*, or fugitives from the eastern zone, should be counted with the *Heimatvertriebene*. The number of *Zugewanderte* increases regularly. Between 1 October, 1949, and 31 December, 1951, 216,000 residents of the eastern zone illegally crossed the demarcation line and requested admittance to the Federal Republic; 69,000 were admitted and 147,000 sent back; 182,000 came over in 1952 and 300,000 in 1953, 80 per cent of them between 15 and 65 years of age. They included 4,000 members of the 'Volkspolizei'. These figures do not include the secret arrivals who refrain from disclosing their presence to the authorities.

When the flood of refugees started pouring into Germany and the agreed transfers of population began, the occupation authorities and their advisers adopted a very simple method of placing the new arrivals. They were directed to the most underpopulated districts—except those in the French zone, for the French commander-in-chief in effect refused to accept refugees on the ground that France was not a signatory of the Potsdam agreement which authorised the transfers of population. The local residents had to do the best they could to make room for them as lodgers; but the overcrowding was such that many had to be accommodated in camps of hastily improvised huts. Once they were installed, it soon became clear that the idea of settling them in under-populated districts, though superficially plausible, was in fact completely mistaken. In a purely geometrical sense there is, of course, more room for new arrivals in a sparsely populated area; but such areas are sparsely inhabited precisely because they are not capable of supporting a larger population. The whole movement of population in the nineteenth and twentieth centuries had been away from the poor districts and the country towards the rich districts and the towns, where the growth of industry and commerce offered more chances of work. But now an impoverished region like Schleswig-Holstein was suddenly to receive a 60 per cent increase of population, and Bavaria, which had little need of more agricultural labourers, an increase of 30 per cent.

It is true that the Potsdam policy, which prescribed a certain de-industrialisation of Germany, was partly responsible for the false steps taken immediately after the war. But it should have been possible to foresee the result, which was that those who sought work were settled far away from the places where they could find it. There are few unemployed in the Ruhr and there is a shortage of labour in many branches of industry and commerce, but the refugees seeking work are in Schleswig or Lower Saxony. For two years the German authorities have been trying to remedy this situation by new transfers of population. At the rate of 300,000 a year the "supernumerary" refugees have moved into the *Länder* which still require more labour. But, in addition to the expense, there is another fundamental obstacle to this process: the shortage of houses. Industry has recovered its stride, and there are plenty of new jobs, but housing has not kept pace, so it is impossible to house the required workers—and still less their families. There are many Germans who have to travel hours by train to their work.

The fact that only 0·6 per cent of the refugees were settled in towns of any size, while eight million were directed to rural areas, has also made the problem of assimilating them almost insoluble. In a large city there is very little communal life; the inhabitants have no deep roots, and new arrivals are accepted without comment. But small towns and villages have their own customs and a more pronounced local speech and style. In them the refugees were usually received not merely as nuisances who deprived you of half your house and shared your kitchen, but as foreigners. And is it surprising? One has only to think of the stolid unprogressive dwellers in some remote Hessian valley, with its pre-capitalist agriculture, and of how they will react to the presence of refugees from a large Sudeten industrial town. The refugees will be skilled workers, tradesmen, or industrialists, having nothing in common with the inhabitants, and their life together will be made up of suspicion and misunderstanding. Similarly in the ultra-Catholic Bavarian villages which had to receive Protestant refugees.

The conflict is so serious that in more than one district a regular class war atmosphere has developed. This description of it is all the more apt because it can truly be said that the refugees have become proletarianised. There having been no agrarian reform, refugees who were formerly peasant-proprietors find themselves compelled to work as hired hands, along with others—intellectuals, tradesmen, artisans—who have no country experience. In the Federal Republic as a whole one quarter of the working peasants are refugees, but by May, 1949, only 4 per cent of the holdings of over an acre had been allotted to them. But it is not only in the country that the refugees have become proletarianised. Of the refugees who are active today, 16 per cent were economically independent and 21 per cent were working in family businesses in 1939. By 1949 this was true of only 5 per cent and 3 per cent respectively. Today 92 per cent of the refugees are working for wages and only too thankful if they can earn enough to feed and house their families. There are still more than 300,000 in the camps of Schleswig and Bavaria, where children are born and grow up knowing no other life than the ugliness and promiscuity and squalor of their huts; and there are young people in the camps who have grown so used to idleness that they prefer to live miserably on a penurious dole rather than look for a well-paid but exacting job.

The Federal Republic's essential problem, as its leaders recognise, is the assimilation of the refugees. Are they doing as much as they could to solve it? Many and various measures have been taken to assist the refugees. There is a special bank whose principal function it is to provide credit for refugees wishing to start a business or workshop; and in 1950 and 1951 refugees were permitted by law to acquire and work 23,000 holdings of more than one acre. The emergency assistance scheme (*Soforthilfe*) and the equalisation of burdens programme (*Lastenausgleich*) have been applied principally for the benefit of refugees.[3] But the *Lastenausgleich* as finally passed by parliament on 16 May, 1952, was so framed as to bear very lightly on the present owners and contained two very questionable principles. Contributions were also levied on the property and capital assets of publicly owned enterprises, that is to say, from the public as a whole, both rich and poor; and allocations were distributed, not according to the beneficiary's present needs but according to his former economic status. The *Vertriebenengesetz* adopted by the Bundestag on 25 February, 1953, was a comprehensive measure confirming, completing, and making uniform the various laws of the individual *Länder* concerning refugees and expelled persons. Can it be said that the results have been satisfactory as a whole? They are as follows: 128,000 new businesses have been started by refugees; 35 per cent of the refugees have found work suitable to their qualifications and skill, and 45 per cent have found jobs, sometimes only seasonal, "below their status"; 20 per cent are still a public charge. Social assimilation is progressing. Mixed marriages (between refugees and old inhabitants) accounted for 20·6 per cent of the total marriages in 1950, 22·1 per cent in 1951, and 23·3 per cent in 1952, the wife being in most cases a native of the district and the husband a refugee. Theodor Oberländer, the minister for refugees in Adenauer's second cabinet, has prepared a two-year plan to speed up the process of assimilation. He proposes in particular that refugees should take in hand a large number of the 250,000 farms now held by women, and especially those owned by women of over 65 (of which there are 51,000).

Taken as a whole, the measures adopted fall far short—considerable though they are—of carrying out the concrete proposals of the Sonne report, which was issued early in 1951 by an American commission of enquiry. But if more has not been done, says the government, it is for lack of money. New credits, and especially foreign credits, would be required for financing the six-year plan proposed, at an estimated cost of 12 milliard marks, in the Sonne report. But there are two other, and deeper, reasons for the government's ineffectiveness.

One of these is the liberal policy of Professor Erhard. The Sonne report considered that "direct measures should be taken to limit construction of buildings that are inconsistent with the refugee program and in case of need to allocate certain basic materials", and went on to say that "It is desirable to force a considerable part of business profits heretofore used for self-financing out into the open market". It ended with the following severe observations: "Some circumstances have made it easy for a few to obtain large incomes. Not enough has yet been done to enable the less fortunate to achieve a satisfactory standard of living. . . . There is a tendency on the part of some elements of the business and financial community in western Germany to be too self-seeking and too little interested in the general welfare. . . . It has been said that, through the lack of courage to stop the dictator in time, the first German Republic was lost. Care must be taken to avoid losing the new Federal Republic through greed."[4]

The other reason is more complex, and derives from the international situation. As early as 1947 the Czech government was protesting vigorously because the Sudeten refugees in the American zone were treated as a distinct category of Germans. It cited in contrast the practice in the Soviet zone where no distinction was recognised between original inhabitants and new arrivals, and where organisations of refugees with newspapers of their own were not allowed.[5] The point at issue was that, according to the eastern view, the expulsions were irreversible and the Oder-Neisse line was a finally established boundary, whereas the west took a much less simple view of the matter. The Federal Republic, as it is entitled to do, refuses to accept the loss of the eastern territories to Poland, for this could only be confirmed by the peace treaty, whose terms Germany will help to draw up. To assimilate the refugees would be to recognise the *fait accompli*. To the best of our knowledge, the problem has never been stated very clearly in this form. Everything suggests, on the contrary, that the possibility of the refugees returning some day to their homes is doing service both as a reason and as an excuse for the delay in assimilating them. The more ineffective the measures taken to assimilate them, the more they are encouraged to believe in their eventual return home; and the more they believe this, the less effort will be made to assimilate them.

Yet the German government knows quite well that the peaceful return home of the populations expelled from the east is practically impossible. The population of Breslau was 650,000 in 1939. Today it is 450,000, of whom barely 1,800 are German. In Hindenburg there remain today 2,000 Germans out of the 1939 population of 150,000, but the town has now become Polish and has a population of 172,000. A return transfer of population back to the former German territories is most improbable, so what likelihood is there of a return to territories which were Polish or Czech before 1937? It may be that Poland and Czechoslovakia will want more of the German industrial and agricultural experts of whom they already have a considerable number; but the Oder-Neisse line is quite certainly a "peace frontier", even though we may not interpret that word as the east does. The matter was correctly summed up by the American congressional commission of enquiry, which investigated the refugee problem in 1950 under the direction of congressman Walter: "The return of the German expulsees and refugees to their former abodes remains within the realm of theory. The American nation, praying and working for peace, rejects outright all suggestions—whispered as they are, rather than voiced—which envisage solutions impossible to achieve without the application of force. . . . The major solution of the problem of the German expellees and refugees must lie in their local assimilation in the German economy."[6]

The refugees themselves find their situation very difficult. On 5 August, 1950, at Cannstatt near Stuttgart, their various organisations jointly adopted a 'Charter of expelled Germans' (Charta der deutschen Heimatvertriebenen) which they still regard as basic. It contains the statement: "We renounce vengeance and retaliation. . . . We will encourage with all our might every attempt to create a united Europe, whose peoples may live without fear or constraint. It is our mission to insist that the right to one's native land must be acknowledged and exercised as one of the fundamental rights bestowed upon men by God. Nevertheless we do not wish, so long as this right is denied to us, to remain condemned to idleness or to hold ourselves aloof." These words imply the hope of a peaceful return to their lost homes, a repudiation of any out-and-out moral and political assimilation to the people of western Germany, and, at the same time, a demand for economic and social integration. But in reality integration leads to assimilation. It is no chance that the refugee organisations are weak wherever the new arrivals have become incorporated with the local population and strong wherever there is material and psychological friction. If the allied and German authorities had had a better policy for integrating the refugees, these organisations would today be wearing quite a different complexion. But even as it is, integration has taken place to a sufficient extent to prevent them from speaking in the name of all, or even the majority of, the refugees.

The first of the refugee organisations to function throughout western Germany has for its essential aim to defend the material interests of all refugees, irrespective of their origin; it tries to facilitate their integration, more especially through the better working of the *Lastenausgleich*. This is the Z.V.D. (*Zentralverband der vertriebenen Deutschen*) or central league of expelled Germans, and its president is a Christian-Democrat deputy, Dr Linus Kather. Dr Kather's influence with the refugees was so great that, in the early summer of 1952, the Chancellor was trying, though without success, to persuade the Federal minister for refugees, Hans Lukaschek, to retire in favour of Kather, who could secure some additional votes for the coalition at the 1953 election. But in August of the same year an event occurred which considerably lessened the influence of the Z.V.D. At Bad Kissingen a federation of Landsmannschaften (V.D.L.) was formed with Dr Lodgmann von Aue, the spokesman (*Sprecher*) of the Sudeten German Landsmannschaft, as its president. In the political field there had already emerged earlier still—on the regional level in January, 1950, and on the Federal level in January, 1951 —the organisation known as the "union of the expelled and dispossessed" (B.H.E.).* The V.D.L. itself is not a political party, but aims only to become the co-ordinating organisation for all the Landsmannschaften. It is the opposition between the Z.V.D. and the Landsmannschaften that has prevented up to now the formation of the comprehensive organisation for refugees which was decided upon in principle in November, 1951.

A Landsmannschaft is a group whose objectives are neither material nor political. It aims to be "the expression and at the same time the representative of the lost homeland (Heimat)

* See chapter vi.

and of the people who dwelt there". Thus there are a dozen Landsmannschaften trying to bring together in groups the former Pomeranians, Silesians, and Brandenburgers, as well as the former German inhabitants of the Carpathians, Hungary or Bukovina. Their chief activity is a sort of cultural propaganda reminding their members, and other Germans, of the material and, above all, the artistic and intellectual riches of the regions they have been compelled to abandon. They issue magnificent booklets setting out the former splendours of Koenigsberg or Breslau, and recall incessantly the men of learning, poets, and thinkers given to Germany by the lost regions. But not given to Germany only—for the emphasis is coming to be laid more and more upon the loss to the world, the damage to "European and western culture", inflicted by the loss of those regions. This is the theme of great meetings, such as the impressive rally of the Sudeten Germans at Frankfurt on 17 and 18 May, 1953. The explanation of this development is to be found in the general political climate. In 1946, when the rupture between east and west was not yet final, the Landsmannschaften were still forbidden by the occupying powers and by some of the *Länder*; but today the Federal government openly encourages them, not only because they are now a power but also because what they assert is coming to be recognised as official truth, namely, that the situation east of the Oder-Neisse line is one of out-and-out barbarity.

This state of mind is disquieting. Not that the nostalgic remembrance of a lost fatherland and the hope of regaining it are in themselves reprehensible, even when there is no reasonable chance of the hope being fulfilled without another war. To suggest that such hopes necessarily imply a will to war is to suggest that the Alsatians and Lorrainers living in France between 1871 and 1914 wanted a war with Germany. Logic and sentiment do not always go hand in hand. At a congress of Landsmannschaften at Frankfurt on 1 July, 1951, the youth organisation of Germans expelled from the east (Deutsche Jugend des Ostens) put forward a "profession of faith" which may be naïve, but we have no a priori justification for doubting its sincerity: ". . . Renouncing vengeance and hatred, we are prepared to work for a new Europe, universal and liberal. Inspired by sincere will and bitter experience, we feel ourselves united with the youth of all liberty-loving peoples, to whom we extend our hand. In the new Europe, we look for the liberation of our brothers and sisters east of the Elbe and the Oder and the Neisse and for our peaceful return to our racial home (angestammte Heimat). For we believe in the victory of reason, the victory of good will, and the victory of justice!"[7]

But the Landsmannschaften seem more and more to regard themselves as the vanguard of the civilised west in its struggle against the barbarous east; and are they not encouraged in this by propagandists elsewhere who no longer remember the monstrous sufferings inflicted on the eastern countries by Hitler's Germany? The Landsmannschaften are even more systematically anti-communist than the average German; and not anti-communist only, for they represent the expulsion of Germans from the east as a sort of Slavic reinvasion which wipes out the effects of centuries of German, and Christian, penetration in eastern Europe. There has been as yet no open call to arms, but the crusading spirit is alive. In a Landsmannschaft notice summoning former inhabitants of East Prussia to a meeting on 3 August, 1952, we may read: "East Prussians, call to mind the words of our Knights' song and you will know what our business is". On the back of the notice are printed the words of the song in question. They are all about cavalry charges and death for the fatherland in the east, oaths of fidelity and clarion calls. Such exhortations may be harmless in themselves, and were bound to be made sooner or later by the more hot-headed refugees. But it becomes dangerous if they can feel they are getting encouragement from the newspapers and if the government lacks the will or courage to call them to order and to state firmly that it recognises no remedy for their plight except a vigorous policy of integration.

The substitution of Theodor Oberländer for Dr Lukaschek in October, 1953, is certainly not a good sign. Oberländer is a specialist in agrarian questions and the problems of the east. He held appointments in the U.S.S.R. on several occasions before becoming professor of agriculture in the university of Danzig. After the attack on Russia he was appointed propaganda adviser to the "Russian liberation movement" or, in other words, Vlassov's army. Previously he had taken part in the "depolonisation" of territories occupied by the German army, writing an article in the review *Neues Bauerntum* in which he advocated drastic expulsion of the Poles as the only means of obtaining "racial purity" in the eastern territories. This article hardly qualifies him to protest against the expulsions of 1945–46. A former Hauptsturmfuehrer of the S.A., since becoming minister he has got rid of the anti-nazi officials brought in by the Christian-Democrat Lukaschek and taken on instead men such as Venzki, a former official propagandist of the Third Reich and recipient of the party's gold badge. Two facts are enough to prove that Oberländer would never contemplate renouncing the eastern territories (and it would be interesting to know just where he would fix their frontiers). The first is that he wants courses on them to be given in every German school and university, and the second is that he wants the best of the refugees not to be sent to the Rhineland or Württemberg but to be kept in the east—even at heavy expense to the state—so that the idea of return can be kept alive and well represented.

* * *

The refugees are the outstanding German social problem, but they are not the only one. Another is the great difference between the various regions. The figures relating to internal population movements are significant of this, even after making allowance for the transfers of refugees. In the period 1950–52 alone, Schleswig-Holstein, Lower Saxony, and Bavaria lost, respectively, 265,000, 278,000, and 131,000 of their inhabitants, while North Rhineland-Westphalia, Hamburg and Württemberg-Baden increased their populations by 715,000, 134,000, and 265,000.

There is, however, another even more significant fact. The word 'proletariat' is usually taken to mean the working class, and the proletariat is thought of as the least privileged group in a population. But in western Germany there is a sub-proletariat so considerable that it makes the working class seem by comparison an authentic middle class. We are not now referring to the difference between salaried employees and wage-earners—although the salaries of the former are 25 per cent lower than the wages of the latter—but to the "economic casualties". These include not only the unrehabilitated refugees but many other categories as well: the old, the widows, the disabled, the ruined rentiers without aptitude or training for new jobs. There are more than twelve million Germans living on pensions or doles, over and above the recipients of unemployment pay; but of course there are many cases where people are entitled to pensions from more than one source. The most reliable estimates put the "economic casualties" at between eight and nine million—not including their children. The pensions and grants are ridiculously small. A monthly wage of less than 250 DM. is considered too low, and yet a war widow receives between 70 and 90 DM. a month, on condition that she is over 40 and has at least one child, plus an extra 31 DM. for each child; and a wounded man with a 75 per cent disability who has a wife and two children gets 107 DM. A man with a similar family and a 100 per cent disability gets 210 DM.[8]

Among the wage-earners we find something that is not typically German—wages are being levelled out and the labour hierarchy broken down. For example, if we take the skilled worker's wage as 100, compared to his pre-war wage, then the figure for the semi-skilled would be 110 and for the unskilled 114. At the end of May, 1952, the index figure for male workers was 152, taking 1936 as 100, and for female workers it was 222. (It should be noted, however, that women's wages as a whole are still less than 67 per cent of men's.) But the important point is the workers' standard of living, and it would appear that by the beginning of 1952 it had reached a level about equal to that of 1936, which was a year of economic hardship. In the course of 1952 and 1953 the level rose by about 15 per cent and reached that of 1938. The rise of wages was irregular and occurred in successive waves, but since 1949 it has been considerable. The trade unions do not contest these figures but they insist that the wage-earners have profited very little from the return of national prosperity and they emphasise—what the government does not deny—that the rate of increase of the social product is slowing down. It was 25 per cent in 1951, 10·6 per cent in 1952, 5·5 per cent in 1953, and will probably be less still in 1954. Wages have always risen very little compared to the increase in production. There was a 25 per cent production increase in 1950, followed by a rise in wages of only 14·7 per cent in 1951, and the production increases of 19·1 per cent and 7·1 per cent in 1951 and 1952 were followed in 1952 and 1953 by rises of only 7·5 per cent and 2·5 per cent in wages. How far is it possible for the trade unions to improve the unfavourable position of the wage-earners?

Trade unionism made considerable progresss in Germany between 1918 and the coming of the nazis. There were three main movements of which the largest was the Socialist "free unions", with three times as many members as the Christian unions and ten times as many as the Liberal unions, whose members were principally office workers. On 1 May, 1933, all three were suppressed by Hitler and replaced by his 'Labour Front'. At the end of the war the allies encouraged the revival of the trade unions, considering them the most hopeful element for the "democratisation" of Germany. The first instructions issued for the American military government, dated 28 April, 1945, before the surrender, banned political activity but provided for the restoration of the unions.[9]

Many of the German trade unionists who began organising after the end of hostilities had been among the leaders before 1933. Whatever their original labels, the fact that they had lived together through the war and the nazi persecution and were now obliged to stand together in dealing with the allies, inclined them to work together to create a unified trade union movement. But there was a serious obstacle. In the Soviet zone a new central organisation had been formed at the outset, but the western powers, wishing to revive gradually the local German administrative and political authorities, insisted that local organisations must be formed first. The British commander-in-chief was the first to allow a central organisation for his entire zone; but his American and French colleagues would only allow organisation in the *Länder*.[10] After 1948 American policy changed fairly rapidly, but in February, 1949, the French were still vetoing a central organisation for the whole of western Germany, and the veto was not lifted until two months later, after the signing of the Atlantic treaty and the fusion of the French zone with the other two. At last it was possible to hold the constituent conference which brought into being the D.G.B. or federation of German trade unions (Deutscher Gewerkschaftsbund). This assembly was held at Munich, 12–14 October, 1949, and the headquarters of the federation was fixed at Düsseldorf. Its president was Hans Böckler, the most respected of the surviving pre-war union leaders.

Today the D.G.B. with its six million members, is the only large German trade union organisation. It includes all the industrial workers' unions and a larger number of office workers than the D.A.G. or clerical union (Deutsche Angestellten-Gewerkschaft), and also more civil servants than the ultra-conservative Deutscher Beamtenbund (public employees' union), which does not admit the practice of strikes. So far, no outside attempt to weaken the D.G.B. by forming a 'factional' organisation with a political or religious "slant" has been successful. In 1950 a Federation of Christian Unions (not to be confused with the Katholischer Arbeiterbund, of which we shall have more to say) was formed at Essen but has not attracted more than a thousand members. We shall have to discuss the problems of maintaining trade union unity, but first it is necessary to examine the aims of German trade union activity, and its methods and achievements.

Like every professional organisation, the German unions seek to improve the living and working conditions of their members. Discussions about wages and hours and security of employment are as common in Germany as elsewhere. But for the D.G.B. all this is only a sort of guerrilla war, concerned with the immediate needs of its members and the defence of their interests within the existing social and economic system. It considers that its real aim is a radical reform of the social structure.[11]

The D.G.B. believes in parliamentary methods, as evolved on the continent in the nineteenth century, and regards universal suffrage and freedom of opinion and association as essential safeguards of parliamentary democracy. It is therefore violently anti-communist. But it considers that democracy is very incomplete while it applies only to the political, or more accurately the electoral, function of its citizens and completely ignores their economic function. What killed the Weimar Republic was precisely the fact that economic power was concentrated in the hands of a few men who used it to help Hitler to destroy political democracy. The workers have gradually achieved political equality, but still today, in the twentieth century, they are as destitute of economic power as they were of political power, in Germany, a hundred years ago. On 6 April, 1839, the first act of social legislation forbade the employment of children under nine years of age, and undoubtedly there has been considerable improvement in the workers' living conditions since then. But the point at issue is not material improvement, but a share of economic power.

A share, but not exclusive possession. The D.G.B. has no desire to destroy capitalism. Although it does demand the nationalisation of basic industries, its real aim is equality between capital and labour and not the abolition of the distinction between them. Empirical rather than theoretical, its campaign is essentially for 'co-determination' on every level of economic power—within each business and professional organisation, in the application of economic policy in each of the *Länder* and in the Federal Republic as a whole. On 22 May, 1950, the D.G.B. presented draft proposals for the complete sharing of economic power and responsibility on a parity basis on every level from the factory management up to a national economic council. In this way, it claims, both political democracy and a new status for the workers are automatically guaranteed. To the objection that "the workers are not competent to assume so much responsibility" the D.G.B. replies that the same thing was said in the nineteenth century about political responsibility—when the citizens were grouped in estates, particularly in Prussia, according to their economic status—whereas today there is no-one who questions the principle of political equality on the ground that the workers are not competent. But there is another objection to which the reply is less clear. The equal sharing of responsibility between capital and labour implies the co-operation of two powers whose nature it seems to be to oppose one another rather than to make decisions in common. We shall have to discuss this fundamental question at greater length, for it actually jeopardises the whole idea of co-determination.

German trade unionism wishes to be able to fight for its

THE SOCIAL BACKGROUND 133

objectives on equal terms with those who oppose them. Both the day-to-day struggle and the long-term objectives of the D.G.B. are served by the maintenance of discipline, and the intellectual training of militants and organisers, and specialists in economic and social problems. The trade union institute of economic studies, to whose work we have already referred, employs permanently at Cologne about fifty economists, social scientists and statisticians; and there are 'social academies' and 'workers' universities' which provide evening classes, lectures, and longer courses on economic, political and social problems for working men, and more especially for the young. Not all these institutions are closely connected with the D.G.B., but there are also special D.G.B. schools for training future trade union organisers and officials. These schools give instruction in labour legislation as well as political economy, and the art of public speaking and conducting discussions as well as the legal aspects of social security. In the wider cultural sphere the D.G.B. organises an annual 'Festival of the Ruhr' (Ruhrfestspiel). The 1952 festival at Recklinghausen included explanatory lectures, round table political discussions, professional and amateur theatrical performances, films, discussions on art, and exhibitions of painting and dancing. This labour cultural festival lasted seven weeks and the total of spectators and participants amounted to 120,000 persons. The seventh festival, in 1953, was on a smaller scale but quite as successful.

The D.G.B. can indulge in these displays because of its considerable wealth, which also enables it to maintain a fairly numerous staff at its large building in Düsseldorf. The sixteen constituent federations have a total membership of more than six millions, and the number is constantly increasing. The central administration gets 15 per cent of all dues collected by the various unions and there is, in addition, a solidarity fund financed by quarterly subscriptions of 0·15 DM. from each individual member. These subscriptions amount to more than 3½ million DM. (about £300,000 or slightly less than a million dollars) a year. The weekly union membership fee is calculated as the value of one hour's work, and members' payments are unlikely to get into arrears because in most cases the sum is deducted in advance from their pay—a method which is undoubtedly beneficial to the D.G.B.'s treasury but not perhaps a perfect example of democratic finance!

Financial power is vital to labour because the threat of a strike has much more weight when the employers know that the unions are rich enough to make it a long one. It is perhaps to prevent any ill-considered use of this threat, and also certainly to maintain the central authority, that the D.G.B.'s 'instructions for the conduct of industrial disputes' are so strict. Article 19 makes it obligatory for union members to obey the instructions. No strike may be declared until every effort at negotiation has been made. A local union may not start a strike without the authority of its national federation; and once the strike has been authorised there must be a referendum of all union members of more than three months' standing and a majority of 75 per cent must be obtained before the strike can commence. Nor will work automatically stop even when this majority has been obtained, for "before resorting to action in a dispute (Arbeitskampf) federations must take into account not only the result of the referendum but also such general considerations as the state of business and the repercussions of a strike upon other sectors of the economy". But in practice authorisation to hold a referendum implies authorisation to apply its verdict.

The return to work is controlled in a similar way, the federation handling the negotiations on behalf of the strikers. The D.G.B. federal council at Düsseldorf (composed of eleven permanent members and one representative of each affiliated federation) has in theory only the right to be informed by the federations before any far-reaching action is undertaken. But according to article 11 of the instructions, headquarters will give financial support only in return for the right of supervision over the development and conclusion of the strike, so it can be said that Düsseldorf, thanks in particular to its possession of the solidarity fund, in effect has the deciding voice. It goes without saying that the D.G.B. tolerates only 'official' strikes. In this connection it is laid down by article 10 that "the representatives of any union within whose sphere a strike occurs, which has not been properly decided upon and authorised, must see that there is a prompt return to work, while safeguarding the workers' interests so far as possible".

There is a loophole in the directives of which the union leaders can take advantage. Should the 75 per cent majority be a majority of all union members, or only of votes cast? In the 1951 metallurgical industry strike in Hesse, for example, the majority at the initial referendum was a majority of votes cast. It was over 75 per cent, so the strike became 'legal'. There was a further vote after the negotiation of a compromise agreement between unions and employers, and it was claimed that the strike should cease because only 65 per cent, or less than three-quarters, of the total membership had voted against the agreement. But of the votes actually cast, 81 per cent had been for a continuation of the strike. Nevertheless, the 70,000 engineering workers obeyed union discipline and returned to work. In general, however, its directives and its financial resources give the D.G.B. such power that the mere threat of a strike often enables it to gain its point without resorting to strike action. There was a notable example of this in connection with the law on co-determination in the coal and metallurgical industries.[12]

Co-determination was introduced by the occupation authorities in 1945, and when the Federal Republic came into being a federal law was necessary to replace the allied legislation. In the course of long discussions every aspect of the problem was examined by the unions, the employers, the political parties and the Churches.* At the beginning of 1951 the question was about to be finally discussed and settled by parliament, when the D.G.B. went into action. It organised a referendum throughout the coal and metallurgical industries and announced, after obtaining 95 per cent support, that there would be a general strike on 1 February unless the government undertook to support a draft law which satisfied the unions' claims. On 25 January there was a decisive interview between the Chancellor and Hans Böckler, which produced agreement. The strike was called off and the Chancellor's party—the Christian Democratic Union—passed a law with the support of the socialist opposition, which was opposed by the other government parties and also by the opposition from the right.

This law, of 21 May, 1951, applies to every coal and metal-

* See chapters v and vi.

lurgical enterprise with more than 1,000 employees. It entrusts the management of each of them to two bodies, a supervisory council (Aufsichtsrat) of eleven members whose function is policy-making, and a management committee (Vorstand) of three members, which is a sort of executive. The method of appointment of the eleven members of the Aufsichtsrat is as follows. There are four representatives of the owner or owners and four of the employees, and to each of these groups is added a fifth member who must not belong to the firm or have any financial interest in it. The 'eleventh man' is nominated jointly by the employers' and workers' representatives, and there is a very complicated procedure for cases where they are unable to agree. It amounts in practice to the appointment of a government nominee, which means, in present conditions, a person who is on the side of the five employers' representatives.

Of the four direct representatives of the workers only two—one manual and one clerical—need be members of the firm. The other two can be full-time union officials. But even the first two have to be approved by the trade union federations concerned. The law does provide that the workers in the firm shall elect them, but candidature is not open to all. Candidates "are proposed by the factory committees after consultation with the unions interested in the firm and with their central organisations. . . . The electors can only vote for candidates proposed by the factory committee and the central organisations." As for the Vorstand, its three members have equal status and are the business manager, the production manager, and the 'Arbeitsdirektor' (literally labour manager, but actually social organiser). The last-named cannot be appointed or dismissed without the majority consent of the five workers' representatives.

It was not only the law itself but the prerogatives it granted to the D.G.B., that incensed the employers and the conservatives in Parliament. They consider it intolerable that trade unionists from outside the business should sit on the supervisory council, and that the trade union federation should have an equal voice with the employees in choosing the employees' own representatives. The controlling power thus acquired by the D.G.B. appears to them exorbitant and they accuse the majority which voted the law of having sanctioned a trade union monopoly which is far more powerful than any trust ever was. The D.G.B. replies that the retired generals and diplomats and the magnates of other businesses who traditionally sat upon directors' boards were also outsiders to the businesses they were called upon to direct; it further points out that the trade union control of candidates eliminates the 'official candidate' on whose behalf the employers may exert pressure. This last argument appears to us illogical, because the procedure it defends is itself strongly weighted in favour of centralisation and bureaucracy in the D.G.B. It lessens the power of the rank and file and increases that of the higher organisations. The fact that some of the employees' representatives come from outside the business is more justifiable. The trade union schools have not yet turned out so many militants that there are sure to be several workers or clerks in every business who are competent to sit upon the supervisory council —competent, that is to say, to examine a balance sheet or judge pricing or investment policies.

The main attack, however, was not against the detailed provisions of the law but against the manner in which it had been passed, a surrender to "mob clamour". For was it not intolerable that the D.G.B., representing only a fraction of the population, should have been able, by the threat of a strike, to blackmail parliament, which represents the whole population, into passing one piece of legislation rather than another? Did this not prove that the D.G.B. was becoming a state within the state and a totalitarian force which threatened the very existence of democracy?

This argument has had some success. On 24 August, 1952, the Cologne labour tribunal upheld the action of the *Kölnische Rundschau* (the largest Cologne newspaper) against the D.G.B. and the federation of printing unions for organising a two-day strike in May of that year. This strike, said the tribunal, was "prejudicial to law and public morality" because it was intended "to influence legislation and obstruct the normal process of law-making". The D.G.B. was inconsistent in its official comment on this judgment. It claimed that there had been only a "demonstration" and not a "strike with a political purpose". But according to its own doctrine it could have rebutted the charge of "undemocratic" action in quite a different way. In the first place, the threat to strike is no worse a form of pressure than that exercised upon parliament by the pressure-groups of well-known economic interests; and, secondly, the strike "intended to influence legislation" is only reprehensible if the existing parliamentary system is to be regarded as the ideal democratic régime. And this is precisely what German trade unionism denies. For it, the exertion of pressure upon legislation is the principal method for transforming a political democracy into a democracy which shall be both political *and* economic.

Why is it, then, that the D.G.B. has given up using the arguments it should use? And why did it not take action in July, 1952, when a general law on works councils was passed which was far from satisfactory to it and one of whose effects was to prevent any general application of the principle of co-determination on a parity basis? Action on a large scale had in fact been announced, so why was it called off?

The first reason, perhaps, is to be found in the general character of the working-class struggle in Germany. Ever since the nineteenth century the line followed by employers and government on the one hand and workers on the other has been very different from that of employers and workers in France, for example. Bismarck was quick to perceive the necessity to grant social reforms rather than let them be extorted from him, and his successors have followed the same policy. As early as the mid-nineteenth century the big German industrialists realised that every advance of their own power ought to bring with it some advantage for their employees, and thanks to these ideas the German workers were the first to enjoy substantial measures of social security and better working and living conditions. So they grew accustomed to being given, rather than fighting for, what they needed.

The employers and the government appeared as embodiments of paternal authority watching over the welfare of their subjects and entitled, if not to absolute obedience, at any rate to respect; and in addition there was the German workman's love of good work for its own sake and his feeling of solidarity with the firm he works for. These sentiments made no small contribution to Germany's recovery and they explain the statement of the president of the national union of German employers' federations, on 14 June, 1951, that "never in our history have relations between employers and their workers and staffs been so good, and even cordial, as they are today".[13]

The idea of class war, therefore, has very little hold in Germany and this explains the trade union formula for co-determination, which presupposes the trustful co-operation between capital and labour without which a business cannot be successfully run. But the D.G.B. is beginning to perceive that the employers do not welcome a form of co-operation which involves the sharing of responsibility. Paternal consultations with employees are approved, but not the "semi-expropriation" which co-determination would imply in the coal and steel industries. This attitude of the employers is the more embarrassing to the D.G.B. because its own behaviour to its members has always been somewhat paternally authoritarian. In this connection the rapid change of outlook of many of the "personnel managers" is characteristic. They have ceased to be working-class representatives and adopted the attitude of managers, displaying a benevolent solicitude towards their former comrades but no longer feeling real solidarity with them. Ought the D.G.B., then, on the one hand to democratise itself, and on the other to take a stronger line and proclaim the necessity of fighting for something more than a share of economic responsibility? Some of its members, especially among the younger element, are pushing it in that direction. But there is another difficulty, which arises from the general trend of political development.

Among the members of the D.G.B. are supporters of more than one political party. It is true that the majority are socialist; and it seems to be an established custom to elect presidents of a socialist tendency and vice-presidents of some denominational affiliation. When Hans Böckler died, on 16 February, 1951, he was succeeded by the moderate socialist, Christian Fette, and not by the intransigent secretary of the metallurgical federation, Walter Freitag. The latter was to be elected in October, 1952, in circumstances which we shall describe later.

In the first years after the war there was no difficulty in maintaining unity. To the occupying powers the trade unions appeared as a genuinely democratic force at a time when it was desired to punish the great industrialists for having helped Hitler to kill democracy. The social conceptions of the two big political parties, the Socialists and the Christian-Democrats, were not very different, although they were already in opposition in the economic and educational spheres; and the views they held in common seemed also to be shared by the churches. Even after the formation of the Federal government and the political rupture between Dr Adenauer's party and Dr Schumacher's Social Democrats, the D.G.B. was able to carry on without too much friction. Its own power was so great that no political party could take it under its wing. Indeed, it was the parties which needed the unions, and not the other way about; and that is how the co-determination law got passed. For the same reason the D.G.B. was able to take a considered and genuinely independent line in the dispute about the Schuman plan; indeed, to some observers the D.G.B. had come to seem not so much a state within the state as a sort of refuge of level-headedness and democratic firmness while the political parties clamorously tried to outbid one another.

Today the situation has changed. For the German Catholic church, as well as for the Christian-Democratic union, the "defence of the west", or more accurately its preservation, is tending to take precedence over social preoccupations.*
This change is itself the consequence of world political developments. For the United States, particularly, it is no longer a question of opposing the forces which made Hitler possible and defining as democratic those which resisted him, but rather of appealing to all Germans alike to rally to the defence of a democracy which is coming to mean little more than militant anti-communism.

Thus whenever the unions emphasise their purpose of transforming political democracy into political and economic and social democracy, they provoke the reaction: "These demands are a sympton of class war; class war equals Marxism; Marxism equals communism; therefore the unions are playing into the

* See chapters v and vi.

hands of communists." Every strike and every demonstration against the existing state of affairs is coming more and more to be regarded as an activity which promotes communism, and as sabotaging the defence of the west. The unions, which were once thought of as the spearhead of democracy, are now looked upon rather as an obstacle to it. In February, 1954, Dr Richard Schmid, president of the court of appeal at Stuttgart, published an article defending the strike as a weapon for wider purposes than wage claims and pointing out that Germany could have been saved from Hitlerism by a general strike. This immediately provoked a violent editorial in the otherwise very moderate economic journal, *Deutsche Zeitung und Wirtschaftszeitung*, attacking and denouncing as "Marxist" the very principle of the strike intended to exert political pressure. This explains the uncertainty of the D.G.B. leaders. They feel themselves on the defensive and are anxious at all costs to avoid being accused of even unintentional communism. Fearing to adopt any general position which might weaken trade union unity, they have avoided any decisive pronouncements on specific problems, thus satisfying nobody and causing discontent among a large section of their members. The debate on rearmament is the best example of this. It revealed violent opposition to the D.G.B. central leadership on the part of rank-and-file militants, especially in Bavaria.

On 17 October, 1952, the D.G.B. congress in Berlin did not re-elect Christian Fette. After a close vote, it was Walter Freitag who succeeded to the presidency. Fette had failed in two ways to satisfy his followers. He had been hesitant and maladroit in the D.G.B.'s campaign to get the principle of co-determination recognised in the law on works councils; and he had exceeded his powers by supporting, in his capacity of president of the D.G.B., the Chancellor's policy of military integration. The Christian-Democrat, Matthias Föcher, was unanimously re-elected to serve with Freitag as vice-president.

The new leaders had to prepare for the approaching general elections. The chief object of attack was the right wing of the government coalition and particularly the minister of justice, Dr Dehler, who had on several occasions made violent speeches against the unions. A few weeks before the elections the D.G.B.

issued the slogan "Vote for a better Bundestag"; whereupon it was criticised for violating the political neutrality of the unions. The Chancellor even wrote an official letter of protest to Walter Freitag, on 30 July, 1953, and complained throughout the campaign about the D.G.B.'s "partisan attitude". Freitag replied that the slogan was essentially directed against the Free Democratic or Liberal party and that it had been adopted by the executive committee unanimously, including the Christian members.

In its first issue after the elections the D.G.B.'s weekly, *Welt der Arbeit*, stated that "the unions of course accept and respect the clear decision by the Federal Republic's electorate announced last Sunday".* At the same time Walter Dirks, whose word is influential with the 'left Christians', was writing in *Michael*, a young Catholics' weekly: "The Christian-Democratic Union has the opportunity to make the second Bundestag a 'better' Bundestag in just the sense intended by the D.G.B." But the victorious parties were not in conciliatory mood, and the less so because the K.A.B. (Katholischer Arbeiterbund), the Catholic workers' association, which is not a trade union, was fanning the flame of controversy. On 16 September the D.G.B. received a letter—emanating from the social commission of the Christian-Democratic party, the K.A.B., and its Protestant equivalent, the E.A.B.—which demanded the co-option of "Christians" to the directing bodies of the D.G.B., both central and local, and of the various federations, and also the formation of specifically "Christian" groups within the D.G.B. On 30 September the D.G.B.'s executive council, which of course included also members with a Christian Union orientation, sent a unanimous reply rejecting these demands as contrary to its statutes, which admit of no denominational or political distinction between its members. It seemed possible that a new trade union organisation would be formed, independent of the D.G.B. and in reality opposed to it; but so far this has not happened. One of the reasons for not disturbing the *status quo* is that it would be a very hazardous operation. The new organisation would certainly have considerable financial resources; but how many union members

* For an account of the elections, see chapter VI.

would leave the D.G.B. in defiance of the plea for unity of all its leaders, "Christians" included? Another reason is the new attitude of the D.G.B. itself, which could be described as complete inaction due to the fear of being accused of political partisanship.

Yet not one of the major demands of the German unions has so far been met—neither full employment, nor a social fiscal policy, nor equality of economic rights. In preparation for May Day, 1954, the D.G.B. did issue a slogan demanding the 40-hour week; but the chances of abolishing the 48-hour week are slight. Perhaps in certain industries the employers will accept a five-day week of 48 hours instead of the six-day week. But the D.G.B.'s offensive weapons are blunted; and the reason for this is essentially that, whereas up to 1951 it was borne on the current of events, it is now, three years later, reduced to stemming a current of which it disapproves.

* * *

Little is known outside Germany about the refugee problem, and German trade unionism is very little studied. But there is a third social group which has been the subject of innumerable enquiries, discourses, and articles ever since 1945—namely, youth. The numerical preponderance of the young seems to justify this preferential treatment, for one-third of the Republic's population is under twenty years old. But it is too often forgotten that this social group is much less homogeneous than the others; and information is sought about the opinions of German youth, as though it were sufficiently homogeneous to be regarded as a collective body with opinions held in common. Moreover, by concentrating on the description of youth's attitude to this or that one ends by completely ignoring the social realities which largely explain the attitude.

Here are some of these realities. The war made 250,000 orphans; 1,250,000 children lost their fathers; more than half the refugees still in camps are children or adolescents ; at least 100,000 young persons are still living by their wits without a permanent job or home; and between 1945 and 1953 "fraternisation" with the occupying forces produced 120,000 illegitimate children, 4,000 of them coloured. Housing conditions are such as to encourage every kind of promiscuity and nervous ailment. There is a shortage of 50,000 classrooms, and those that do exist are for the most part not particularly hygienic or suitable. Finally, even if the children do manage to reach the age of fourteen with the full educational equipment prescribed, the prospect that opens before them is not a brilliant one.

In 1951, 780,000 children left the elementary schools. In 1952 the number was 830,000; in 1953, 880,000; and in 1954, 900,000. In the next years the number will diminish, to begin increasing again in 1960. Today, scarcely a fifth of these continue their education after the age of 14. The remainder, especially the boys, have to learn a trade; but this is not always possible. There are several candidates for every apprenticeship available, the proportion varying regionally and reaching eight or ten for every apprenticeship in the Länder with a big refugee population, such as Schleswig, Lower Saxony, or Bavaria. At about the age of 18 a youth needs a secure and normally well-paid job, but there is a considerable risk of his not finding it. About a quarter of all the unemployed are men under 25. It is doubtless very interesting to discuss whether German youth is nationalistic or not, but it is well to bear in mind that the urgent problem which concerns the majority of young Germans is how to acquire a trade and find employment.

The one-fifth of elementary school pupils who pass on to secondary education contains very few working-class children, and in higher education the disproportion is even more marked. In 1953, out of every hundred students, only four youths and one girl were children of manual workers.[14] But this does not mean that the 110,000 students in Germany (of whom 17 per cent are girls or young women) lead on the whole a comfortable life. In 1953, only 31·6 per cent of the male and 51 per cent of the female students were entirely supported by their families, and 39 per cent of the former and 34·5 per cent of the latter were getting no family help at all. That the situation has deteriorated is shown by the fact that in 1953 45·4 per cent of the male and 24·4 per cent of the female students were supporting themselves by other work during their studies, whereas the corresponding figures for 1951 were 36·2 and 21·6 per cent. But it is chiefly during the vacations that students work, so as to have enough to live on during the term; and 67·4 per cent of the boys and 44·4 per cent of the girls get themselves paid jobs during their vacations. There are also the students who are called Spätheimkehrer (demobilised soldiers who returned from captivity after 1 January, 1948). These still account for 8·2 per cent of all students, and for them the resumption of their studies must require an extra effort of will-power.

The consideration of their case enables us to raise the question: up to what age can a person be called "young"? In France the transformation of the young into the adult occurs at about the age of legal majority, and the members of youth groups are young people of not more than 20 or 22, except for a few leaders who may be considerably older. But in Germany the position is less simple.

During the first post-war years the denazification procedure set a standard for classifying the generations. A person was young if he had not reached the age of reason in 1933 and could therefore disclaim any share in helping or failing to oppose Hitler's assumption of power. But the allies' amnesty law did not go quite so far. In 1946, it fixed the age limit at 27 years, that is, for Germans born after 1919, although many men of 30 and 35 considered themselves members of the younger generation, and the more so because they felt that the war had in a sense sterilised the best years of their youth. By 1954 the criterion of having reached the age of responsibility in 1933 had become almost obsolete, and there is now a new standard about which much less is said but which is of considerable importance for understanding the behaviour of German youth. Nearly all those born before 1928, that is to say those who are 26 or older, were soldiers, while the rest knew the war only as children or adolescent civilians. As more and more of the former soldiers leave, a perceptibly different outlook is developing in the universities and the youth movements. In a general way, however, all the arbitrary classifications due to past events are disappearing, and the traditional boundaries between the generations are reasserting themselves.

Maturity comes later in Germany than for instance in France. It is not by chance that two-thirds of the deputies in the first Bundestag were over fifty and nine-tenths over forty, and that the average age in the second is very high: 53 for the Liberals, 52 for the Christian-Democrats, 49 for the Socialists, and 48 for the Refugees. In France, lecturers of 23 or 24, with full qualifications, are appointed every year to the *Lycées*, but a German *Studienrat* of the same age would be almost sensational. A German author will still be classing himself as one of the "young" writers at an age when St Exupéry or Sartre or Malraux or Camus were looked upon by French youth as masters. This German characteristic is worth examining more closely. We believe that the principal reason for it is to be found in that quality which Goethe ranked so high—the sense of reverence. Age, in Germany, has long enjoyed an authority before which it was necessary to bow; and there are not a few young Germans today who tend to refer to some representative of the older generation when trying to form an opinion. Flattered by the confidence reposed in them, the elders feel justified in holding on to their positions while paternally assisting the young men of twenty, thirty and even forty to prepare to replace them in ten or twenty or thirty years' time.

They either forget or are simply unaware that the majority of the young have lost this deferential attitude. But the fact is that when they look at the disastrous heritage bequeathed to them, the young are beginning to find it impossible to believe in their elders' infallibility. Thanks to the collapse in 1945, and also to certain efforts by the occupying powers and by German democrats, a spirit of free reflection and criticism has been aroused, and many of the young are becoming impatient at being kept out of things. Their pretended political indifference is often no more than distrust and disgust for a gerontocracy which seems impregnable. In reality, it seems to us, there are four age groups to be distinguished in the Federal Republic: first, the 'elders' who already held positions before 1933 and who occupied most of the responsible posts from 1945 to about 1952; second, the men of mature age, who were profoundly marked by nazism in its heyday and who are now taking over from the first group;* third, those who were still young in 1945, but old enough to experience the shock of the collapse and who are now responsible for the revival of the student and

* See chapter VI.

youth movements; and finally, the young people of 18 to 20 who were not permanently marked by the events of 1945 and who are influenced by their elders of the second group. This is of course only a rough description, and far from accurate; but it does go some way towards explaining the developments which we shall have to describe later.

The Federal Republic does a good deal to assist the young. There is a *Bundesjugendplan* (Federal Youth Plan) which has financed since 1950 the construction of workshops and hostels; it tries to mitigate the hardships of the young in the neediest areas (Notstandgebiete) and subsidises the national and international activities of youth movements and organisations; and there are other subsidy schemes which supplement the work of the Bundesjugendplan in the Länder and smaller administrative units. The Jugendaufbauwerk (Youth Reconstruction Scheme) has also built workshops and hostels, and many of the larger towns have started "Youth Houses". Most of the important municipalities and urban and rural districts employ a Jugendpfleger, an official specially concerned with the work of the young. But all these efforts remain very inadequate from the social point of view, and especially as regards lodgings and apprenticeship; and, moreover, in spite of the excellent administrative work done by a few officials, there is still a note of paternalism which is resisted by the youth leaders.

Who are these leaders? There are about four million young Germans who are organised—that is to say, they are members of some youth group or movement or association. Four-fifths of these belong to one or other of the educational organisations affiliated to the Bundesjugendring (Federal Youth Council). These organisations are: the Catholic Youth and the Protestant Youth, both of which are composed of a large number of groups with a total membership of about 900,000 in each case; the D.G.B.'s Trade Union Youth, with about 650,000 members (some of whom also belong to a religious group); the Young Clerical Workers, of the D.A.G., with 40,000; the socialist "Falcons" with about 100,000; the socialistic "Friends of Nature", with 60,000, and the Youth Sports Associations, with 1,500,000. The Bundesjugendring is merely the co-ordinating body, and its decisions must be unanimous, which means that each of the affiliated organisations possesses in effect the right of veto. Up to 1952 its president was Josef Rommerskirchen, the Catholic Youth president, and the vice-president was the president of the "Falcons". Rommerskirchen was succeeded by the socialist Willi Ginhold, president of the Trade Union Youth, and he in turn was succeeded by Pastor Dannemann, the leader of the Protestant Youth. Corresponding to the Bundesjugendring in the smaller administrative spheres of Land, district, and town, there are Landesjugendringe, Kreisjugendringe and Stadtjugendringe to co-ordinate the activities of the diverse groups within their areas.

The Bundesjugendring's opponents deny it the right to speak for German youth—first, because only one-third of all the young people of an age to belong to a youth group are in fact organised and, second, because the leaders of the various movements have become bureaucrats, cut off from the mass of their members. To the first criticism the Bundesjugendring replies by comparing itself to the trade unions. Just as the D.G.B. can speak for all the workers, whether union members or not, because it works on behalf of all of them, so the Bundesjugendring has the right to speak for youth as a whole. This controversy is familiar elsewhere than in Germany. The second criticism is more difficult to refute. The membership of the central directing bodies is renewed very slowly, if at all; and the Bundesjugendring representatives who sit on innumerable commissions and committees are often the same ones who were there when the organisation was first formed. It must be added, however, that it is impossible to read the Bundesjugendring's excellent monthly review, *Deutsche Jugend*, without being struck by the great ability of its editorial board.

Another problem is the relations of the youth movements with their seniors. The Catholic Youth is more influenced by the church than by the Christian-Democratic union, but its leaders were able to win considerable freedom of action even from the church hierarchy. However, the pressure from that quarter is always increasing. The Protestant central body, in a little office in Stuttgart, has no more than a co-ordinating function, and its powers are less than those of the Bund Katholischer Jugend at the Altenburg Catholic centre near Cologne. The "Falcons", whose office is at Hanover, are the most directly dependent upon a parent body. They are closely tied to the Socialist party and it is the party's power, and not their own numerical weight, that accounts for their influence within the Bundesjugendring. They are the only group to be affiliated to a solidly established International, the I.U.S.Y. (International Union of Socialist Youth); and it was not until early in 1954 that they lifted their veto upon the Bundesjugendring's affiliation to the W.A.Y. (World Assembly of Youth), which is composed of the co-ordinating councils of youth movements of forty different countries. Disagreements between the I.U.S.Y. and the W.A.Y. came near to preventing the formation, by U.N.E.S.C.O., of the first international institute of youth, which is now in operation at Munich.

All the movements have made strenuous efforts to instil into their members the sense of international co-operation, in connection with which they organise courses, lectures, and exchanges. For example, in 1951 the Bundesjugendring organised, in liaison with the French authorities, a great international camp at the Lorelei rock, which was a highly spectacular occasion and also a valuable experience for the participants. It is the aim of the youth movements to be educational rather than propagandist, and their internationalism is largely a growth from the idea of Europeanism. In this matter their tendency is the same as that of more specialised bodies such as the Bund europäischer Jugend—an organisation which they criticise for not performing any fundamental educational work.

Less ideological and recreational, but more immediately effective, is the work of the numerous international associations for practical reconstruction. Such a body may be the German branch of an international organisation like the Quakers, the International Civil Service, and others, or it may be a German organisation of international tendency, such as the remarkable Internationaler Jugendgemeinschaftsdienst (I.J.G.D.), but the principle on which all of them act is that physical labour in common in the service of some needy social group is the best way of promoting sympathy between the young of different nations. The purely political youth organisations (Young Christian-Democrats, Young Socialists—older than the Falcons—and Young Liberals) have few members and their methods are different; but they, too, aspire to work for international understanding. Indeed, the efforts of organised German youth to create and develop foreign contacts and exchanges are quite amazingly multiple and various.[15]

The students' organisations also are interested in international contacts. There is a member responsible for international relations in every A.S.A. (Allgemeiner Studenten-Ausschuss, or university students' council) and this member devotes practically the whole of one term to his work for the council. The V.D.S. (national union of students) also runs a comprehensive service of international exchanges, and the various colleges and students' hostels show a keen desire to welcome as many foreigners as possible and to cultivate relations with other countries.[16] The World University Service has a branch in Germany and there are several girl students' organisations whose sole purpose is the development of international contacts. Like the Bundesjugendring, the V.D.S. has fought hitherto not only against nationalism but also against the plague of anti-semitism. There was a campaign, sometimes violent, against the return of Veit Harlan,* the producer of *Jew Süss*, which was led by the youth movements and the A.S.A.; and at the V.D.S. congress at Berlin in 1952 the new president received an ovation when he denounced anti-semitism in his first speech. His successor in 1953 is also a first-rate leader who vigorously opposes the revival of past evils.

But there is unfortunately a danger that this encouraging picture will soon cease to correspond to the facts; and the reason for this has nothing to do with German youth. For several years now there has been profound disagreement between the Bundesjugendring and certain American authorities on the question of how to be an anti-communist. All the German youth movements are anti-communist except the communist "Free German Youth" (F.D.J.), which could not join the Bundesjugendring because it does not recognise the Federal Republic. Its small membership is mainly in the Ruhr. But the

* See chapter v.

Bundesjugendring is opposed to any purely negative propaganda and therefore certain German and American industrial and business firms, with some official backing, financed a new "German Youth Union" (Bund Deutscher Jugend). This organisation attracted only an insignificant number of members, but its funds enabled it to plaster the whole country with virulent slogans against the east. Some leaders of the B.D.J. were arrested in Hesse in October, 1952, for having formed secret shock brigades with the mission of liquidating socialist leaders as probable "collaborators", in the event of an attack by Russia. The B.D.J. was banned in Hesse in January, 1953, and later in Bremen, Hamburg, Lower Saxony, and Württemberg-Baden, and finally it disbanded, after having received subsidies of 500,000 DM. in the course of 1952. This story would have no great importance if it did not coincide so significantly with the rearmament situation and the return of the "alte Herren".

German youth is profoundly troubled by the problem of rearmament, and innumerable discussions, "forums", and polls have been conducted by organisations of every kind. What emerges in every case is a hesitant and contradictory attitude, varying from categorical refusal to resigned acceptance of a necessary evil. It is easy to understand the confusion of a young man who has sincerely accepted demilitarisation ever since 1945 and who now finds himself in disgrace for not wanting to bear arms! Yesterday even gliding was forbidden as a warlike sport, and today compulsory military service is on the way. We shall have more to say about German reactions to rearmament. But we may as well point out here that there were always some of the young who refused to take democracy and internationalism seriously and who observe with a smile today that it would have been better to help Hitler in 1945 instead of getting excited about the alleged wickedness of German soldiers—and rearmament has the appearance of justifying their attitude.

The new social situation includes a revival of the resources and influence of the "alte Herren"—the old members of the student corps (Burschenschaften) and the corps themselves are flourishing more and more vigorously. While cultural and political associations languish in holes and corners, the student corps possess smart villas put at their disposal by some "alter Herr". Their essential characteristics, which are gradually reasserting themselves, include a sort of ritual libation of huge quantities of beer, and duelling, which enables the most "virile" students to win admiration for their scarred countenances, and a strict and narrow nationalism. The student corps were originally banned, but now, in one university after another, they are regaining the right to fly their colours and display their scars. They exert their influence to confine the A.S.A. within the narrowest possible sphere of activity and even succeed in getting control of them through the election of corps members. Not, of course, that all the student corps are objectionable; many of them encourage activities which satisfy the most legitimate of the students' communal aspirations. But nevertheless it does appear that the student corps as a whole are rapidly developing, under the influence of the "alte Herren", towards a complete revival of the habits and ideas of the past.

At Tübingen in 1949 the rectors of all the German universities unanimously condemned the corps. But their united front has sadly fallen apart since then. In 1953 the rector of Munich university (a theologian who demonstrated, during the nazi régime, that the gospel and *Mein Kampf* were complementary) offered a warm welcome at Munich to all corps members who might be having difficulties elsewhere. The duel with bare weapons (scharfe Mensuren) would be allowed, for was not its purpose—as the 1953 *Bruderschaften-Handbuch* put it—to alert the student and bring out the right spirit in him ("Die scharfe Mensur soll ihn zur Einsatzbereitschaft und zu wahrhaftem Geist erziehen")? At the annual festival at Hamburg, in 1953, of the 'Coburger Convent', which includes a large number of the student corps, the principal speaker informed his audience of teachers, wearing corps colours, that there are 250,000 alte Herren in the Federal Republic watching over 30,000 students who are grouped in a thousand corps, possessing five hundred beautiful houses. These statistics prove that only one student in four is "incorporated"; but they also prove that the alte Herren are a force to be reckoned with. Not a few students are induced to join a corps simply as an investment for their future career.

The trend is not confined to student circles, but it has so far touched only a small section of the young. It is vital that the efforts of the younger generation, which we have been describing, to influence their juniors in the right direction, should not be counteracted by reactionary adult influences; and in this connection the editorial of *Deutsche Jugend* for April, 1954, makes sad reading. This is the gist of it:

"Has any general assembly of the Bundesjugendring or any other democratic organisation ever attracted such a galaxy of political personalities as was seen at the reunion at Bonn in mid-March of the German Soldiers' Union—the president of the Bundestag, three Federal ministers, two Minister-Presidents of Länder, and a number of deputies of all parties? That some of the distinguished guests made use exclusively all through their speeches of the comradely term "we soldiers" might pass without comment. But what must be noted is that throughout nearly all these leading politicians' speeches a tendency was discernible which could be summed up in the formula: Hands off the German soldier! Stop criticising, and learn to appreciate his worth! ... So was the Bundesjugendring inspired by mere spiteful calumnies of the German soldier when it included in its constitution the aim of preventing any revival of militarism? It seems now that we are being told there never was any militarism and the new watchword is: Honour our military past, cultivate tradition, and stop all discussion!"*

---

* German text: Hat man etwa je schon bei einer Vollversammlung des Bundesjugendrings oder bei einer anderen demokratischen Organisation ein so grosses Aufgebot politischer Prominenz gesehen, wie es sich zur Vertreterversammlung des Verbandes der deutscher Soldaten Mitte März in Bonn einfand: Der Bundestagpräsident, drei Bundesminister, zwei Ministerpräsidenten und zahlreiche Bundestagabgeordnete aus allen Parteien.

Dass manche dieser hohen Gäste bei ihren Reden sich ausschliesslich des kameradschaftlichen "wir Soldaten" bedienten, damit mag man sich abfinden. Bedenklich aber ist, dass fast durch alle Reden dieser führenden Politiker eine Tendenz spürbar war, die man etwa auf die Formel bringen kann: Schluss mit der Kritik an dem deutschen Militär, positive Würdigung des deutschen Soldatentums!

... Ist also auch der Deutsche Bundesjugendring nur einer böswilligen Hetze gegen das deutsche Militär zum Opfer gefallen, wenn er sich in seinen Satzungen zur Aufgabe stellte, ein Wiederaufleben des Militarismus zu verhindern? Es scheint, als hätte es diesen Militarismus nie gegeben, und die neue Parole heisst: Achtung vor der militärischen Vergangenheit, Pflege der Tradition, Schluss mit jeder Diskussion!

NOTES TO CHAPTER IV

[1] These figures are taken from *Statistisches Jahrbuch für die Bundesrepublik Deutschland* (Stuttgart 1952) and *Sozialtaschenbuch* 1952: *Deutsche Sozialstatistik für die Praxis* (Frankfurt, 1952).

[2] On this question see the book by the Federal Minister for Refugees, Hans Lukaschek, *Die deutschen Heimatvertriebene als zentrales deutsches Problem* (Bonn, 1951); *Das Vertriebenen-Problem* (Bonn, 1951); P. J. Bouman, *The Refugee Problem in Western Germany* (The Hague, 1950). To study it against a broader background see G. Frumkin, *Population Changes in Europe since 1939* (London, 1951); H. Wander, *Die Bedeutung der Auswanderung für die Lösung europäischer Flüchtlings- und Bevölkerungsprobleme* (Kiel, 1951); and, above all, P. Frings, *Das internationale Flüchtlingsproblem, 1919-1950* (Frankfurt, 1951). Attempts to analyse the European aspect of the question can be found in E. Lemberg, *Die Ausweisung als Schicksal und Aufgabe* (Munich, 1949), for the Germans, and H. Lukaschek, *Die deutschen Heimatvertriebenen und ihre Bedeutung für Europa* (Bonn, 1952) for other countries.

A basic study of the facts and of the possibilities of a solution is to be found in *The Integration of Refugees into German Life*, a report of the E.C.A. Technical Assistance Commission (1951), known as the Sonne report after the chairman of the commission. This is much more thorough than the well-documented report on *Expellees and Refugees of German Ethnic Origin* (Washington, 1950), submitted by a special sub-committee of the House of Representatives Committee on the judiciary under the chairmanship of Mr F. E. Walter.

Revealing sociological investigations into the integration of refugees are to be found in Lemberg-Krecher, *Die Entstehung eines neuen Volkes aus Binnendeutschen und Ostvertriebenen* (Marburg, 1950), and *Zeitschrift für Raumforschung: Das deutsche Flüchtlingsproblem* (Bielefeld, 1950). The economic aspects of the question are treated in Friedrich Edding, op. cit., W. Albers, *Die Kapitalausstattung der Flüchtlingsbetriebe in Westdeutschland* (Kiel, 1951); Zitzewitz-Muttrin, *Vertriebenes Landvolk* (Hamburg, 1952); and above all in the 1951 and 1952 annual reports of the *Vertriebenen-Bank A.G.* The juridical aspects have been treated in Fritz Thomas, *Das Recht der Vertriebenen* (Dortmund, 1950), now partly outdated by more recent legislation.

See also Göttinger Arbeitskreis, *Die ostdeutschen Landsmannschaften* (Göttingen, 1951), and Vereinigte Ostdeutsche Landsmannschaften, *Reden und Vorträge gehalten auf dem ersten Bundeskongress der V.D.L. am 1.7.51*. An inadequate and rather superficial account of the more recent refugees from the Soviet zone is given in H. Kuelz, *Die Flüchtlinge aus der sowjetischen Besatzungszone* (Frankfurt, 1950).

[3] See Wilhelm Conrad, *Von der Soforthilfe zum Lastenausgleich* (Göttingen, 1951).

[4] Sonne Report, pp. 65, 54, 62.

[5] Statement made by Dr Vl. Clementis, p.21 *et seq.*

[6] *Expellees and Refugees of German Ethnic Origin*, p. 86.

[7] The text is given in *Reden und Vorträge* (note 2).

[8] The most useful sociological study is undoubtedly the compilation edited by Helmut Schelsky. *Wandlungen der deutschen Familie in der Gegenwart* (Dortmund, 1953).

[9] The text is given in Hajo Holborn, op. cit., pp. 135, 143.

[10] See in particular Deutscher Gewerkschaftsbund, *Die Gewerkschaftsbewegung in der britischen Besatzungszone* (Cologne, 1949), a valuable source of historical and statistical information.

[11] A concise account of the economic and social views of the trade unions is given in Matthias Foecher (vice-president of the D.G.B.), *Die deutschen Gewerkschaften in*

THE SOCIAL BACKGROUND 155

Wirtschaft, Staat und Gesellschaft (Munich, 1952), and Franz Grosse, *Gewerkschäfte, und soziale Neugestaltung* (Munich, 1951). On the present legal position of the D.G.B. see Ulrich Brisch, *Die Rechtsstellung der deutschen Gewerkschaften* (Göttingen, 1951), which reproduces the Statutes and the 'directives on the conduct of labour struggles'.

A good introduction to the trade unions is provided by Richard Seidel, *Die Gewerkschaftsbewegung in Deutschland: ein ABC der Gewerkschaftskunde* (Cologne, 1952).

[12] The text of the law, and a long but valuable legal commentary, are given in Gerhard Boldt, *Mitbestimmungsgesetz Eisen und Kohle* (Munich, 1952), and Mueller-Lehmann, *Kommentar zum Mitbestimmungsrecht Bergbau und Eisen* (Heidelberg, 1952). There is a good bibliography in Waldo Loesch, *Leitung, Mitbestimmung und Arbeitnehmerhaftung* (Mannheim, 1951, thesis). For a comparison of the powers exercised by workers within factories in Germany before 1933, and in France in 1937, see Alexander Lorch, *Trends in European Social Legislation between the two World Wars* (New York, 1943).

[13] For the text see p. 196 of the 1952 section of Bundesvereinigung der deutschen Arbeitgeberverbände, *Jahresberichte* (Cologne); and also the *Jahresbericht* of the Bundesverband der deutschen Industrie.

[14] See Gerhard Kash, *Das soziale Bild der Studentenschaft in Westdeutschland und Berlin* (Frankfurt, 1952), which gives the results of an enquiry carried out in 1951 by the Verband deutschen Studentenwerke. (Our figures have been taken from the 1953 enquiry to be published shortly.) See also Bondy and Eyferth, *Bindungslose Jugend* (Munich-Düsseldorf, 1952); for young workers the study by Karl Bednarik, *Der junge Arbeiter von Heute—ein neuer Typ* (Stuttgart, 1953), with its highly debatable conclusions. The most striking presentation of the social problems of youth is given in Helmut Schelsky and others, *Arbeitslosigkeit und Berufsnot der Jugend* (Cologne, 1952).

[15] See for example the annual report for Bavaria in Bayrischer Jugendring, *Blick in die Welt* (Munich, 1952).

[16] For communal student life see Walter Killy, *Studium generale und studentisches Gemeinschaftsleben* (Berlin, 1952). On the attitude of young Germans at the time see Robert d'Harcourt, *Visage de l'Allemagne actuelle* (Paris, 1950), which is also useful for the following chapters.

CHAPTER V

THE MORAL BACKGROUND

IT is not surprising that there are a large number of religious youth movements in Germany, because the influence of the churches is still strongly felt in every sphere of intellectual and moral life. In France, since the separation of church and state, it has become a purely personal affair to belong or not belong to a church, and it is not mentioned in official forms. But in Germany, where there has been no separation, a person has to state his religion in almost every form he fills up. Every baptised German belongs in principle to some church and is taxed for its support; and to leave one's church it is not sufficient to cease religious practice. It is necessary to notify the fact officially and obtain exemption from the *Kirchensteuer*. In western Germany 96 per cent of the population belong to some church— 45 per cent to the Catholic church and 51 per cent to one or other of the Protestant denominations.

How many are practising churchgoers is difficult to ascertain, and varies by region and social environment; but it is incontestable that the churches have had since 1945 an influx of members such as they had not known for many years. In other countries too religious practice becomes more general after a national disaster. Whether because people are driven back to the essential truths or because they are simply seeking consolation, it is not our business to decide here. But in Germany there has been still another reason for the return to the churches. In the chaos of 1945 they appeared to be the only institutions still unshaken, the only refuge to which people could turn for material and moral support, the only voice that could speak for a shattered Germany. And what were these churches to which people turned for protection and help?[1]

On 23 August, 1945, the bishops assembled at Fulda issued a declaration giving an account of Catholic life in Germany under the Hitler régime. They recalled how they had "intervened on behalf of the rights of the person" and "resisted the state's encroachments upon the life of the Church"; and they thanked those parents who had "made a courageous stand for the Catholic schools". At the same time they regretfully acknowledged that "many Germans, including some in our own ranks, allowed themselves to be deceived by the false doctrines of nationalsocialism and looked on with indifference while crimes were committed against freedom and human dignity; many lent support to the criminals by their attitude, and many became criminals themselves. A heavy responsibility lies upon those who might, by their influence, have prevented these crimes and who not only did not do so but actually helped to make them possible and thereby became the criminals' accomplices".

This text gave a true and balanced account of the attitude of German Catholics since 1933. The church had failed to give an immediate warning of the dangers of nazism. On 20 July, 1933, it signed a concordat with Hitler's government completing and extending to the Reich as a whole the concordats of 1924, 1929 and 1932 with the Länder of Bavaria, Prussia, and Baden. According to this agreement there was to be a papal nuncio at Berlin and a German ambassador at the Vatican, the Roman curia was to have untrammelled contact with German Catholics, and the freedom of religious schools and communities was guaranteed; bishops were to swear fidelity to the Reich, and a weekly prayer was to be said in every church 'for Reich and people'.

It soon became clear that the national-socialist régime respected neither the letter nor the spirit of the concordat. The application of racial doctrines and the tightening grip of the party upon the schools created an ever-increasing tension between church and state. In the encyclical of 14 March, 1937, *Mit brennender Sorge*, Pope Pius XI described the bitter trials endured by the church in Germany in its fight against the government's school policy, and emphasised, in opposition to Hitler's anti-semitism, the importance of the Old Testament for every true Christian. From this moment the conflict continually widened until there was a regular persecution of Catholics, in which priests who spoke out too frankly were the chief sufferers. Nevertheless it cannot be said that the Catholic

church carried on any systematic or organised opposition to
Hitler. Cardinals, archbishops and bishops formed no sort of
united front but fought against nazism more or less individually
and with varying degrees of energy. Some of them appeared
to have no quarrel with the secular authorities except where
they challenged the church's prerogatives.

German Protestants made a deeper but less general examination of conscience. The church dignitaries who met in 1945 to
lay the foundations for a new union of evangelical churches in
Germany went further than the Catholic bishops along the
path of introspection and humility; but they themselves represented only one aspect of what Protestantism had been in
the Third Reich.

The confession of sin was carried out according to Jeremiah's
precept "Let us search and try our ways". The leaders of the
new evangelical church in Germany, founded at Treysa on 31
August, 1945, received the delegates of the ecumenical church
council at Stuttgart on 18 October with the words: "We
accuse ourselves for not having confessed our faith with more
courage and for not having prayed with more faith, believed
with more joy, and loved with more fervour". In a message
of January, 1946, Pastor Niemöller said: "We cannot excuse
ourselves on the ground that to speak out might have cost our
lives. In my Bible it says that I must defend truth even unto
death". Niemöller himself had been interned in a concentration
camp in 1937, but, he said, "the camps were started in 1933 and
it was communists who were put into them. What did we care?
. . . We thought "Communists, enemies of religion. . . ." It
was not until later that the church was directly attacked, and
then we did speak out, until they stopped our mouths. . . ."
If the 14,000 pastors had protested in 1933 and 1934, perhaps
30,000 or 40,000 Protestants would have been killed—but
thirty or forty million human beings might have been saved.[2]
At Treysa the fundamental error was expounded: "A mistaken
view of Lutheranism allowed us to think that we had only one
responsibility towards the state, namely, obedience; and that
it was our duty to preach obedience to Christians and teach
them to obey, except only if the state commanded a manifest
sin".[3] The men who said this were among the founders and

leaders of the small body of German Protestants who did fight against nazism.

The 'German Christian' movement, which adopted the ideas of blood and race and believed in a 'heroic Saviour, suitable for German piety', was born in 1932.[4] When Hitler came to power he backed these 'Deutsche Christen' in their attempt to found a Reichskirche which should represent the union of all the twenty-nine German Protestant churches; and the first 'Reich bishop' was a German Christian who enjoyed the Fuehrer's confidence. The movement became more and more pagan until in the end it was nothing but an instrument of the nazi dictatorship. But from 1933 onwards it had to meet the opposition of Protestant leaders and of a whole group of young theologians with men like Martin Niemöller and Hanns Lilje at their head. In May, 1934, at the synod of Barmen, the Confessional church (Bekennende Kirche) was brought into being and proclaimed itself the only authentic German Protestant church. The Lutheran, the reformed, and the 'united' churches were combined in it, and there were internal dissensions which culminated in a schism in 1936. However, each of the two groups into which it split continued to fight against the German Christians and national socialism.

It was the leaders of these groups who assembled at Treysa in 1945, and the new name they chose for the Church (Evangelische Kirche in Deutschland) was profoundly significant. From 1933 to 1945 the German evangelical church (Deutsche Evangelische Kirche) implied by its name a specifically German type of Protestantism; but the new name implied the evangelical church *in* Germany—in other words, the German branch of world Protestantism. The presence of foreign churchmen at Stuttgart, and their fraternal attitude—refusing to act as accusers and anxious publicly to examine their own consciences —enabled the E.K.D. to begin its life inspired by the ecumenical spirit which it has not since lost.

The organisation of the E.K.D. was not completed until 1948. It is a rather strongly centralised federation of twenty-seven provincial churches—thirteen of them Lutheran, two reformed, eleven united, and one other which is not easily classifiable. It has three controlling bodies: the synod, which consists of delegates from the synods of the member churches, the churches' conference, which has one representative from each member church. and the elected council, one of whose three permanent bureaux—the Kirchliches Aussenamt—is a sort of foreign office of the E.K.D. Lay activities are co-ordinated by the Deutscher Evangelischer Kirchentag, which has functioned since 1949 and whose annual 'week' is attended by as many as 200,000 of the faithful.

In spite of this seeming unity among German Protestants, which has never existed before, some disagreement and friction still remain. There are theological differences between Lutherans and Calvinists, and between both of them and the united church. There is pressure from the laity for a more complete fusion of the churches and for more power for the Kirchentag; while some of the church authorities, especially among the Lutherans, want to diminish the influence both of the Kirchentag and of the laity. But these are small troubles compared to the one great problem that faces the E.K.D. The 1951 Kirchentag was held in Berlin with the motto: 'We are brothers all the same', and was attended by almost as many Germans from the east as from the west. But at Stuttgart in 1952 there were only forty from the east. The next Kirchentag was held at Hamburg, 7–11 July, 1953, and a larger number of east Germans were able to come. But there was great difficulty in making arrangements for 1954. Leipzig, in the Democratic Republic, was chosen as the locale and the motto was: 'Be joyful in hope'.

The E.K.D. makes no distinction between its members in the two Germanies. 'We are brothers all the same'. Thus the Lutheran provincial churches in Hanover or Bavaria are considered in theory to be closer to the Lutheran churches of Saxony and Thuringia than to the united churches in the Palatinate or Baden. The population of the Federal Republic is three times that of the Democratic Republic; but 80 per cent of the population east of the Elbe belong to the E.K.D., and they represent 43 per cent of all German Protestants. The political schism in Germany, therefore, is keenly felt by the Evangelical church, whose major preoccupation is to prevent it from becoming more complete. This preoccupation corresponds to that of world Protestantism to prevent the cutting of the world in two. At the ecumenical conference held at Lund, in Sweden, in August, 1952, delegates from the eastern countries seemed surprised by the 'fraternal spirit' they encountered. The most prominent of them, the Czech theologian Hromadka, declared after the meeting that "several of the German delegates had manifested a remarkable spirit of solidarity"; yet in the political sphere the delegates from behind the iron curtain, and Hromadka in particular, had expressed their confidence in the governments of the 'people's democracies'. It would seem that the ecumenical movement is above all anxious to maintain its spiritual unity in spite of political differences, on the principle that the same evangelical premisses can lead to varying political conclusions.

The same principle is maintained by the leaders of the E.K.D., who continually repeat that when they express political opinions they are speaking only for themselves as individuals. Nevertheless, there are criticisms both in Germany and abroad of Pastor Niemöller, head of the church in Hesse and director of the E.K.D.'s foreign affairs bureau, or of Dr Heinemann, lay president of the synod, for expressing even their personal political opinions instead of confining themselves to purely religious matters. The leaders thus criticised reply by referring to their examination of conscience in 1945. The fault of German Protestantism lay in too strict a distinction between the spiritual and the temporal, in having understood too late that the Christian has political responsibilities. To limit themselves to the care of souls, they consider, would be to repeat the sin of omission they committed in 1933. The campaign against rearmament conducted by Niemöller after his open letter of 4 October, 1950, to the Chancellor, and by Dr Heinemann since his resignation in September, 1950, from the post of minister of the interior, is far from being approved, either in its manner or its theme, by all the E.K.D. leaders; and the less so because the pastor's uncontrolled vehemence and the former statesman's lack of political realism often betray them into inopportune statements which the press can easily convert into inflammatory slogans.

In his very vulnerable position, Niemöller is certainly a

figurehead of the E.K.D., but he is much less representative of its main tendency than the president of the council of churches, Bishop Dibelius of Berlin, who succeeded Theophil Wurm in 1949. At the Berlin synod in August, 1952, Dibelius sharply criticised educational methods in the eastern zone, the rifle exercises for boys of under 18, and the pressure exerted upon the churches by the Democratic Republic. In September, however, he accepted an invitation to go to Moscow for conversations with the leaders of the Russian church—though the invitation was cancelled a few weeks later, before he had started. Dibelius considers it is the mission of the E.K.D. to act as a link between the two Germanies.

In his view, the revived German unity for which he hopes must be a synthesis which rejects both a complete reversal of policy in the east and also the bolshevisation of the west. From this standpoint, rearmament can only increase tension and make reunification almost impossible. We shall see later what the differences are between Dibelius' conception, which is always expressed with discretion and reserve, and that of the Socialist party; and we shall also have to ask whether the expressed opinion of a section of their spiritual leaders has any profound influence upon the political attitude of the mass of German Protestants.* We shall find that this was the case only in 1950–51, and that the 1953 elections were a crushing defeat for Heinemann and Niemöller. But one fact is already clear. Whatever importance the E.K.D. may attach to theological questions or to social problems (which dominated particularly the first Kirchentag at Essen in 1950), it is the division of Germany which remains the principal problem for a church which will not reconcile itself to being the church of the Federal Republic alone.

For German Catholicism the priorities are not the same. The church certainly suffers from the splitting in two of the world, and of Germany. But its very structure, and the Holy See's authority over its clergy, make it less vulnerable in world politics and less embarrassed than the Protestant churches by the problem of how to deal with the various governments. The hostility between the Vatican and the people's demo-

* See chapter VI.

cracies, and the persecution of Catholics in the eastern countries scarcely predispose the church to act as mediator between the rival blocks. And there is also a purely statistical consideration. The line of demarcation between the Federal Republic and the Democratic Republic splits German Protestantism into two almost equal parts, whereas only one-tenth of the Catholic population is in the eastern zone. The church certainly desires the reunification of the country, but does not need to regard it as a fundamental and almost physical necessity.

In so far as it is possible to make national distinctions in Catholicism, it could be said that Catholic Germany belies its geographical position by coming somewhere between France and Spain. This is true as regards the relation between church and state, as regards tolerance, and also as regards educational and social questions. 'Left Catholicism', which has developed so rapidly in France since 1945, is much less important in Germany, although it appeared to be developing there up to 1949. In that year the Catholic congress (Katholikentag) at Bochum made a solemn declaration in favour of the right of co-determination: "The right of co-determination belongs to natural right under the order of providence and it should be recognised equally with the right of property." The Bochum resolutions were strongly influenced by the group responsible for the magazine, *Frankfurter Hefte*.

But after Bochum an opposite trend began to appear. Cardinal Frings, Archbishop of Cologne, who is unquestionably the most influential prelate in the German Catholic church, had not altogether approved of the Kirchentag's formulations. He published a book in the same year which was much more guarded and not unreservedly in favour of equal participation by employees in the management of industry and business.[5] Appealing rather to the generosity and charitable feelings of employers, he called for the opportunity of social advancement for "working class children especially gifted in intellect and morals". The book also touched upon the question of working class disaffection, but the existing structure of society was left unquestioned.

Subsequent Katholikentage have devoted much less time to problems of social justice and the hierarchy's attitude towards 'left Catholics' has grown much more reserved. The *Frankfurter Hefte* appears to have lost a good deal of its influence, while the ultra-conservative *Rheinische Merkur* assumes the right to speak for the whole of German Catholicism. Nor have high church dignitaries ever supported a strike in the name of social justice, as has very often happened in France in recent years; and whereas in France a large part of the clergy still believes that Catholic action among the working class should be such as to prove that the church is not, or is no longer, for the bourgeoisie alone, the emphasis in Germany is upon the purely evangelising aspect of such activities.

The truth is that the German Catholic church does not seem to think that its essential vocation lies in the social domain. It regards tensions between social groups as secondary compared to the religious and moral formation of each individual, and its main effort is concentrated upon the education of children and adolescents. The principle it adheres to is a simple one: Catholic schools for Catholic children, with teachers trained in exclusively Catholic institutions. It considers the denominational school (Bekenntnisschule) in every way preferable to the mixed school (Simultanschule or Gemeinschaftsschule) in which Protestant and Catholic children are mingled.

Relations between the Catholic and Protestant churches improved considerably during the nazi oppression and their common struggle against the national misery after the war; and the cordial atmosphere was still apparent in August, 1952, when the Archbishop of Munich stayed with Pastor Dibelius in Berlin during the Catholic congress. But on the schools question Catholicism remains intransigent. It opposes the Simultanschule (in which each child, unless specially excused, has to attend religious instruction in its own faith) as strongly as it opposes the secular schools which are advocated by the Socialists in certain districts.

It is impossible to give a simple summary of the schools controversy in the Federal Republic as a whole, for each Land is in effect responsible for education within its own administrative area. Thus when there is a new majority in the Land the schools system may be altered, and this is what happened at Hamburg in March, 1954, after the November, 1953, local elections. Within a single Land there may be more than one system in operation, as for example in Lower Saxony where the Gemeinschaftsschule (mixed school) is the norm except in Oldenburg, where the schools are denominational. But schools regulations are being prepared for application throughout the Land, and this has given rise to the sharpest conflict on the subject since the war. Protesting against the new regulations, which would extend the prevailing system to Oldenburg, the Archbishop of Osnabrück wrote, in 1952, to the minister for education: "If necessary we shall call upon our Catholic people to fight for their most sacred and incontestable rights." Demonstrations took place in March, 1954, and one bishop denounced "a return of the ideas of the Third Reich". The papal nuncio made representations at Bonn to the effect that the denominational school alone is in conformity with the 1933 concordat—which raises the question, as yet undecided, of whether that concordat is still in force.

In other Länder the situation is simpler. Hesse has only Gemeinschaftsschulen, whereas in Bavaria, where 72 per cent of the population is Catholic, as against only 19 per cent in Lower Saxony, the denominational school prevails and any teacher would risk his chance of promotion if he refused to give religious instruction, although he is legally entitled to refuse. The teacher who was openly an unbeliever would be unlikely to get a job at all. In Rhineland-Westphalia the opposing parties are more or less equal and the majority vote of 110 to 94 for the schools bill of 2 April, 1953, was a limited victory for the supporters of the Catholic view.

It would appear that the elections of 1953 have introduced a new phase in which confessional disputes will again become prominent. On 8 March, 1954, the 72-year old diplomat, Wolfgang Jaenicke (who was dismissed by the nazis, and had been Bavarian commissioner for refugees since 1945 and ambassador to Pakistan since 1952) was appointed ambassador to the Vatican in accordance with the German diplomatic practice of appointing a Protestant to this post. But this has led to violent protests, in spite of the fact that his deputy, Herr Rudolf Salat (hitherto head of the foreign office cultural department) is a leading figure in the international Catholic movement, Pax Romana. Bavaria, fortified by its own separate concordat, even proposes to send a special Bavarian representative to the Holy See. Another sign of contention is the policy of Dr Würmeling, the new minister for family affairs, which is causing considerable anxiety to non-catholics.*

As for the schools controversy—even though it is muffled under the federal structure of western Germany, its effects are sinister. It draws attention away from that important function of a school, the general education of the country's future electors. The question whether literature and history should be taught from a religious point of view, and if so which, is not the only question. It is also important to educate the pupils to understand the age they live in and play the active part required of its citizens by a democracy.

* * *

The national-socialist influence in education has left profound traces. How many young adults there are today who are sincerely convinced of being anti-nazi but who still retain, without knowing it, ideas and ways of thought which they imbibed as children between 1933 and 1945! The post-war school generation is doubtless in no danger of that sort of contamination, and yet the picture it is being given of its country and of the world is also a distorted one. The readers (Lesebücher) used in German schools are strangely out of date although they were compiled and published only recently. They present a romantic and rural Germany, still unsullied by noisy towns and factory chimneys—a land of forest and heath where war and its ruins are unknown. There are very few passages from contemporary writers, for the books are composed almost entirely of extracts from the works of nineteenth-century novelists and story-tellers. Thus the child's mind is constantly steeped in a dream world, although it knows by experience at home the problems and hardships caused by the war, and although the school itself is crowded and uncomfortable. The Lesebücher either offer an escape from reality or else they awaken vain

* See chapter VI.

hopes of a future resembling the idyllic past which they falsely describe.

Many of the teachers find a sort of relief in doling out this threadbare teaching. The older ones look back with regret to their own young days, when the Wandervögel disseminated a romanticism similar to that of today's Lesebücher; the younger are often themselves disoriented and feel unable to act as guides to their pupils; and the intermediate generation includes a good many who have been 'denazified' and, having learnt their lesson, prefer to keep away from any controversial topics. This last attitude seems even commoner among history teachers in the secondary schools. Since 1933 the truths of history have been rewritten so often in the text-books, and there are many who believe that they will change again as the political situation changes. Suppose the Russians come, or suppose nationalism revives—then it will be a crime to have taught modern history according to the fashion of today, just as it was a crime in 1933, and again in 1945, to have taught it according to the previous fashion. So the teachers keep as much as possible to the study of the distant past. The situation in the universities is much the same.[6] To judge by most of the curricula, one might think that German history ended before Bismarck; and to judge by the subjects discussed by the majority of professors, neither German nor foreign literature seems to have produced anything of importance for a very long time.

The picture given above of the German educational attitude to the contemporary world is, of course, incomplete and misleading. There are also a number of encouraging developments. In Hesse, for example, political instruction is a compulsory subject in both primary and secondary schools; and this includes a study of the administrative, political, and economic structure of Germany both today and in the immediate past, including the concentration camps, and also of the interdependence of modern nations. And there are many professors and teachers who try to arrange foreign contacts for their students. Then there are the school broadcasts (Schulfunk), to which nothing in France corresponds, whose organisers often succeed in opening windows upon the real world. These broadcasts, which are received in the classroom itself, are of enormous assistance to teachers and are able to bring life to the dryest subjects. In each Land a commission of educationalists, ministry officials and radio experts prepares the programmes and issues them six months in advance with abundant explanatory material.[7] In about a thousand towns there are people's universities, sometimes attended by as much as 10 per cent of the population, which give courses and lectures on topical German problems and on foreign countries. German pedagogues are working in collaboration with Scandinavian, Swiss, and French colleagues to bring teaching methods up to date; and under the influence of the International Institute of Historical Study at Brunswick, directed by Professor Eckert, professors of history have compiled a number of manuals intended to widen their students' international outlook.

But before education can be radically reformed, educators are required for the educators themselves; an intellectual élite should set to work in Germany to tackle in a new spirit the new problems that have arisen in every domain—and there is scarcely a sign of such an élite. In France for the past ten years there has been an extraordinary intellectual ferment— Catholics re-examining their attitude to the church, writers and dramatists re-examining the foundations of literature and drama, all of them probing the fundamental problems of culture and politics; and research groups have grown up around magazines and study circles. But in Germany we see an accumulation of detailed analyses and synthetic compilations— which certainly have their use, but they are not sufficiently made use of, and the existence of a few outstanding individuals cannot compensate for a considerable poverty of intellectual life. There has in fact been no revival in the field of thought to correspond to the extraordinary effort of material reconstruction and the advance of scientific and industrial techniques. Before examining two particular examples of the deficiency we must try to ascertain the general reasons for it.

After 1933 the German intellectuals were decimated by emigration and the nazi repression. Those who stayed in Germany without being interned had either to keep quiet or else to abase themselves. For twelve years freedom of research was suspended, the rising generation had nothing on which to sharpen its wits, and foreign contacts became steadily more difficult. Then the drainage of life in the war and the misery and confusion that followed it still further weakened Germany's intellectual resources. In the general collapse, a new impetus might perhaps have come from even a small group of intellectuals closely in touch with one another; but in fact one of the chief difficulties in reconstituting an élite has been their geographical dispersion. Thanks to decentralisation, a number of small German towns enjoy a cultural life which might often be the envy of provincial France; but the disadvantage of centralisation in Paris is compensated by the opportunity it offers to intellectual specialists of every type to meet and discuss and stimulate one another. In Germany there is no centre comparable to Paris. Even in a large city like Cologne, Munich, or Hamburg an intellectual may feel isolated and abandoned to his own resources. He may read the publications of others, and meet them at congresses or through very costly travel, but he will lack their daily stimulus as neighbours.

But the scarcity of intellectual centres in Germany is not completely explained by the effects of nazism, or chaos, or geographical dispersion. There is another reason, of longer standing and more fundamental. In Germany there has always been a gulf between the world of intellect and the economic and political worlds. Whether from contempt or ignorance, German intellectuals have always held aloof from political life; and the profound metaphysician has sometimes been the most cravenly pusillanimous of citizens. Writers have engaged with zest in the pursuit of the 'eternal human' while completely ignoring certain realities—transient, no doubt, but assuredly not without some importance. The indifference of the universities, shuttered in their ivory tower of pure learning, contributed not a little to the ease with which Hitler captured power; and today again, when the young are anxious to understand the times they live in, the professors mostly prefer abstract speculation to concrete analysis. While in France the men of the universities have plunged as one man into the literature of 'engagement', only a few rare 'Dozenten' participate in the daily life of German letters—whose slow revival is due to the efforts of isolated young writers who have great difficulty in obtaining a hearing.

Books are once again produced in large numbers. Many new publishing firms have appeared and German books are now as luxuriously bound and excellently printed as in the past. It is true that they are very expensive, but several publishers have taken to issuing pocket editions. There are now, as before, from 14,000 to 17,000 books published in a year in the Federal Republic (as against 18,000 in Britain, and 11,000 in France and the United States) and their total circulation is 100 million. On top of this there were in 1951 about 2,500 works catalogued as 'schöne Literatur'. But which authors are being printed, or reprinted? A great many nineteenth-century novelists and story-writers (the same whose works are anthologised in the Lesebücher), important contemporary writers like Hermann Hesse or Ernst Wiechert, some foreign authors and a small number of newcomers.

We shall not attempt a sketch of German literature since the war, because the purpose of this book is not to assess the cultural situation but to try to explain the political facts. We could wish it were otherwise, for it would be pleasant to describe such engaging literary figures as Heinrich Böll, Luise Rinser, Alfred Andersch and Rudolf Bongs. But in the circumstances only a few general remarks seem to be required.

Apart from stories in a vein of symbolism, which is sometimes of considerable profundity, the younger German authors mainly write novels of lived experience—a 'literature of the ruins' which revives the sufferings of the war, the material and moral misery of the camps, and the painful struggle towards a more normal life. It is these books that foreigners find the most interesting, but at home they meet with a two-fold opposition. The majority of critics object to a type of literature which can be called journalism rather than art, and publishers show a growing disinclination to publish this kind of book because it appeals to too few readers. It is true that the demand for such books is small, and the reason, no doubt, is that the public has had its fill of stories which retrace the familiar difficulties it has had to contend with and now wishes to forget. The kind of book that strongly appeals to it is Ernst von Salomon's

Fragebogen, which gives vent to all the rancour accumulated during the long years of disaster. Most people only read to take their minds off their daily life.

But even the more open-minded section of the public seems to be tiring of 'Ruinenliteratur', and this may be because the authors have not yet succeeded in going much beyond pure description. To bear witness is not necessarily to illuminate a subject, still less to explain it; and we can scarcely cite a single recent German book dealing with contemporary fact which enables the reader to transcend his personal experience or effectively enlightens him about his present condition. Yet the existence of a considerable public in Germany for works of the first order is proved by the warm welcome accorded to certain foreign works. In the theatre the inferiority of German plays is even more conspicuous, but the capacity audiences which applaud contemporary foreign pieces bear witness to the fact that the inadequacy of German work is not due simply to the public's lack of comprehension.

The same problem is seen even more clearly in the cinema, which is now one of the most important cultural media in most countries. Good German films are few, and do not even get mentioned when the prizes are distributed at Cannes or Venice. If you ask producers the reason their reply is always the same. The public only care for sentimental stories, costume romances, and tasteless comedies. With experienced producers directing well-tried players, the audience dissolves in happy tears. Keep away from thorny problems and unhappy endings, and from anything that could make the story real to the spectator. It must be admitted that the box-office takings, and the style of certain films regarded as triumphs, seem to prove that the producers understand their business perfectly well.

A good example of a film that was hailed as an altogether exceptional achievement is the war film *Es kommt ein Tag* (A day will come), which deals with Franco-German relations. In this film the discovery is made by some lovable French civilians and some pleasing German officers that their two countries are at bottom indissolubly united—and the war which serves as background to this tear-jerking fantasy is not the war of 1939, nor yet of 1914, but the war of 1870! The plot is as implausible as a pulp-magazine story and the politics and psychology of the film are of a naïvety almost beyond belief. The contrast with the classic French war film, *La grande Illusion*, is devastating. We will mention one other typical German production—*Der fallende Stern* (The shooting star). The first ten minutes of this film portray the glacial reception of some liberated prisoners at a hostel and the story seems to be going to deal with the problems of rehabilitating demobilised soldiers; but suddenly the scenario skips back thirty years to a crudely symbolic fable about the struggle for a child's soul between an angel called Luciano and a demon called Monsieur Lenoir (in French in the original).

Can the German public, then, really appreciate only second-rate thought and crude sentiment? The answer is certainly 'yes' for a large part of the regular film-goers, though one may ask whether the education they have had is not chiefly responsible. Moreover, when the best English, Italian and French films are shown—which happens very rarely—there is always an appreciative public to fill the house; and would there not be a still larger public for German films of the same quality as the Italian *Bicycle Thieves*, the American *From Here to Eternity*, the English *Brief Encounter*, or the French *Justice est faite*? In any case, and above all, is it not conceivable that the taste of the film-goer might be gradually improved?

In France too it is melodrama and light entertainment that make the most money, but an appreciable number of superior films can be produced without financial disaster thanks to the influence of film clubs and of the critics, and the discussion provoked by an important film. The cinema has become a recognised form of artistic and intellectual expression, and a film institute has been established at the Sorbonne. The best writers work for the cinema and the style of a producer is discussed with the same respect as a poet's choice of words. A debate on a film dealing with some social problem may attract an audience of as many as three thousand to the big university amphitheatre.

The lack of any intellectual support for the cinema in Germany is partly accounted for by the reasons we have enumerated: the promise of the first post-war period was blighted by

Hitler and the talents it produced were lost to Germany either through emigration or through dictatorship and war, and the same causes prevented the growth of any new talent. But the overriding cause of the backwardness of the German cinema is a more permanent one. It is the characteristic German separation between the realms of spirit and matter, between the conception of art as eternal and the humble day-to-day reality of life. The short life of a film, the industrial and commercial methods of its production, the very fact that it is addressed to a great mass of spectators, all this is taken to prove that the thing is entertainment rather than art; and the fact that the greater number of intellectuals hold contemptuously aloof naturally makes the film industry even more commercial and the films even more mediocre, while the public taste grows more and more insensitive.

We have dealt at some length with the state of the cinema because it seems more useful than literature as a test of the intellectual climate; and, further, it is the film-spectators and not the cultured amateurs of belles-lettres who will have the biggest say in determining Germany's political future. The films they see certainly influence the spectators' attitude, if not also their opinion, concerning events and people; and the diffusion of a sickly sentimentality is not apt to develop the sense of civic responsibility. On the credit side it can be said that the few thought-provoking German films (such as *Marriage in the Shadows* or *In those Days*) that have been made since the war have been more effective influences for 'democratisation' than a great many articles and speeches. The existence of these films, and the new development of film clubs among the young, and the fact that some educationalists are beginning to attach importance to the cinema, may justify us in hoping that the quality of German film production will improve in the not too distant future.

* * *

Though novels and films are an influence in developing or drugging a people's political consciousness, they do not act so directly in forming opinion as the press does; and in Germany as in other countries the press has long been established as the fourth estate. The way in which politics evolve depends very largely upon the standards and structure of the nation's press. The readers' attitudes are moulded by the way in which news is selected and presented; and, conversely, in its attempts to please its readers and increase its circulation the newspaper comes to reflect public opinion. Clearly, then, we must study the German press if we wish to understand the development of Germany.

In 1945 all the newspapers had ceased to appear, but in May of that year the allies decided to authorise new publications whose editorial boards had to be licensed in each zone by the occupying power. In principle, the new journals were supposed to confine themselves to impartial reporting with no definite political or ideological bias, but in practice, as we have seen,* the American military government was the only one to insist upon the appointment of representatives of different tendencies to the board of each newspaper. It had some difficulty later in getting rid of communists from the boards to which it had appointed them. The journalistic profession was exhaustively purged, and as a result a number of completely inexperienced men received editorial appointments. The printing works, however, had remained in the hands of their former owners, who, when taxed with what they had printed in the past, replied that they had been acting under duress. They were ordered by the occupying powers to sign contracts with the new licensed newspapers, and these contracts were replaced later on by new ones much more favourable to the printers.

Until the currency reform in June, 1948, the papers could not keep pace with a demand that was greatly enlarged both by the public's thirst for news and information, and also by the fact that old papers could be sold. Starting as twice-weekly sheets of only four pages, they gradually increased in size and frequency of appearance, at the same time acquiring a certain freedom from allied supervision. The number of licences increased and the hundred-and-fortieth was about to be granted when control was withdrawn. But the currency reform hit the press in two ways. First, it became possible to buy things which

* See chapter II.

were more immediately necessary than a newspaper and, second, the faithful readers among people with small savings were ruined. Reviews and weeklies suffered even more seriously and a number of interesting publications disappeared in 1948, partly because the return of abundance and facility of distribution gave an advantage to the illustrated light magazines of which we shall speak later.

When the licensing system was abolished in 1949 and it became possible freely to start a new paper, the economic basis of the licensed press was not yet solidly established. Capital was still lacking and it was often impossible to buy office fixtures and printing presses. Moreover, the presses were now free to print rival newspapers, which were in effect partly financed by the high rents paid by the licensed press. Quite often a compromise solution was found by admitting the printer-publisher to the editorial board—and sometimes with a controlling voice—which seemed to mean a return of the old influences; and this tendency was soon reinforced by the return of various editors who had been 'denazified' after the war. But, contrary to the expectations of those who feared a spectacular revival of the nazi press and the collapse of the papers fostered by the occupation, the return of freedom did not too greatly damage the licensed press. There are today more than 1,200 papers, but 52 per cent of them have a circulation of less than 10,000 and the former licensed press accounts for more than eight million of the twelve or thirteen million copies printed.

The principal German dailies have balanced budgets. They have a high proportion of subscriptions, sometimes 80 per cent of total circulation; and sales to subscribers greatly reduce distribution costs, which absorb almost the whole profit when papers are sold in the streets or at news stalls. Further, businesses and even individuals go in much more for publicity and small advertisements than in France or England. German newspapers currently run two pages of small advertisements five days a week and eight pages on the sixth. Thus, for a price approximately the same as a French daily, they can offer their readers twelve pages of reading matter every day with numerous weekly supplements, including sometimes eight pages of illustrations. But the importance of the advertiser threatens editorial independence, for the articles must not offend too many clients and above all must not displease the most important ones.

As in all departments of intellectual life, the press has always been decentralised in Germany. Great Berlin dailies like the *Berliner Tageblatt* and the *Vossische Zeitung* were of no greater national or international importance than the *Kölnische Zeitung* or the *Frankfurter Zeitung*; and today Berlin's special situation has further diminished its importance. In fully ten of the 930 centres which have at least one newspaper there are two or three superior dailies, each of them with an experienced editorial staff and its own correspondents abroad. It is true, on the other hand, that the little local papers are run in such a small way that they have to make use of syndicated stereotypes. This system, which is used by 50 per cent of all the German newspapers, consists in setting up sheets with unsigned articles in a central office and distributing them to dozens of small daily newspapers, often with no staff except the editor himself, which then issue them without so much as changing a comma but merely adding two pages of advertisements and local announcements. The ostensible purpose of these newspapers is to express the spirit of neighbourhood and local attachment (heimatverbunden und bodenständig), but in fact it is the central offices where the stereotypes are set up that acquire influence, and all the more so because they are subject to no serious control.

Nearly all the dailies, both large and small, claim to be independent. Barely 13 per cent of them are party organs, and these have as difficult a life as their French counterparts. The German public wants its newspapers to be 'above party' (überparteilich), and the Socialists understand this so well that they much prefer to work upon public opinion through newspapers which they can influence than through specifically party organs. It is in fact true that the editorial boards enjoy a considerable degree of freedom. Naturally, the reader of any newspaper can detect some general political or religious bias, but the influence of powers behind the scene, particularly economic powers, is not increasing at all rapidly.

How does the press make use of its liberty? For one thing,

it defends it vigorously against the state. In March, 1952, the ministry of the interior proposed legislation, on the pretext of safeguarding the dignity of journalism, whose adoption would have paved the way for a control amounting to censorship, but the combined protests of all the press caused it to be withdrawn.[8] Several newspapers have shown great courage in denouncing political and administrative abuses and in some cases, for example the *Frankfurter Rundschau*'s campaign against the presence of nazis in the foreign office, they have caused parliamentary commissions of enquiry to be set up. But in most cases the department concerned brings an action for defamation, which nearly always succeeds; and even if the newspaper does win the action, it has to spend a lot of time and money and incur a lot of trouble. It may also happen that a too accommodating judge will order the confiscation of a whole issue of a paper in which some public figure is attacked, before any calumny has been proved. So there is a tendency for press campaigns to grow rarer. Instead, the editors publish letters from readers—which are sometimes written in the office.

Towards their readers, too, the big morning dailies like the *Frankfurter Allgemeine* and the *Süddeutsche Zeitung* maintain their independence, in the sense that they do not concede much to the taste for sensationalism and crime. Leaving it to the evening papers to indulge in screaming headlines and blood-curdling reports, they are both serious and dignified in their presentation of news and in their informative articles. A good deal of space is devoted to international news, and trivial news items are not permitted to crowd out the commentary of local events. Culture is given an important place, and it is rare for political articles to be inspired by the cheap demagogy which appeals to hatred or fans delusive hopes.

Nevertheless, it is difficult to read the German daily newspapers without some feeling of dissatisfaction, and why is this? Foreign problems are sometimes presented with imperfect comprehension but, allowing for the fact that German editors have not yet had much time, since Germany emerged from her isolation, to get the hang of foreign affairs, the effort at objectivity by the greater part of the press seems remarkable. Nor is it the almost complete lack of special investigations and reports that explains our dissatisfaction. Rather is it a certain effect of grey monotony which obscures the individual characteristics of each newspaper and makes them all a little too drab and indistinguishable from each other. Here again, doubtless, the lack of a new intellectual élite is partly responsible, but the main reason for dissatisfaction seems to lie rather in the way the editors appear to interpret the idea of impartiality.

Every newspaper which aims to provide its readers with objective information has the duty of reporting the activities and decisions of the government. But the first difficulty arises with the problem of commenting upon them. To pass judgment upon a speech or an official action within a general political context suggests that one has taken a political stand and made a definite choice. But to make such a choice is to cease to be 'above party'. So it is more prudent to comment upon the fact in isolation and to say as little as possible about its context of political principle. Then the reader will remain convinced that his newspaper is only in disagreement with official policy on a question of detail. The next difficulty concerns the presentation of news about non-official activities. To give much space to information about some unorthodox trend of opinion seems to attribute importance to it, and might suggest lack of impartiality and implicit support of the trend in question. So it seems better not to say too much about anything that might savour of communism, for example, or neutralism, or defeatism. In this way there has grown up around a number of subjects a taboo which nearly all the newspapers respect.

It is this timid conception of impartiality, we believe, and not so much the pressure of hidden forces, that explains the increasingly conformist attitude of the German press and makes it doubtful whether it represents the views of the public. If the daily newspapers have lost about three million readers in three years, may it not be partly because people have become disgusted by their timidity? And yet Chancellor Adenauer and Dr Ehlers, the late president of the Bundestag, have complained on several occasions, and notably before the Association of German journalists (Deutscher Journalistenverband) in April,

1954, that the German press is still much too critical and unsympathetic towards the authorities.

The weeklies can be classified in four categories: serious publications, illustrateds, neo-nationalist organs, and the *Spiegel*. To the first category most of what has been said about the daily press applies, but the journals are addressed to a smaller public and their tendencies are more marked. The *Rheinische Merkur* is conservative Catholic; the twice-weekly *Deutsche Zeitung und Wirtschaftszeitung* is upper-bourgeois Liberal; *Christ und Welt* is Protestant in a somewhat 'geopolitical' manner; and *Welt der Arbeit*, published by the D.G.B., is trade unionist. All of them are extremely well produced and edited, but none has a circulation comparable to that of the illustrateds —some of which have a weekly circulation of over 500,000.

These illustrated weeklies are bulky, with even more pages of close-printed text than of photographs, but they give little space to political events. On the other hand, the space occupied by allegedly true historical memoirs is ever increasing. Sometimes it is the highly romanticised lives of the kings, princesses and statesmen of yesterday and today, which gratify the same desire for escape and facile sentiment as the majority of German films. Others exploit the nazi period and print the memoirs of generals, officers, ministers and, less often, resisters —most often of all, secretaries and valets of the great men of the régime. Hitler and Eva Braun, Goering at home, or the family life of Himmler, are dished up again and again. It would not be true to say that the past is exactly glorified, but the criminals are, so to speak, whitewashed with their family virtues. The atrocities of the régime are admitted, but are passed over in pointing out that one of the leaders hanged at Nuremberg was a good husband and father, whose disconsolate widow is a sufficient proof that, although he may have sinned, he was not really such a bad man. The same treatment is applied to the living, especially the military and S.S. who were condemned for war crimes; and this kind of sentimental rehabilitation is much more dangerous than the violent articles in the more frankly militaristic and neo-nazi magazines, such as the *Stahlhelm* and the *Deutsche Soldatenzeitung*. These publications have a small circulation, restricted to embittered groups of former military men, and they would stagnate and finally disappear, provided their readers were never reinvolved in active politics. The rearmament policy, which encouraged their reappearance, makes their disappearance less likely.*

The *Spiegel* (Mirror), which is often quoted in the French press, is on the way to becoming an institution of Germany's political life. In style it is an imitation of the American weekly, *Time*, but its content is its own. The articles are written in an ostensibly casual and detached style, which is in fact expertly lethal. Sometimes disingenuous, but always extremely well informed, it reveals everything that the other papers hush up or ignore. It spares nobody, and convinces many readers of its absolute intellectual honesty. Its influence is at once salutary and harmful, and it can certainly claim to have shown up more than one scandal or anomaly which would otherwise have passed unnoticed. From one point of view, it appears as a perfect example of the freedom of the press; but its comment is so often destructive and denunciatory, instead of constructive, and its malice in foreign affairs is so constant, that its influence upon the public mind is not always very healthy. Rather, it reinforces the view that 'politics is a dirty business', when what the citizens of the new Federal Republic need is precisely to be encouraged to take a more active part in public life.

* See chapter VI.

NOTES TO CHAPTER V

[1] See Centre d'Études de politique étrangère, *Les églises en Allemagne* (1949). On the German Catholic Church under Nazism cf. Nathaniel Micklem, *National Socialism and the Roman Catholic Church* (Oxford, 1939), well documented; Robert d'Harcourt, *Catholiques d'Allemagne* (Paris, 1938), with more human interest; the English text of the encyclical *Mit brennender Sorge* is published in *Selected Papal Encyclicals and Letters*, Vol. II, *1931–1937* (London, 1939). On the Protestant Churches see Arthur Frey, *Le culte de l'État et le témoignage de l'Église* (Geneva, n.d.), a French translation of an account of the efforts of the Confessional Church written by a Swiss pastor while the struggle was going on, and also Stewart Herman, *The Rebirth of the German Church* (London, 1946), extremely valuable both for the period before 1945 and for the first stage of post-war reconstruction.

On the resistance of the Churches, see the three series of collections, *Das Christliche Deutschland, 1933–1945* (Catholic, Fribourg; Protestant, Tübingen; joint series, Fribourg and Tübingen, 1946). For Catholic resistance, see the massive

THE MORAL BACKGROUND 181

work of Johannes Neuhaussler, *Kreuz und Hakenkreuz*, and, on the Protestant side, Heinrich Hermelink, *Kirche im Kampf* (Tübingen, 1950). See also the account of the Protestant bishop Hanns Lilje, *Im finstern Tal* (Nuremberg, 1947).

On the Protestant Church after 1945, in particular the development of the Confessional church, see Karl Barth, op. cit., Martin Niemöller, op. cit., Karl Barth, *Die evangelische Kirche in Deutschland nach dem Zusammenbruch des dritten Reichs* (Stuttgart, 1946), *Bekennende Kirche. Martin Niemöller zum 60ten Geburtstag* (Munich, 1952), a symposium containing a number of most interesting contributions. The book by the retired general who acts as private secretary to Niemöller, Franz Beyer, *Menschen warten. Aus dem politischen Wirken Martin Niemöllers seit 1945* (Siegen, 1952), seems to have been written to justify all those who accuse Niemöller of being 'Prussian'. *Evangelisches Laien-ABC* (Hamburg, 1952), is very informative on Protestant life in Germany.

[2] M. Niemöller, *De la Culpabilité allemande*, pp. 11–12.

[3] *Les églises en Allemagne*, p. 56.

[4] For the history and the role of Protestantism in the development of Germany up to 1945 see Edmond Vermeil, op. cit., and *L'Allemagne contemporaine*.

[5] Cardinal Frings, *Verantwortung und Mitverantwortung in der Wirtschaft* (Cologne, 1949), edited by the Dominican Father P. Welty.

[6] A technical and administrative survey of higher education is given in Verband deutscher Studentenschaften, *Deutscher Hochschulführer* (Bonn, 1952).

[7] See, for example, Hessischer Rundfunk, *Fünf Jahre Schulfunk in Hessen* (Frankfurt, 1951), and Hermann Schneider, *Wege zur Methodik des Schulfunks* (Berlin, 1950). For the teaching of history see *Internationales Jahrbuch für Geschichtsunterricht*, vol. 1 (Brunswick, 1951).

[8] The text is given in C. H. Luders, *Presse und Rundfunkrecht* (Berlin and Frankfurt, 1952). For general information on the press see *Handbuch der deutschen Presse*, 2nd ed. (Bielefeld, 1951), and H. P. Pilgert, *Press, Radio and Film in West Germany, 1945–1953* (Bad Godesberg, 1953).

CHAPTER VI

POLITICS SINCE THE WAR

THE BONN REPUBLIC is a federal state which was composed, from its inception, of eleven Länder: Bavaria, Bremen, Hamburg, Hesse, Lower Saxony, North Rhineland-Westphalia, North Württemberg-Baden, Rhineland-Palatinate, Schleswig-Holstein, South Baden, Württemberg-Hohenzollern; and these Länder for the most part already possessed institutions of their own.[1] The Grundgesetz, or basic law, passed on 8 May, 1949, by the parliamentary council at Bonn* provided an interim constitution which is valid until such time as Germany is in a position to adopt a definitive constitution. It represents a laborious compromise between the most diverse theories of the degree of autonomy proper to a Land. In principle the Länder possess the right to legislate in every domain except those specified in the basic law as coming within the competence of the Bund, or federal authority—namely, foreign affairs, customs, currency, railways, and postal, telegraph and telephone services. But other domains are listed, under twenty-four headings, in which the Bund possesses concurrent rights of legislation with the Länder, and this list includes labour and industrial legislation and also civil law, traffic legislation, and scientific research. In addition, the Bund may declare itself competent in any case which cannot be 'effectively dealt with by the Länder in isolation' and in cases where the juridical or economic unity of the federal state—especially the uniformity of living standards—is threatened. The compromise, therefore, clearly favours the centralising tendency.

And could it have done otherwise? The Länder could only have been given a large autonomy on the supposition that each of them represented an ethnic, historical and cultural unit. But the demarcation of the Länder carried out after 1945 took less account of German traditions, than of the boundaries of

* See chapter 1.

the occupation zones. Bremen was made a Land solely because the Americans needed a free port within the British zone; Baden, Württemberg and Hesse were cut in two by the boundary between the French and American zones; and the Rhineland was divided between French and British. The Länder thus created were an ill-assorted patchwork, and the more so because of the influx of refugees and the displacements of population in Western Germany during the war. The populations of Bavaria and Württemberg became so diluted that their local characteristics were largely submerged; and if the regional authorities had been stronger there would have been even worse discrimination against the newcomers. In short, the economic and social problems of a ruined Germany were difficult enough on the level of the Bund, but on the level of each individual Land they were completely insoluble.

The arbitrary boundaries presented a troublesome problem to the parliamentary council, and in the end the basic law was so framed as to allow for a reorganisation, which has already led to the creation of a new south-western state. After long debate this new Land is to receive the name of Baden-Württemberg. It only came into being after years of complicated discussion and arduous negotiations in which the occupation authorities played an important part. By merging together the Länder of Baden, Württemberg-Baden, and Württemberg-Hohenzollern, it reduces from eleven to nine the total number of Länder which compose the Federal Republic. The final decision was made by the populations concerned, through a referendum which was contested by Baden, the principal opponent of the new Südweststaat. Baden's objection was primarily religious. Its own population being 70 per cent Catholic, and its régime being under fairly strong clerical influence, it feared the influence of Württemberg Protestantism in the new state. It might perhaps have been possible to avoid combining two regions with such different traditions by creating two new Länder—Württemberg and Greater Baden—instead of only one, to replace the original three of 1945. But the partisans of the Südweststaat urged the necessity of creating in the south of the Federal Republic, alongside Bavaria, a second important counterweight to Rhineland-Westphalia—which, with its 13 million inhabitants and its industrial power, is liable to become, as the politicians of other Länder put it, the 'Prussia of the new Germany'. It was not until 19 November, 1953, that the Landtag, functioning as a constituent assembly, finally adoped the constitution of Baden-Württemberg.

The choice of Bonn as federal capital has been regarded as symbolic of the Rhineland's predominance. It was the result of a vote obtained by somewhat obscure methods, and although Bonn is a charming little place for a parliament and administrative centre, it is itself far from central and not particularly well equipped for the building of offices and an important telephone installation, or for providing accommodation for members of parliament and government officials. It was only by a very narrow margin that it was preferred to Frankfurt, which is a large town situated in the middle of the Federal Republic, is an important road and rail centre, and had been capital of the western zone since 1947. Historically, Bonn stands for a particularist and romantic Germany, while Frankfurt represents both the industrial and commercial expansion and the unifying liberal and democratic movement of 1848. There is little doubt that Frankfurt would have been chosen in spite of the pressure exerted by Rhineland-Westphalia, if there had not been a government of socialistic and anti-clerical tendency in Hesse, of which Frankfurt is the principal urban centre, and if Dr Adenauer, the Christian-Democrat candidate for the chancellorship, had not been a citizen of Rhöndorf, which is a little village only a few miles from Bonn.

Each Land has its own constitution and its own parliament (Landtag) and government, which is not necessarily of the same complexion as the Federal government. Thus, while the Socialists are in opposition at Bonn, in Lower Saxony they are in power jointly with the Refugee party. At Hamburg until November, 1953, the Socialists had an absolute majority; in Bavaria they are allied with the Christian-social union, although the latter support the Chancellor in the Bonn parliament; and in Baden-Württemberg they first shared power with the Liberals, while the Christian-Democrats were in opposition, but since the general election of 1953, there is a coalition at Stuttgart which embraces all three parties. Ever since 1951, however, a new political development has been proceeding which is due to something more than the nation-wide accentuation of party differences. The Socialist party, which was in favour of centralisation during the debates of the parliamentary council, has begun to defend the independence of regional parliaments, while the leaders of the Christian-Democratic party have argued in the regional federations that alliances in the Landtags should reflect the party alignments at Bonn. The Chancellor himself has exerted his influence on several occasions to obtain the dissolution in Rhineland-Westphalia of the alliance between Socialists and Christian-Democrats. As for the leaders of the Liberal party, which is very decentralised although it is in favour of a highly centralised Federal Republic, they nearly succeeded in 1952 in getting the Minister-President of the Südweststaat out of office for not having formed his government on the same pattern as Bonn. There is nothing surprising in these changes of attitude. Every central government will always prefer that the Länder should follow the same road as itself, and if the Socialists should ever come to power on the federal level there would no doubt be another general reversal of attitudes.

In any case, there has certainly been an increase of independence since the general elections of 6 September, 1953. Not that the Chancellor has weakened on the principle that the governments of the Länder should be composed in conformity with the Bonn government. On the contrary—and the coming to power at Hamburg of a coalition similar to the coalition at Bonn has been a marked success for him. But the Länder are defending themselves more and more stubbornly, and selfishly, in the financial field, refusing to increase the proportion of their revenue contributed to the Bund or to admit the need for the richer Länder to contribute more to the poorer ones.* In December, 1953, Dr Hans Ehard, the Minister-President of Bavaria, paid a solemn visit to his colleague in Württemberg-Baden, Dr Gebhard Müller, to assert, as it were, the existence of a South Germany opposed to the centralising tendencies of

* The differences of revenue are considerable. Taking the index for receipts from taxation per head as 100, the figure for the richest Land is 137 and for the poorest 53 (see chapters III and IV).

Bonn—and opposed also to the actual composition of the Federal coalition; and in February, 1954, he called a meeting at Munich of all the Minister-Presidents. The results were not revolutionary, but were a proof that the Länder insisted on co-ordinating their action among themselves, without interference from Bonn.

If the Chancellor is very anxious that the governments of the Länder should have the same political composition as the Federal government, it is because—contrary to the classic principle of separation of executive and legislative powers— the executives of the Länder determine the composition of one of the Bund's legislative bodies. Federal legislative power is in fact vested in two bodies of very different character. The first, the Bundestag, is elected for four years by direct universal suffrage; but the second, the Bundesrat, is composed of ministers or delegates from each Land and represents the governments of the Länder. There are five representatives from each Land with a population of over 6 million, four from each Land with a population of over 2 million, and the remaining Länder have three each. Laws are passed by the Bundestag, and the Bundesrat has merely the right to refer back for a second reading any law of whose terms it disapproves. If the Bundesrat votes the reference back by a simple majority, then the Bundestag requires only a simple majority to pass the law as it stands; but if the reference back is voted by a majority of two-thirds or more, the Bundestag requires a two-thirds, or at least an absolute, majority before it can confirm the law against the opposition of the upper chamber. In practice, conflict between the two chambers usually ends either in the immediate defeat of the Bundesrat or else in the convoking of the joint conciliation commission, which is prescribed by the basic law and has rendered very valuable service. The basic law itself cannot be modified without a two-thirds majority in both chambers, and the importance of this provision was clearly demonstrated in the debates concerning the constitutional amendments required for 'legalising' the ratification of E.D.C. In effect, although there is dual legislative power, the balance is definitely weighted against the Bundesrat, which represents the federalist attitude, and the Bundestag, which is elected by the nation's voters as a whole and therefore represents the unifying tendency, has almost all the power.

The only political act performed on a footing of equality by national and regional representatives is the election of the President of the Republic, who is appointed for a five-year term by a special assembly composed of delegates of the Bundestag and delegates from the parliaments of the Länder, in equal numbers. But the President's powers are very limited and his influence upon the country's political life is intended to be based upon his personality and not upon written law. It is thanks to his human qualities, his good nature, modesty, and moderation—and thanks also to his wife, whose death in July, 1952, was a national sorrow—that President Heuss, who was elected on 12 September, 1949, has become such a popular figure. It is true that since the end of 1952, when he may have appeared too ready to defer to the Chancellor's decisions on every occasion, his political prestige has declined. But he still stands as the embodiment of enlightened liberalism and unostentatious civic virtue.

Executive power is in the hands of the government, consisting of the Chancellor and his ministers. The Chancellor, who determines the general lines of policy on his own responsibility, is elected by the Bundestag, by absolute majority. Ministers are appointed and dismissed by the President, on the Chancellor's advice. Executive power is thus based on the same principle as in France, whose 1946 constitution considerably modified in this respect the constitution of 1875. But the German Chancellor is much more secure in his office than a French prime minister, for article 66 of the basic law lays it down that the Bundestag can only express lack of confidence in him by electing a new Chancellor by absolute majority and then requesting the President to dismiss the present one. 'The President must comply with this request and appoint the newly elected candidate.' In other words, a Chancellor cannot be got rid of until a successor to him has been found. Should the majority in the Bundestag lose confidence in the Chancellor but fail to agree on his successor, the President of the Republic has the right, if the Chancellor advises him to do so, to dissolve the assembly within three weeks of the first hostile vote.

These clauses were inserted in the basic law with a view to two contingencies of unequal importance. Their purpose is to ensure the continuity of the executive power but also, and much more, to avoid a repetition of the progressive paralysis which overtook the Weimar Republic when two incompatible extremes combined against the governments of the centre. Article 66 ensures that the Chancellor cannot be turned out by a 'negative' majority composed of groups which would be unable to unite as a government after their victory. It also protects him against the fluctuations of opinion of individual deputies and makes lobby manœuvres more difficult. Such fluctuations of opinion are in any case restrained by the system of compact parliamentary groups which impose a more or less rigid voting discipline (Fraktionszwang). This rigidity is essentially the result of the method of electing deputies, which is not part of the constitution but was determined by legislation. In 1949, 60 per cent of the deputies were elected by straight majority vote and 40 per cent were appointed by the political parties of the Länder according to an original system by which second votes are proportionately distributed. In 1953, as we shall see, only 50 per cent were elected by direct vote.

In the basic law the parties are given the modest task of 'contributing to the formation of the people's political will'; and article 21 continues as follows: 'They [political parties] may be created freely. Their internal organisation must be founded on democratic principles. They shall make public the sources of the funds at their disposal.' But the legislation to enforce this last obligation has not yet been framed and therefore, of course, has not become operative. 'Any party which, by its aims or by the behaviour of its members, tends to prejudice or destroy the basic liberal and democratic organisation of the Federal Republic, or to endanger its existence, is unconstitutional.' This ban has already been invoked against a neo-nazi party and there are demands from various quarters that it should be used against the communist party. The judge of a party's democratic character is the Federal Constitutional Tribunal, which sits at Karlsruhe. The functions of this tribunal are comparable alike to those of the United States' Supreme Court and the French Conseil d'État. Its members are nominated half by the Bundestag and half by the Bundesrat, and it is certainly the most original institution of the new German state. Apart from the dispute over the constitutionality of the Bonn and Paris treaties, the Federal Constitutional Tribunal has had to take cognisance of other fundamental problems, and it has effectively done so. It can be said, indeed, that the rationale of its judgments of 17 December, 1953, and 26 February, 1954, concerning, respectively, denazified or expelled officials and employees and former military personnel, has a historical importance for the Federal Republic equal to that of the basic law itself.

Such, in outline, is the Federal Republic's structure, which it is necessary to know in order to understand German political life. But it is only the frame, and the value of parliament, government, and regional assemblies depends much less upon their constitutional structure than upon the men and parties which give them life.

* * *

Twenty-four and a half million voters, or 80 per cent of the total registered electorate, voted in the general election of 14 August, 1949, for the first Bundestag. The Christian-Democrats obtained 31 per cent of the votes and 139 seats, the Socialists 29·2 per cent (131 seats), the Liberals 11·9 per cent (52 seats), the Communists 5·7 per cent (15 seats), the Bavarian Party (Bayernpartei) 4·2 per cent (17 seats), the German Party (Deutsche Partei) 4 per cent (17 seats), the Centre Party (Zentrum) 3·1 per cent (10 seats), and the Union for Economic Reconstruction (Wirtschaftliche Aufbau-Vereinigung) 2·9 per cent (12 seats). 4·8 per cent of the votes went to independent candidates, but, as the electoral law worked, only three independents were elected. The German Conservative Party obtained five seats and the Union of South Schleswig Electors (Südschleswiger Wählerverband) one. Let us examine these parties.

The 1949 election was a severe defeat for the German Communist Party (K.P.D.) and confirmed its previous setbacks in the municipal and regional elections of 1946. Even in the great industrial centres it failed to recover its pre-1933 position.

In Duisburg, for example, the communists had twice as many votes as the socialists in 1932, but in 1946 they got only 87,000 as against the socialists' 214,000, and at Essen and Düsseldorf there was the same shift of power. It is true that communists suffered more than others from Hitler's persecution, and this partly explains their weakness after 1945, but the essential reasons for their decline are other. In France communists and non-communists took power together at the liberation because they had fought side by side in the resistance, and France and the U.S.S.R. had been fighting against a common enemy. But in Germany in 1945 the German communists appeared as the 'collaborators' of a detested conqueror and occupying power. The extent of the outrages, particularly rape, committed by Soviet troops against German civilians cannot be established with certainty; but there seems no doubt that they were on a great scale and that an atmosphere of terror accompanied the passage of the Red Army. However, it very soon ceased and never approached in horror the atrocities committed in Russia by the Germans. Its repercussions would not have been so widespread if it had not been preceded by twelve years of Hitler's propaganda and followed by an inhuman Soviet policy. The Berlin riots of 17 June, 1953, and the accounts given by the new refugees further confirmed western Germany's anti-communism. Generally, communist doctrine and propaganda have no appeal to the average German, for to him communism is nothing more than the totalitarian régime which keeps Eastern Germany in bonds.

Of the main German parties now in existence the Social Democratic Party of Germany (S.P.D.) is by far the oldest. It was brought into existence in 1875, as the 'German socialist workers' party', by the fusion of two already existing groups, one Marxist and the other reformist. Its activities were under an interdict until 1890, but from that date it was able to develop without restrictions under the name it bears today.[2] On the eve of the first world war it was the largest political block in Germany, in membership, voting strength, and numbers elected. Though its programme was strictly Marxist, its predominant tendency was moderate. It voted for the military credits on 4 August 1914, and accepted William II's policy of national union. After 1916 its extreme left wing split off, but in 1919 it obtained 38 per cent of the total vote and was again the largest party. Its chiefs, who had played a leading role in repressing the revolutionary movement of November, 1918, directed the party back into the moderate reformist channel; and throughout the Weimar Republic it worked to 'republicanise' the administration, the army, and the law, and to obtain social reforms—sometimes in opposition and sometimes in coalition with the bourgeois parties. The Marxist theoretical side of its programme adopted at Heidelberg in 1925 was never more than an accessory. Between 1928 and 1933 the party lost two million votes but it was still able to muster 7·2 million, or 18·3 per cent of the total vote, at the elections of 5 March, 1933, although these were controlled by the national-socialist government. Hitler suppressed the party on 23 July, 1933, and dismissed its members from the Reichstag, on the pretext that its leaders in exile abroad were working against the nation.

On 6 October, 1945, the surviving socialist leaders met at the convent of Wennigsen near Hanover to prepare the reconstruction of the party. Their debates were dominated by three personalities: Kurt Schumacher, who had been in one concentration camp after another ever since June, 1933; Erich Ollenhauer, who arrived from London representing the leadership in exile; and Otto Grotewohl from Berlin, who was head of the Socialist party in the Soviet zone. Grotewohl proposed the immediate appointment of a new executive committee and that steps should be taken towards a fusion with the communist party, but Schumacher, supported by Ollenhauer, succeeded in getting the election of the new body postponed until the congress that had been arranged for the following year and declared for an independent S.P.D. Grotewohl's Socialist Unity party (S.E.D.) was duly formed on 22 April, 1946, in the eastern zone, and on 10 May the S.P.D. congress at Hanover elected Schumacher president and Ollenhauer vice-president of a party which now existed only in the west. Unlike the Socialists, the Christian-Democrats were not split by the rupture between east and west until December, 1947, and even then the C.D.U. did not disappear in the eastern zone.

The S.P.D. was not only the first political organisation to suffer from the rupture between east and west Germany but also the one most weakened by the limitation to the western zone of its membership and activity. Up to 1933 Prussia had been the stronghold of German socialism. In 1946 the S.P.D. could still obtain 48·7 per cent of the Berlin vote, and west Berlin remains today one of its most important centres. Before Hitler, 34 per cent of the electorate outside greater Berlin and east of the Elbe used to vote socialist and, moreover, a large number of the 'western' leaders of the S.P.D. came originally from the east—Schumacher from Kulm, south of Danzig, Ollenhauer from Magdeburg, and as many as 50 of the 131 Socialist deputies in the first Bundestag from places outside the Federal Republic. Among the Christian-Democrats, on the other hand, this was true of only 15 deputies out of 139. (In the second Bundestag the corresponding figures are 51 out of 151 for the Socialists and 19 out of 244 for the Christian-Democrats.) For the S.P.D., then, as for the Protestant church, the division of Germany was a crippling blow. But the brutal manner of its liquidation in the east, and also its fundamental anti-communism, give to its desire for reunification a very different colour from that of the Protestant leaders.* The S.P.D. does not envisage a synthesis of the two Germanies but hopes, like all the other big western parties, for an extension eastwards of the Federal Republic. This essential difference between the S.P.D. and the Protestant outlook has been kept in the background since 1950 by the party leaders, for tactical reasons, in their bid for the Protestant vote.

The S.P.D. is the only mass party in the Federal Republic, that is to say it is the only one which possesses not only organisers and voters but also a large number of regular party members. It is true, however, that after a rapid growth between 1945 and 1947 the membership figures have continually dropped, though this has not been reflected in the voting at elections. There were 875,000 members in December, 1947, and only 845,000 twelve months later, with a further fall to 736,000 in December, 1949, 688,000 in September, 1950, and 650,000 in September, 1952, after the Dortmund congress. At the present time only 3 per

* See chapter v.

cent of the paying members are less than twenty-five years old and 68 per cent are more than forty-five. General reasons, such as the disillusionment of the young with political parties, are not sufficient to explain this simultaneous shrinkage of numbers and growth of age-disproportion in the membership, and it seems probable that the rigid bureaucratic organisation of the party is also an important factor.

The S.P.D. is highly centralised and much under the influence of its president, even when his character is not so authoritarian as Dr Schumacher's. The congress (Parteitag) which is the party's final authority meets only once in two years and in the interval power is in the hands of the executive committee (Parteivorstand), a group consisting of twenty unpaid and seven paid members including the president and vice-president. The unpaid members live in all the four corners of Germany and scarcely see their fellow members more than one day in a month. The five full-time members have each their own specific and limited tasks, and the vice-president is especially concerned with problems of internal organisation. It required the illness of Dr Schumacher, his personal friendship with Erich Ollenhauer, and the latter's exceptional qualities, to make it possible for the second-ranking figure in the party to play the leading role. Wilhelm Mellies, who became vice-president when Ollenhauer was promoted to the presidency after the death of Dr Schumacher, on 2 August, 1952, has hardly followed this example. The president is thus the only member of the Vorstand who is in a position to define the party's attitude to the general questions which arise every day. The parliamentary group is under strict voting discipline and some forty of its members are financially dependent on the party, holding important positions in its official hierarchy. The party headquarters has a controlling influence upon the parliamentary group's decisions.

Though it is a proletarian party, essentially based upon the working class (in 1949 the monthly income of 95 per cent of its members was less than 300 DM.), the S.P.D. is neither the party of all the disinherited, since it has not succeeded in attracting the unassimilated refugees, nor yet a revolutionary party. Its economic aim, which is reformist and no longer derives from Marx, is the nationalisation of basic industries and the planned control of credit and raw material distribution; and socially it stands for a genuine equalisation of burdens, meaning levies on capital instead of small charges upon income only. Its view of co-determination is similar to that of the trade unions, and there is reciprocal influence in this field between the party and the D.G.B. In the schools question it favours the interdenominational or even the undenominational school, and its traditional anti-clericalism was still in evidence in 1949 although, for various reasons, it had lost some of its venom. The reasons include friendships formed during the common opposition to Hitler, the rise of the inclusive trade union, a decline of aggressive clericalism in the church, and the desire not to antagonise Catholic voters who support the S.P.D. in order to avoid voting for the C.D.U., while at the same time not wasting their votes. Recently, however, political developments both at home and abroad have tended once again to stiffen the party's attitude towards the church. Taken as a whole, it is difficult to deduce any firmly established doctrine from the programme and opinions of the S.P.D., as we shall see again when we come to discuss the 1953 elections; but cannot the same be said of the other European socialist parties?

In judging the S.P.D.'S foreign policy it is necessary to bear in mind two factors, the first of which operates also for the C.D.U. It is this: on two occasions a parliamentary régime has been introduced in Germany as a consequence of national disaster, and for many Germans the words 'democracy' and 'capitulation' are synonymous. Among the reasons for the defeat of the parties that supported the Weimar Republic was the criticism from the extreme right that they were too 'internationalist' and were weakening Germany for the benefit of the victors of 1918. This explains why a politician like Dr Schumacher, who had lived through 1918, adopted in 1945 a sort of preventive nationalism, which involved an intransigent attitude towards the occupying powers, in order to prevent history repeating itself. In his anxiety to avoid being called a 'collaborator' he sometimes carried the nationalist bravado to extremes.

The other factor goes far towards explaining the reserve

shown by the S.P.D. towards the Europe of the Schuman plan. The German Socialist party would like to see the Federal Republic co-operate particularly with those countries where there is a strong socialist party—that is to say, a party which represents the mass of the workers inside the country and is also influential in foreign affairs. The S.P.D. leaders do not consider that the Socialist Party in France or Signor Saragat's Italian socialist party at all fulfill these requirements. It is the British Labour Party and the Scandinavian socialists who are the true fraternal colleagues with whom the S.P.D. would like to collaborate, and this in spite of all the ruffled susceptibilities due to Dr. Schumacher's nationalism and the lack of comprehension displayed towards Germany by Mr Hugh Dalton. The S.P.D. regards itself as the only solid representative of international socialism in the Europe of 'the Six', which includes the three great Christian-Democratic parties of Italy, France, and Germany.

The Christian-Democratic Union was formed on the initiative of a group of anti-nazi resisters who had been interned in the Moabit prison in Berlin. The first nucleus was composed of Christian trade unionists, Protestants of various political backgrounds, and members of the former Catholic Zentrum. They wished to build a new Germany with a completely transformed social and economic structure and purged of all the poisons of national-socialism. But the purity of the C.D.U.'s first programme, the 'Guiding Principles' laid down at Cologne, became somewhat tarnished when it was brought down into the electoral arena. In 1946, when for the first time since 1933 Germans had a choice of parties to vote for, the C.D.U. represented a right wing choice. The Liberals were still unorganised and their anti-clericalism was distasteful to electors who wanted to vote 'Christian', so those who were anti-socialist and anti-communist had no choice between abstention or a vote for the C.D.U. Among those who voted were no doubt many who believed in the social and political ideals of the C.D.U.'s leaders, but there were also a number of conservatives and former fellow-travellers of nazism who were still imbued with the Hitler ideology. Like the meteoric rise of the M.R.P. in France, the rapid growth of the C.D.U. was partly due to the lack of any party which really corresponded to the desires of some of its supporters. Such a situation cannot last indefinitely, and the party which profits by it will sooner or later be faced with a choice. Either it will lose votes when the unsatisfied section of its supporters finds another party to vote for, or else it will modify its principles so as to keep their support.

The C.D.U. has not got a large membership and it depends financially upon a few big supporters. It is in the true sense of the word a union, that is to say, its constituent elements are loosely grouped together with little centralisation. Whereas the S.P.D., as we have seen, held its first Parteitag in April, 1946, and set up a rigid hierarchical structure, the first national congress of the C.D.U., at Goslar, was not held until October, 1948, and the powers of the party Executive are still today strictly limited and do not even extend to all Christian-Democrats. Bavarian Christian-Democrats still form a distinct group, the Christian-Social Union, which in principle co-operates with the C.D.U. on terms of equality on the basis of work for a common purpose. The correct name for what is usually called the C.D.U. is Arbeitsgemeinschaft (Co-operative union) C.D.U.-C.S.U., and the distinction becomes important whenever the question of federalism arises. Thus the nineteen C.D.U. members of the parliamentary council voted for the basic law while six of the eight C.S.U. members opposed it as being too centralist; and the C.S.U. Minister-President of Bavaria, Hans Ehard, has led more than one revolt in the Bundesrat against the Chancellor's practical anti-federalism. But Dr Adenauer himself is the president of the C.D.U.-C.S.U. and his personal authority has given it a unity which the leaders of other more centralised parties fail to impose. When he became Chancellor this authority increased; but Christian-Democrats remain divided, both in religion and in social and economic opinion.

It is the aim of the C.D.U. to be a Christian party, but not a sectarian party more or less directly controlled by the Catholic church. In the first Bundestag 40 per cent of its members were Protestants—among them the President of the Bundestag himself, and the consistorial counsellor (Kirchenrat), Hermann Ehlers, who is certainly the C.D.U.'s strongest personality after the Chancellor and who became its vice-president on 19 October, 1952, and Eugen Gerstenmaier, the Protestant church's director of social work (Hilfswerk der E.K.D.); and it was as a leading member of the C.D.U. that Dr Heinemann became minister of the interior. The latter's resignation brought to a head the problem of co-operation between the two faiths within the party, a problem which we shall have to examine in connection with the general policy of the Bonn government.

The economic and social programme of the Christian-Democrats in the British zone, which was adopted at Ahlen on 9 February, 1947, was inspired by Karl Arnold, the Minister-President of Rhineland-Westphalia, and his trade unionist and 'Left Catholic' friends. It gave equal importance to political liberty and economic liberty, asserting in measured terms the failure of capitalism and condemning both monopolies and state capitalism; and it called for economic planning and control through a system of economic corporative organs functioning under parliamentary supervision, whose principle was not unlike that of the agencies proposed by the D.G.B. But the Düsseldorf programme of 15 July, 1949, rejected all planning, whether of production, labour supply, or internal and external markets; the only governmental economic action it envisaged was through taxation and import policy. In effect what it proposed was Professor Erhard's Soziale Marktwirtschaft, and its adoption was a definite victory for the liberal as against the 'socialising' wing of the party. But the C.D.U. could not finally fix its economic and social orientation until it had made a political choice. After the elections of August, 1949, should it ally itself with the S.P.D. or with the right? And if with the right, how far should it extend the alliance?

The F.D.P. (Free Democratic Party) was not established in all three western zones until November, 1948, and its first congress was held in June, 1949. A democratic liberal party (L.D.P.) had been formed in the Soviet zone in 1945; and in Württemberg-Baden in January, 1946, a popular-democratic party (D.V.P.), which became, without changing its name, a regional constituent of the F.D.P. In its origins the F.D.P. was at one and the same time the party of the republican liberals, who derive from the political tradition of 1848, and the party of the great industrialists who demand an undiluted liberalism in the economic field, but because of the ambiguity of the word 'liberal', this dualism can usually pass unnoticed. The former tendency is strongest in south-west Germany, where it is exemplified in men like Reinhold Maier and President Heuss himself; and the centre of gravity of the second tendency is in the Ruhr, where the vice-Chancellor Franz Blücher is one of its outstanding representatives. The second tendency has been predominant ever since 1949, and was still growing up to the time of the Naumann affair, which we shall describe later.

In the fields of religion and education the F.D.P. was much more united. It "combated the false modern doctrines of Marxist and biological materialism" and was opposed to the non-denominational or secular school "because it exposes the youth of wide social strata in the big towns to the danger of growing up insufficiently informed about Christian religious and cultural values, and consequently without a proper understanding of the western tradition". But at the same time it condemned clericalism and opposed the denominational school, preferring an extension of the Simultanschule whose teaching "is linked with the cultural and religious heritage of the west wherever it applies".[3] The views of the F.D.P. in these matters, therefore, were somewhere between those of the S.P.D. and the C.D.U. though in the economic sphere the C.D.U. came between it and the S.P.D.

Two of the parliamentary groups set up in 1949 were exclusively Bavarian. The Union for Economic Reconstruction (W.A.V.) was led by the demagogic Alfred Loritz who never became important and lost his popularity as suddenly as he had gained it; nor were the deputies of his group to prove more faithful to him than the electors. The Bavarian Party (Bayern-Partei) has more solid electoral support. Its programme calls for "an autonomous Bavarian state within the framework of a German and European community"; it favours a corporative social system and wishes to establish "a culture flowing from the traditions of the Bavarian people".[4] This particularist and traditionalist party allied itself towards the end of 1951 with another party from which it might have seemed to be poles apart—namely, the Centre party.

The name Zentrum was revived in October, 1945, by a group of eminent Catholics who wanted to reconstitute one of the oldest and most influential of German political parties. Under the Weimar Republic this party had been the keystone of a number of government coalitions. Dr Brüning, who fell in May, 1932, was the fourth Chancellor to come from the Zentrum, in which there had always been conflict between conservative and socialistic elements. It was some of the latter who revived the party in 1945; but they were unable to check the rival growth of the C.D.U.—many of whose members, and notably Dr Adenauer himself, had been members of the pre-war Zentrum. There were several attempts to unite the two parties, but they broke down because the Zentrum finally decided that conservative influence was too strong in the C.D.U. Moreover, although it is a Christian, and more especially a Catholic, party, the Zentrum feared that a two-party political system of S.P.D. versus C.D.U. would inevitably lead to a disastrous alternation of clerical and anti-clerical governments; it therefore became a party of the left, strongly opposed to capitalism and fairly close to the S.P.D., except in religious matters. In 1951 its president, Frau Helene Wessel, resigned in order to devote all her time to the campaign against rearmament in the course of which she founded, with Dr Heinemann, the Gesamtdeutsche Volkspartei (G.V.P.), a vocal but small group apparently led by idealists but in effect exhibiting most of the pro-Communist tendencies of "front" organisations and usually repeating the political slogans of the East German government. By making an alliance with the Bavarian Party it would seem that the Zentrum was reverting to its federalist tendencies of the early years of the century, which had been maintained during the Weimar Republic by the Bavarian People's Party —a group which split off from the Zentrum in 1920 in protest against the latter's centralising and leftist tendencies at that time.

The seventeen deputies of the German Party (Deutsche Partei) came from the north-east of the Federal Republic, from Schleswig, Lower Saxony, Hamburg, and Bremen; and the party's original name, when it was founded in June, 1945, was the Niedersächsische Landespartei (Lower-Saxony Party). Hanover being the capital of Lower Saxony, the party became the champion of the Guelph particularists who used previously to rely for support upon the Hanoverian aristocracy, clergy and peasants; but its extension beyond Hanover was inspired by a much less regionalist ideology. It was indeed the explicit aim of the D.P. to become a right conservative party, and it showed from the first a strong predilection for the imperial black, white and red flag which had been the rallying symbol during the Weimar Republic for nationalists who disliked the democratic and republican associations of the black, red and gold. The party very soon began to organise public meetings with processions and military music.

The five extreme-right deputies were elected in the same parts of Germany as those of the D.P. Their principal leader, who was arrested in 1951 for having furnished himself with a false identity, was in reality a former nazi leader. His programme-speech in the Bundestag on 22 September, 1949, had been a long diatribe against the east and against denazification, which ended with an appeal to the west: "Do you want to save Europe? You will only be able to save Europe if you first save Germany".

At the time of the 1949 elections the Refugees' party (B.H.E.) did not yet exist. As we have seen, it was only in January, 1950, that the 'union of the expelled and dispossessed' was founded in Schleswig and only in January, 1951, that it was extended to the Federal Republic as a whole.* Defending the interests of a precisely defined section of the population, it has no general doctrine, but it has become a force in all those Länder where the refugees are inadequately assimilated. It has been sometimes in opposition and sometimes in power with the most diverse allies, and its position is often incomprehensible except by reference to regional problems; but essentially it is more dependent than the parties with comprehensive programmes are upon the general development of the Federal Republic as a whole.

* * *

On 15 September, 1949, Dr Konrad Adenauer, president of

* See chapter v.

the C.D.U. in the British zone and of the C.D.U.-C.S.U. parliamentary group, presented himself before the Bundestag as the Chancellor designate of President Heuss. There being 402 deputies, he required 202 votes in order to be elected, and he just succeeded in obtaining them. It had been for his party and himself to decide how to produce the requisite majority. The C.D.U.-C.S.U. held 139 seats of which a few were occupied by Bavarian deputies whose voting discipline could not be relied on. Where were the remaining votes to be sought? One alternative was the 'great coalition' with the Socialists, which would have produced 270 votes and a comfortable governing majority, and the other was the 'little coalition', excluding the S.P.D. but including the 52 Liberals. The little coalition, however, required to be fortified by the addition of either the Bavarian Party or the German Party, since the Zentrum refused to join any coalition without the Socialists. The Chancellor and his friends decided for the little coalition.

They justified this choice by two reasons of unequal value, neither of which revealed all the motives behind it. The main issues at the election had been economic and the C.D.U. had fought on its Düsseldorf programme, which was acceptable in the main to the F.D.P. but was anathema to the S.P.D. Therefore, said the Chancellor and his advisers, the great coalition between Christian-Democrats and Socialists would have been a betrayal of the electorate, for an economic policy framed jointly by "liberals" and "planners" would at best be incoherent and at worst would simply fail to materialise. And, further, would it be right in such critical times for the two big democratic parties to govern together and leave all the responsibility of opposition to the extreme left and the extreme right—thus giving them the chance to repeat the tactics they had used against the Weimar Republic by exploiting the grievances of the electorate as weapons against parliamentary democracy? The latter argument had substance, whereas the first rested upon a premiss whose acceptance implied a previous choice. It presupposed that economic policy was more important than social policy, for the differences between C.D.U. and F.D.P. concerning social policy were at least as great as those between C.D.U. and S.P.D. concerning economic policy.

In any case, whatever weight we may attach to the C.D.U.'s official arguments, there were other reasons for its rejection of the great alliance. A C.D.U.-S.P.D. government supported by the trade unions would inevitably have alienated the conservative supporters of the C.D.U. without bringing it any new votes from the left, since the left already voted for the S.P.D.; and this consideration had all the more weight with the Chancellor because it offered a political justification for his personal sympathies and antipathies. But a much more important reason still was the hostility, and even hatred, between the Chancellor and Dr Schumacher, the president of the S.P.D.

Everything seemed to conspire to set the two men in opposition. Adenauer came from the Rhine and Schumacher from the Vistula; the former's Catholicism alienated the Protestant Schumacher, whose faith was political and not religious. Having been a leader in the parliamentary group of a great centralised party ever since 1930, Schumacher criticised his opponent, who had been a municipal councillor of Cologne, his home town, since 1906 and mayor from 1917 to 1933, for conducting major political business as though it were municipal administration. Schumacher had a gift of passionate eloquence and withering sarcasm; and having lost an arm in the first war and a leg as a result of his sufferings in concentration camps, his physical appearance was arrestingly tragic. He seemed to incarnate the destiny of a mangled and butchered Germany. Adenauer, on the contrary, has always had a horror of pathos and seldom departs from a cold formalism in speech and manner. And above all both men loved power and wished to wield it alone. Each of them had been in favour of wide powers for the Chancellor in the basic law, for each of them counted upon victory in the election, which would enable him to rule alone. They both knew, too, that the one who failed could probably not afford to wait for the next election. Adenauer was already 73 and Schumacher, although nearly twenty years younger, knew that it was only his vigorous spirit which kept his shattered body alive. Seldom has a country suffered such heavy political consequences from the antipathy between two men.

The Chancellor presented his cabinet to the Bundestag and

delivered his policy speech on 20 September, 1949. Eight of the thirteen ministries went to the C.D.U.-C.S.U.—namely, the interior, finance, economy, agriculture, labour, the post office, refugees, and finally 'all-German questions' (Gesamtdeutsche Fragen), which were entrusted to Jakob Kaiser, leader of the east German C.D.U. in exile. The vice-chancellor, who was in charge of Marshall Aid affairs, and the ministers of justice and reconstruction were Liberals and the minister of transport and the minister for relations with the Bundesrat were members of the German Party. Each of the ministers could prepare long-term plans, since the terms of the basic law made it highly probable that the cabinet would remain in office until the next election in 1953. But for the death of Eberhard Wildermuth, who was a great minister of reconstruction, and the resignation of Dr Heinemann, the Adenauer cabinet would have been the same at the end of its legislative term as on the first day.

The Chancellor has always been the unchallenged head of the cabinet. No important decision has ever been taken in his absence, and when he goes on holiday to Burgenstock, near Lucerne, vice-chancellor Blücher can never assume the prerogatives granted him by the basic law because ministers and high officials go from Bonn to Switzerland to consult the holiday-maker. Yet Dr Adenauer has clearly shown that his chief interest is in foreign affairs, and after the first revision of the occupation statute he became his own foreign minister. In internal affairs he leaves his ministers a free hand, being content simply to arbitrate when necessary, as in the periodic disagreements between Professor Erhard and Dr Schaeffer, the finance minister. The Chancellor's personal point of view can be summed up in a sentence: he favours the economic policy of the right and the social policy of the trade unions in order to secure the support of both for his own foreign policy. His greatest triumph was the almost simultaneous adoption of the co-determination law and a fiscal reform favouring large incomes. Since then, the increasing influence of the right has caused the D.G.B. to lean more and more towards the socialists.*

* See chapter IV.

For a government, to be dependent upon the votes of a small parliamentary group is to be in its power, even if it is a group of only a handful of members. Since the Bavarian Party was usually in opposition, the Chancellor was obliged continually to depend upon the German Party in resisting the attacks of the Socialists, the Zentrum, and the extreme right; and this led to such incidents as the Krebs affair. In 1952 Krebs, the former nazi mayor of Frankfurt, was elected to the city's municipal council as a member of the D.P. (German Party), after a campaign whose atmosphere and slogans were strongly reminiscent of the 1930's. The majority in the council, representing the C.D.U., the socialists, and the refugees' party, declared that it had "no desire to work for the reconstruction of the city side by side and on terms of equality with conspicuous representatives of the régime which had brought about the city's ruin". Incidents occurred at the municipal council and at a D.P. meeting, whereupon the party's parliamentary group made an accusation in the Bundestag, on 13 June, 1952, that democratic freedom had been violated at Frankfurt. A part of the C.D.U. joined with the socialists and a few members of the F.D.P. in a counter-attack to the effect that the former mayor would do better to seek obscurity, even though he had been whitewashed by a denazification tribunal. However, as a result of Dr Seebohm's intervention in the debate, the government and the C.D.U. parliamentary group refrained from committing themselves either way.

In any case, and even if the coalition had not been threatened, many deputies of the C.D.U.-C.S.U. group would have avoided publicly criticising the D.P.'s attitude, for in several Länder the C.D.U. and the D.P. were at the same time competitors and allies, appealing to a section of the electorate which felt no aversion for a former nazi like Krebs. In Schleswig and Lower Saxony the two parties had formed a close alliance, which constituted the majority of the government coalition in the former Land and was the most active nucleus of opposition in the latter, where the government was made up of Socialists, Zentrum, and Refugee Party. In the attempt to overthrow this government the two parties went so far as to treat with thirteen of the Landtag deputies who had become "independents" in September, 1952, after the self-dissolution of their party—which was the S.R.P. (Reich Socialist Party). This party had been founded in 1950 and met with great success in the regional elections in Lower Saxony, but in July, 1952, the constitutional tribunal at Karlsruhe placed a ban on its propaganda and it was finally declared to be a neo-nazi group, and therefore unconstitutional. That the C.D.U.-D.P. block should have made advances to a group of deputies whose party clearly drew its inspiration from the nazi past was the cause of lively protests not only from the Socialists but also from the Lower Saxon Liberals, although they were in opposition in the Landtag, alongside the D.P. and the C.D.U. The incident is significant, although it had no immediate consequences. It shows that the same party can wear two very different faces, for the charge against the S.R.P. at Karlsruhe was entered by the federal minister of the interior, who is a member of the C.D.U.—and yet the C.D.U. in the Lower Saxon Landtag sought the co-operation of deputies who had represented the condemned party.

In the time of Hitler the film producer Veit Harlan produced a film, *Jew Süss*, which was an incitement to massacre. When brought before a denazification tribunal, he was acquitted on the ground that he had acted under duress, whereupon he immediately wanted to resume film-making. He had plenty of capital, for he knows his business and his new films have struck the sentimental and edifying note which pleases the great public; but a vigorous campaign was launched against him, in the first instance by Senator Lüth, who is responsible for the press in the state of Hamburg, but supported in a large number of towns by trade unionists, students, and youth movements of every colour. They asserted that the producer of *Jew Süss* had forfeited the moral right to make films in Germany. But they found themselves up against the forces of Order. Lüth, who had urged a boycott of Harlan's films, was accused of interfering with liberty of opinion and condemned to pay a heavy fine—which was paid for him by a collection. When the president of the tribunal told him to be "reconciled" with Harlan he had replied that it was not a question of himself but of six million massacred Jews. In January, 1952, at Freiburg some students who were making an orderly demonstration against one of Harlan's films were attacked by counter-demonstrators and then cudgelled by the police; but the film was withdrawn. In July, however, it was shown again and there was another demonstration organised by Socialist, Liberal and Christian-Democrat student associations. On this occasion the police protected the demonstrators, who numbered about 800, against the attacks of a crowd of some 4,000 people yelling anti-semitic slogans. But on 28 and 29 July the trial took place of a student who had been arrested in February, and he was convicted of "obstructing an official", although all he had done was to protect himself—unsuccessfully—against the police truncheons and manhandling. The tribunal took no account of the police violence, on the ground that "such things do not in reality happen"; and the fact that it was former nazi officials, who had been suspended from 1945 to 1948, who were responsible for the police intervention, had no effect, in the minds of the Freiburg magistrates, upon the reliability of their evidence. In the same trial a policeman accused by the students of inflicting physical injury was acquitted.

At a meeting in the great hall of the university the students' spokesman answered the charge that his friends were acting aggressively by demonstrating against Harlan. "We desire peace", he said, "but peace with Israel is more important to us than peace with Herr Harlan! . . . We are simply trying to fulfil our duty as citizens, and if we become conspicuous in so doing it is no credit to us, but a disgrace to our fellow-citizens." 'Peace with Israel' has become the motto of the movement initiated by Senator Lüth, whose scope greatly exceeds the Harlan affair. It raises the whole problem of anti-semitism; and one may agree with Dr Schumacher that "Hitler's barbarity has brought shame on the German people by the extermination of six million Jewish human beings"[5], and that the struggle against anti-semitism is the test of a genuinely reformed Germany.

The churches, both Catholic and Protestant, have always emphasised the need to acknowledge clearly the extent of the crime and to make reparation—in so far as it is possible for atrocities to be "repaired", and the Catholic congresses at Mainz and Bochum in 1948 and 1949 were particularly insistent upon this point. In 1950 the synod of the Evangelical church repeated: "We proclaim that by our inaction and silence we are guilty before the God of mercy for the crimes committed against the Jews by men of our nation." The German-Israel negotiations* were preceded on 27 September, 1951, by a statement from the Chancellor to the Bundestag in which Dr Adenauer recalled that "in the German people's name unspeakable crimes have been committed, which demand material and moral reparation", and the statement was greeted with approval by every group in the parliament.[6] At the Frankfurt book fair on 25 September, 1952, the president of the publishers' association appealed for a gift of books to Israel; and in November, 1953, in special articles and in some dignified and moving ceremonies, there was a commemoration of the 'Reichskristallnacht' of 9 November, 1938, when the worst anti-semitic persecutions began. Moreover, as we have already said, the national union of students and the various youth movements are campaigning against anti-semitism. It would therefore be a serious mistake and a grave injustice to say that anti-semitism is reappearing in Germany without being denounced and opposed. But it would equally have been a mistake to expect a sudden and total disappearance of anti-semitism after 1945. The fact that the anti-semites were silent implied no change in their sentiments, even though of the original 600,000 there were only 30,000 Jews left in Germany for them to hate; but what may well cause anxiety is the encouragement they have received from the authorities. It is true that the outcry provoked in Germany and abroad by the behaviour of the Freiburg police in January, 1952, led to different behaviour in July—but the outbreak of an anti-semitic mob in July was encouraged by the police brutality in January; and the tribunal's judgment was not such as to diminish the likelihood of further anti-semitic demonstrations. It was typical, however, of the attitude of many German magistrates since 1950. They have begun to dismiss the libel actions brought by survivors of the plot of 20 July, 1944, against those who call them traitors and to acquit S.S. officers who are accused of the execution of political prisoners.

* See chapter III.

At the same time, in certain places and in certain circles it was becoming fashionable to recall that one had been a member, or even a dignitary, of the nazi party and the height of bad taste to mention that one had been persecuted, or involved in a plot against Hitler, or interned in a camp. Parliamentary circles were not immune to this change of fashion and in the 1952 edition of the Bundestag year-book the biographical details of the deputies, supplied by themselves, underwent some significant re-editing. Dr Dehler, the Federal minister of justice, deleted all reference to his past as a resister; another Liberal deputy suppressed the statement that he had been "persecuted for political reasons between 1933 and 1945"; a socialist deputy deleted the words "arrested in May, 1933, interned at Dachau"; and others now inserted the fact that they had been officers, and gave their war records. But this new development passed as unimportant compared to the economic revival and the serious problems of foreign policy to which government and opposition alike accorded first priority.

In his address of 20 September, 1949, Chancellor Adenauer defined his government's objectives—the recovery of national sovereignty and equal rights with other nations, participation in the work of creating a united Europe, and the reunification of Germany. On the first point he affirmed that "the only road to national freedom is the recovery of our liberties and powers one by one and in agreement with the allied high commission". On the second point he quoted article 24 of the basic law: "The Bund may vest elements of its sovereignty, by legislation, in international institutions. In order to safeguard peace, it may integrate itself within a system of mutual collective security. For that purpose it will accept such limitations of sovereignty as will conduce to and ensure a peaceful and enduring order in Europe and between the peoples of the world". He expressed his conviction that Franco-German relations could improve and that the Saar need not be an insurmountable problem for the two countries. As for the reuniting of the two Germanies, he hoped for it but pointed out that only the allies were in a position to make it possible.[7]

The opposition's programme was set forth by Dr Schumacher on 24 September in his reply to the government statement, and again a few days later by Professor Carlo Schmid. The latter, a brilliant speaker, able politician, and jurist of distinction, was to become vice-president of the chamber and a specialist in foreign affairs influential with the S.P.D., but without ever manifesting any fundamental divergence from the opinions of his party leader. The objectives of the opposition were those of the government—sovereignty, Europe, unity—but their relative importance and the means to be employed for attaining them were different.[8] Co-operation with the allied high commission? Certainly—but "to say *No* at the right moment often contributes more to good relations than to say *Yes* all the time". Creation of a united Europe? Of course—"but not the Europe of the Holy Alliance, nor a Big Business Europe, but a genuine Commonwealth, a federation of European nations. It must be a complete Europe and not a restricted one, for the restricted Europe would be no more than an American bridge-head or a temptation to the east". The reuniting of Germany should be the main objective, and the first step towards it, although the allied veto might make it legally impracticable, would be to treat Berlin as the twelfth of the Länder.

From September, 1949, to May, 1952, the differences between government and opposition appeared to widen. The S.P.D. opposed the Schuman plan on the ground that the coal and steel pool would accentuate the division of Germany and give control of Europe to the Christian-Democrats. It continually reproached the Chancellor for having signed away German independence with no effective compensation, for accepting the division of Germany, and for making no serious effort to promote renewed four-power discussions. Rearmament was also violently opposed by the Socialists, with special emphasis on the argument that it could not be legally undertaken without a revision of the constitution (in other words, without socialist consent, because a constitutional revision requires a two-thirds majority in the Bundestag). An appeal was made to the constitutional tribunal at Karlsruhe to settle the debate on the legality of the European army treaty, in which debate the government relied on article 24 of the basic law and the opposition on the point that none of the legislative or executive bodies envisaged in the basic law are endowed with military prerogatives. In the event, therefore, every part of the Chancellor's policy has been categorically rejected by the Socialists.

Yet the disagreement was in reality much less profound than it appears. In the contractual agreements the Chancellor obtained for the Federal Republic equal rights and national sovereignty, with only the two restrictions which we have previously discussed,* and these restrictions were considerably relaxed by a two-fold promise which the three powers made. They undertook always to consult the Federal government when negotiating with the east and never to accept any settlement that would infringe the rights already acquired by the Federal Republic. In this way they allayed the German fear that an east-west détente might be accompanied by a "return to Potsdam" with a consequent isolation and permanent weakening of Germany. Could the Socialists have obtained more than this?

On the Saar question the Chancellor's attitude was certainly much more conciliatory than the S.P.D.'s; but on one essential point his view coincided with theirs. He was against any settlement which would irrevocably confirm the political separation of the Saar from Germany. He considered in fact, as the Socialists did, that to allow Germany's western frontier to be finally fixed before the signing of the general peace treaty would amount to abandoning the right to repudiate eastern Germany's agreement with Poland over the territories east of the Oder-Neisse line. No German party can acquiesce in the loss of those territories, even though it may have no plan to suggest for their recovery; and the same is true of the division of Germany. The Chancellor's formula, "the unity of western Europe is the precondition of the reunification of Germany", is of the nature of a gratuitous assumption, and the opposition had no difficulty in showing that it hardly fitted the facts. But the S.P.D. had no alternative to suggest, and all it could do was to oppose every development which it thought would diminish the chances of reunification — for example, the Schuman plan. But their speeches at the Dortmund congress in September, 1952, proved that the Socialist leaders no longer

* See chapter 1.

believed that the Big Four could reach agreement. Had they really believed until then that reunification in the form in which they desire it—namely, the withdrawal of Soviet influence, at least as far as the Oder—could ever take place unless Russia received a substantial *quid pro quo*?

On rearmament the S.P.D.'s opposition was never absolute, but was based upon a number of considerations which can be summarised as follows. To rearm Germany would be to provoke the Soviet Union and encourage it to attack before the rearmament was complete. Western Germany ought not to be used as a battle-field for rearguard actions, and rearmament should not be undertaken without the certainty that allied troops would be fighting in force on the Elbe alongside the Germans. The Federal Republic should not merely provide mercenaries but should be a member of all international military and political bodies, on equal terms with the other countries. The cost of rearmament ought to be distributed equitably among all the population, and this could not be the case within the political and economic structure imposed by the Adenauer government. And, finally, rearmament would accelerate that return of undesirable elements in German life against which the Socialists were protesting. But at the Dortmund congress these arguments were not pressed with so much vigour as formerly; and although the resolutions adopted did not express any very coherent attitude, they did nevertheless envisage Germany's entry into a system of collective security—which implies that they accepted rearmament, although they called for a coalition of national armies instead of a single integrated European army.

It was at the Dortmund congress that the outlines of the S.P.D.'s election campaign were drawn up, and the result of the election was to prove that its foreign policy had not been emphatically enough defined.

* * *

Fully to understand the significance of the elections of 9 September, 1953, it is necessary first to tabulate the results and then examine them in detail.

ELECTORATE

	14 Aug. 1949	6 Sept. 1953
Registered	31·2 million	33 million
Voted	24·5 million	28·5 million
	(78·5 per cent)*	(86·2 per cent)

RESULTS

	1949			1953		
	Votes	Percentage	Seats (402)	Votes	Percentage	Seats (487)
	million			million		
C.D.U.-C.S.U.	7·4	31·0	139	12·4	45·2	243+1†
S.P.D.	6·9	29·2	131	7·9	28·8	151
F.D.P.-D.V.P. (Liberal)	2·8	11·9	52	2·6	9·5	48
D.P.	0·9	4·0	17	0·9	3·3	15
D.R.P. (Neo-nazi)	0·4	1·8	5	0·3	1·1	—
K.P.D. (Communist)	1·4	5·7	15	0·6	2·2	—
B.P.	1·0	4·2	17	0·5	1·7	—
Zentrum	0·7	3·1	10	0·2	0·8	3-1†
W.A.V.	0·9	4·0	12	—	—	—
B.H.E. (Refugees)	—	—	—	1·6	5·9	27
G.V.P. ("Neutralist")	—	—	—	0·3	1·2	—

* Percentages calculated from exact figures.
† The only candidate from the Zentrum list elected by direct vote in Rhineland-Westphalia was a Christian-Democrat.

It must be noted first of all that the electoral law effects a very fair mathematical distribution of seats. The percentage of seats allotted to each party corresponds very closely to its percentage of the total vote. The three largest parties, although the law works in their favour, gained respectively only 4·7, 2·0 and 0·4 per cent more seats than votes; but if the revised electoral law had been adopted, as proposed by the C.D.U. and long and forcefully championed by the Chancellor, the C.D.U. would have gained 26 per cent and thus obtained 71 per cent of all the seats in the Bundestag, while the S.P.D. would have *lost* about 9 per cent and been allotted only 19 per cent of the seats!

The law as applied gave two votes to each elector in the 242 constituencies. The first vote was cast for an individual candidate and the second for a party, and in each constituency the candidate receiving the highest number of 'first votes' was elected to the Bundestag. But only 50 per cent of the candidates were elected by direct suffrage, so in the end the total number of seats gained by a party depended upon the number of 'second votes' it obtained in each Land. The other 50 per cent were drawn from lists established by the different parties in the Länder. They were appointed on the principle that each party in the Land ought to have a number of deputies proportional to the number of 'second votes' it had obtained, irrespective of the number of its 'direct' seats and 'first votes'. This proportional distribution, however, is subject to a restriction as regards the small parties. In order to have a share in it, they must either have obtained 5 per cent of the second votes in the nation as a whole or else have gained at least one seat on first votes. The first of these rules was intended to prevent the parliament from becoming composed of tiny and intractable groups, and it seems entirely reasonable. It has been said that its real purpose was to keep the neutralists, neo-nazis and communists out of the Bundestag, and this was no doubt the case, but it does not necessarily condemn the rule. In fact, it also hit the Bavarian Party; and the B.H.E. (Refugees Party) very nearly found itself with no seats, instead of 27, because it had failed to secure any victories by direct suffrage. The second rule, on the other hand, was framed solely in order to secure the continued parliamentary existence of the Zentrum. In the safe constituency of Oberhausen the C.D.U. refrained from putting up a candidate against the Zentrum—at no cost to itself, because it asked its supporters to give it their second votes;* and thus enabled the Zentrum to benefit from the proportional distribution in North Rhineland-Westphalia although it had obtained only 0·8 per cent of the total national vote!

One of the most interesting features of this system of the double vote is that it reveals, in certain constituencies where the Christian-Democrats refrained from putting up a candidate against some member of a friendly party, the way in which the C.D.U. achieved its success. In the Cuxhaven constituency in Lower Saxony the C.D.U. wanted to secure the election of the D.P. candidate, who was in fact an easy winner; but an analysis of the first and second votes shows that by no means all the

* They did so. The Zentrum got nearly 50 per cent of the first votes; but the C.D.U. got 44·3 per cent of the second and the Zentrum only 11·9 per cent.

C.D.U.'s 25,300 votes came from electors whose first votes had been for the D.P.; 2,200 of them came from electors whose first vote had been socialist, and 2,400 from those whose first vote had been for the B.H.E., while 3,800 preferred not to use their first vote at all rather than to give it to any candidate other than a Christian-Democrat. And in Oberhausen, which we have already mentioned, the situation was similar. Not all the C.D.U. supporters gave their first votes to the Zentrum candidate, but 1,800 voted Liberal, 2,900 abstained, and 3,100 voted Socialist—which shows clearly that in this election voters of very different sympathies were determined, and strongly determined, to vote for the Chancellor's party. But we must now consider the most important political aspects of the voting.

The rapid decline of the Communist Party continues. Before 1933 Essen was one of its strongholds; but in 1949 in the three constituencies of this great industrial town it obtained only 13·1, 14·0, and 6·3 per cent of the total vote, and these percentages have now fallen to 4·3, 2·6 and 2·1. The party's hopes were centred on the Remscheid-Solingen constituency, where its leader, Max Reimann, was the candidate and where in 1949 he had obtained 20 per cent of the vote, which was more than the Liberal obtained and almost as much as the Christian-Democrat and the Socialist. But in 1953 he got only 12 per cent, losing 10,000 votes, although the electorate had increased by 25,000.

The neo-nazis had had some success in the Lower Saxon municipal elections and hoped to repeat it on 6 September, at least in the constituencies of Aurich-Emden and Lüneburg, where they had particularly "colourful" candidates. But they were annihilated, obtaining only 7·9 per cent of the vote in the first constituency and 6·6 per cent in the second. At Wilhelmshaven they got 5·4 per cent (in 1949, 23·7), at Uelzen 7·7 per cent (in 1949, 15·3), and at Brunswick 1·4 per cent (in 1949, 12·3). The only exception was Hameln, where the ultranationalist R.S.F. (Radical Social Freedom Party) got 14·7 per cent of the vote and the D.R.P. 3·3 per cent.

Before the election there were two big questions. First, how would the refugees vote—especially in regions like Schleswig where they had not yet been assimilated? And second, how would the populations of the great industrial centres vote? The answer in both cases was satisfactory for the C.D.U. Its most striking success with the refugees was in Lauenburg, where they accounted for 39 per cent of the population, and where 21·8 per cent of the ablebodied workers were still unemployed at the beginning of 1953—though this had fallen to 13·3 per cent by 30 June. The C.D.U. had collapsed at the regional election in 1950, losing nearly half its votes of the year before; and yet the result on 6 September gave it 47·9 per cent of the total vote and only 26·9 per cent to the Socialists (as against 22·9 and 28·6 in 1949), and although the B.H.E., which did not exist in 1949, got 14·4 per cent, this was less than two-fifths of the refugee vote and in fact much of its vote came from former supporters of the D.P., whose vote fell from 20·6 to 3·3 per cent. Even allowing for the fact that the candidate's name was Prince Otto von Bismarck and that his wife has considerable influence in refugee circles, the C.D.U.'s triumph is still remarkable. The B.H.E. candidate was the president of the party himself, Waldemar Kraft, and the B.H.E.'s percentage of votes in this election was the highest it attained anywhere in Schleswig except at Oldenburg, where it was 16·5 per cent.

In the Ruhr the S.P.D. can point to the results at Gelsenkirchen and Dortmund II and III to prove that it is advancing slightly. Its percentages in the three constituencies were 42·5, 45·2, and 47·0 respectively, compared with 36·5, 41·0 and 44·8 in 1949. The C.D.U., however, can point in reply to Essen II and Remscheid-Solingen, where they made big gains in working-class votes. At Essen the Communist disaster (from 14 to 2 per cent) cannot hide the fact that the Socialists also suffered a severe setback (from 38·9 to 32·7 per cent) while the Christian Democrats doubled their share of the vote (from 25·0 to 49·9 per cent). At Remscheid-Solingen, to which we have already referred, the results were as follows (in percentages of total vote):

	1949	1953
K.P.D.	20·9	12·0
S.P.D.	25·0	29·1
C.D.U.	21·4	36·4
F.D.P.	20·0	16·9

We see clearly here how the C.D.U. exercised a double attraction, upon both the right and the left, while the S.P.D. gained almost nothing from the Communists' losses. The same conclusion could be drawn from the results at Essen I and Mülheim-on-Ruhr—at least if it is granted that the newly registered electors as well as the previous abstainers should be expected to vote for the various parties in the same proportions as the electorate of 1949; and this assumption seems correct for the new voters, who are chiefly the young, but more doubtful for the former abstainers because elections in other European countries, and notably France, have shown that they would be likely to support the "parties of order" rather than the "parties of movement".

Religious and social influences frequently interact, and it is usually in Protestant areas that the socialist strongholds are found. But from this point of view the most interesting of the Länder—apart from Bremen, where the C.D.U. more than regained its losses of 1951, and Hamburg where, for the first time, the government coalition parties won a majority—is inevitably the Südweststaat, or rather its Protestant region, Württemberg. In the Land as a whole the C.D.U., which had been in opposition since 1949, gained 52·4 per cent of the total vote, as against 42·7 per cent in 1949, while Dr Reinhold Maier's three parties polled as follows: S.P.D. 23·1 per cent (in 1949, 27·3), F.D.P. 12·7 per cent (in 1949, 18·2) and B.H.E. 5·4 per cent. The results in detail are even more revealing because there is no particular significance in the C.D.U.'s gains in a Catholic and agricultural district like Baden; but let us examine the results for the town of Mannheim, where Carlo Schmid was the socialist candidate and which was considered such a safe socialist constituency that the S.P.D. did not even take the precaution of including Schmid in the list for the Land as well:

	1949 (Percentages)	*1953*
C.D.U.	24·6	36·9 (52,744 votes)
S.P.D.	38·3	37.4 (53,528 votes)
F.D.P.	12.8	10.1
K.P.D.	18.7	7·3

If only 800 more voters had remained faithful to the Communist Party the vice-president of the Bundestag would have failed to secure re-election, such were the gains made by the C.D.U. both from the right and the left in that predominantly Protestant town. At Heidelberg the C.D.U. considerably increased its majority—from 36·7 to 47·8 per cent. At Waiblingen the F.D.P. candidate was Dr Pfleiderer, who is a strong personality, and he obtained 32·9 per cent of the first votes, thus defeating the C.D.U. candidate, who got only 30·9 per cent; but no more than 22·6 per cent of the second votes went to the F.D.P. as against 37·7 per cent to the C.D.U., which emphasises that the electors had a very sound grasp of the working of the electoral law. In both Heidelberg and Waiblingen the great majority of the population is Protestant.

Dr Heinemann's party (G.V.P.) suffered total defeat. In the three divisions of Frankfurt, where he had the help of wholehearted propaganda by his friends, the G.V.P. obtained only 3·9, 3·9 and 4·7 per cent of the vote; but the constituency on which Dr Heinemann chiefly counted was Siegen in Westphalia, and the results there are very revealing:

	1949 (Percentages)	*1953*
C.D.U.	38·0	44·7
S.P.D.	29·6	24·0
F.D.P.	7·7	15·5
K.P.D.	3·0	0·8
B.H.E.	—	5·2
G.V.P.	—	8·3
D.R.P.	12·6	—

These results show that while the Liberals, the Christian-Democrats, and also, no doubt, to some extent the Refugees shared the former neo-nazi votes, the G.V.P. not only absorbed the Communist vote but also took some votes away from the S.P.D., though it took none from the government parties. We may compare this result at Siegen with the result at Borken-Bocholt, where the C.D.U. candidate was Theodor Blank, the head of the Federal government's office of military affairs. He raised the C.D.U. vote from 48·1 to 75 per cent—mainly, it is true, at the expense of the Zentrum, but also defeating the S.P.D. (whose vote fell from 16·2 to 13·5 per cent) and completely pulverising the Communist Party (from 2·5 to 0·6 per cent) and the G.V.P., whose poll was only 477 in an electorate of 114,599.

* * *

The Chancellor's triumph was principally due to Germany's two-fold recovery: its economic expansion and its resumption of an active role in diplomacy. The rapid improvement of living conditions between 1949 and 1953 blunted many of the arguments of an opposition whose pessimistic prophecies have proved untrue and which now found itself the victim of a very simple psychological reaction. When people become more comfortable than they were, they are less conscious of the injustice of privilege. And as for foreign policy, the feeling of the great majority of the electorate was expressed in one of the government's election posters. It showed the Chancellor raising his top-hat against a background where Bonn was seen linked with Brussels, London, Washington, Paris, etc., and the caption stated simply: "He has renewed our links with the free world". The Federal Republic of 1953 was no longer a passive object in international politics and no longer outside the comity of nations; and it was for this above all that Dr Adenauer had won the gratitude of the electors.

On 9 October he was re-elected Chancellor, this time by 305 votes to 148; and after somewhat prolonged negotiations he was able to present his cabinet and read his inaugural address on the twentieth. In order to ensure the two-thirds majority necessary for the constitutional amendments he required for dealing with rearmament problems, he had decided to associate the B.H.E. (Refugees Party) with the government; and the B.H.E. had demanded in return, and finally obtained, two ministries including the ministry for refugees, whose scope was to be considerably enlarged under its new name of "ministry for refugees, expelled persons, and victims of the war". Out of eighteen ministers, seven came from the F.D.P., D.P. or B.H.E., although these three parties had only 26 per cent of the deputies in the Bundestag. But most of the important ministries, particularly finance, economy, labour, and all-German affairs remained in the same hands, all of them belonging to the C.D.U. Dr Lehr left the ministry of the interior, to be replaced by another Christian-Democrat, Dr Gerhard Schröder. Though only 43, Dr Schröder, who is a protégé of Dr Pferdmenges, was not the youngest member of the cabinet, for Dr Preusker, the Liberal minister of reconstruction, was 40 and Franz-Josef Strauss, the C.S.U. minister without portfolio, only 38. The impetuous Bavarian Strauss would have liked to be minister of defence, but the Chancellor was unwilling to create such a ministry, both on account of possible reactions abroad and also in order not to have to make a choice between Strauss and Blank, who is at present in charge of rearmament problems.

There was keen competition for the ministry of justice, and a solution was postponed by asking Dr Neumayer, a 70-year old Christian-Democrat from the Palatinate, to take on the job for a year. The postmaster-general was not appointed for several weeks, and the final selection was the Bavarian S. Balke, who is a director of the chemical industry and only joined the C.D.U. after being nominated. There were two other Christian-Democratic appointments, however, which created more interest: Dr Tillmanns, a member of the Evangelical church synod and Berlin observer in the Bundestag, became a minister without portfolio although he was not a Federal Republic deputy; and a new ministry for family affairs, which was to cause some talk, was created for the ultra-catholic Dr Würmeling from the Rhineland.

From the religious point of view the cabinet is partly balanced and partly unbalanced. In the C.D.U. parliamentary group Catholics outnumber Protestants by no more than three to two, but out of eleven C.D.U. ministers only three are Protestants. However, as the two D.P., the two F.D.P., and the two B.H.E. ministers are all Protestants, the total number of Protestant ministers is eleven out of eighteen. But what has been more remarked abroad in Dr Adenauer's second cabinet is the rather questionable past of some of the new ministers. In the House of Commons a Labour member asked if the British government had made any observations at Bonn about the past contacts with nazism of Messrs Oberländer, Preusker, Schröder, and Kraft, and the case of Kraft, president of the

B.H.E. and a former high S.S. official, was so flagrant that the Chancellor himself first refused to include him in his team and finally gave him only a ministry without portfolio. Of Dr Theodor Oberländer, the new minister for refugees, we have already spoken in this connection.*

It was not without a certain embarrassment that the B.H.E. found itself a part of the majority and in the government, although it had already changed its name some months before the election to 'Gesamtdeutscher Block', as a sign that it aimed to represent all strata of society and not solely the 'refugees and the dispossessed'. The question of how far a permanent attachment to the claims of the refugees is compatible with governmental responsibility was posed at the party congress at Bielefeld in May, 1954; and a provisional solution was found by electing Dr Oberländer to the party presidency in place of Waldemar Kraft. The reasons for this change appeared clearly in the public debates, and still more so in the lobby discussions. Kraft was criticised for being too much "Adenauer's man", especially in foreign policy, for identifying himself too much with the government and forgetting the specific claims of the B.H.E. In contrast, Oberländer was considered "tough"; he had laid down conditions before accepting his portfolio and his subsequent independent and forceful language had further enhanced his prestige with his party. What the party's electoral future will be is not easy to guess, for it has still no coherent structure or definite programme; but its latest congress has shown that it remains true to its original name and that it will still appeal to the expelled persons to keep alive their hope of return and to the expropriated to demand reparation. Need it be added that the "expropriated" in question are not those who were plundered during Hitler's régime, about whom the congress said nothing, but rather the "victims of denazification"? It looks, therefore, as though the B.H.E. may take the place of the German Party as the *enfant terrible* of the government coalition. The latter party has not been much heard of since the election. Weakened by its failure at the polls, it owes whatever electoral importance it still possesses entirely to its alliance with the C.D.U., its only representatives in the

* See chapter IV.

government are the gentle Dr Hellwege, responsible for liaison with the Bundesrat, and the minister of transport, the violent but politically ineffective Dr Seebohm; in the circumstances, therefore, the D.P. has been obliged to renounce its pre-election dream of forming the nucleus for a great "national rally" of the right, which should include the Liberals but not the Christian-Democrats.

The F.D.P. was in bad shape when the election came. At its congress at Bad Ems in November, 1952, the right wing seemed to have carried the day and the star of Dr Middelhauve—a more vigorous representative of North Rhine-Westphalia than the colourless vice-chancellor Blücher—had risen to its zenith. But on 15 January, 1953, the Naumann scandal broke out. On the night of the fourteenth the British authorities arrested on a charge of conspiracy Dr Walter Naumann, former secretary of state in Goebbels' propaganda ministry, and five other notorious former nazis; and the evidence of Naumann's own diary certainly does suggest that he was planning to get control of the F.D.P. as a preliminary to capturing the government. Two of the F.D.P.'s leading personalities were compromised by their relations with Naumann: Dr Middelhauve himself and his friend Dr Achenbach, a Düsseldorf lawyer who had been a high official of the German occupation in France and possessed close contacts in industrial circles. As a result the party was violently agitated and the right wing found itself so much weakened that Reinhold Maier, the Minister-President of Württemberg-Baden, could appear at the Lübeck congress in June as candidate for the chancellorship in a contemplated governmental coalition with the socialists. Meanwhile Naumann had been transferred from an English to a German prison and his release on 28 July on an order of the Constitutional Court passed almost without notice. The right wing of the F.D.P. made the best of a bad job and accepted the bargain offered it by the left at Lübeck: oblivion for the Naumann affair in return for a united election campaign on a moderate programme.

But the ostensibly reunited F.D.P. did not succeed in attracting a very large number of voters—partly, perhaps, because of the Naumann affair, but partly also because the F.D.P.

regarded as a government party had little to distinguish it politically from the C.D.U., and that being so, people preferred to vote for the Chancellor's party. The F.D.P. leaders were well aware of this situation and at the Wiesbaden congress in early March, 1954, they tried to find a way of meeting it. The first step was to choose as president a personality who would be capable, if not of rivalling the Chancellor, at least of impressing himself upon the public. By 228 votes out of 243 the choice fell upon Dr Dehler, who had been dropped from the ministry of justice by the Chancellor precisely on account of his strong personality. A Bavarian of the moderate F.D.P. school, famous for his anti-trade-union diatribes, but also anticlerical, Dr Dehler is undoubtedly the brilliant orator and dynamic figure which the F.D.P. has hitherto lacked both in parliament and in the country; and, what is more, he is now able to speak in the name of an apparently united party, for his two vice-presidents are Dr Schäfer, the very moderate vice-president of the Bundestag, and Dr Middelhauve—who was nominated by the Württemberg-Baden federation! Reinhold Maier, however, had held aloof at Wiesbaden, largely because he was aggrieved at the serious setback which his followers had suffered in his own Land—a setback which has certainly put an end to his political career.

Under Dr Dehler's influence the F.D.P. is concentrating upon religious questions, in the hope of attracting those voters who are offended by the C.D.U.'s clerical tendencies; and in foreign policy it tries to play the nationalist hand, taking a strong line on the Saar and in favour of negotiations for reunification without waiting for the Europe of "the six powers" to materialise. This line of opposition to the Chancellor is developed by the party's best foreign affairs specialist, Dr Pfleiderer. But what is remarkable about the post-election policies of the F.D.P., both in home and foreign affairs, is that they are often identical with those of the S.P.D.—the very party which Liberals have most often attacked. The result is a sort of *de facto* alliance between the F.D.P. and the S.P.D., more especially when the Bundestag is debating either cultural questions or the problem of the Saar, and also an intensified rivalry between them in the competition for electoral support.

The truth is that Socialists and Liberals are now compelled to seek for votes from the same section of the electorate. The F.D.P. no longer hopes to win votes away from the C.D.U., the D.P., or the B.H.E. by advertising conservative ideas or the appeal to the past, and must therefore woo the petty bourgeois class, which is liberal in religious and cultural outlook and also tolerably nationalist. It would be more or less true to say that the F.D.P., having failed in the last election to make any gains on the right, is now hoping to advance on the left—while the Socialists, now that the Communist Party has almost disappeared, have won all they can on the left and are hoping to advance on the right by an appeal to the same petty bourgeois whom the F.D.P. are wooing, and with almost the same arguments.

Erich Ollenhauer's programme speech in the Bundestag on 28 October, 1953, attacked the government for setting up a ministry for family affairs, for its projected ministry of information, and for the limitations of sovereignty implied in the Bonn agreements. The speech was quite well received by the F.D.P.; and the Socialists, for their part, applauded several passages in Dr Dehler's speech for the F.D.P. On the same day Radio Württemberg re-broadcast an address by Professor Carlo Schmid which had been somewhat played down during the election as being insufficiently orthodox. It contained a phrase which was destined to release torrents of ink, urging the party "to throw overboard the deadweight of old errors" (den fehlerhaften und toten Ballast abwerfen). This suggested the rejection of Marxism in favour of a sort of genial Liberalism, and although Carlo Schmid's address was neither expressly repudiated nor endorsed by the party, it brought into the open the theoretical problem which faces a party when it can only make further electoral progress by abandoning an important part of its traditional ideology. The S.P.D. leaders, however, are beginning to see that even this is not the chief and most urgent of their problems. What matters even more is that many potential young supporters are repelled by the party's rigid and almost bureaucratic structure. The elaboration of a coherent doctrine, then, and a new and more flexible organisation—these are the prerequisites if the S.P.D. is to make any real progress instead of continuing indefinitely to represent a full third, but never much more than a third, of the electorate.

The C.D.U., for its part, looks forward to achieving some day an absolute majority, not only in the Bundestag but in the country as well. Without the Chancellor, however, this would hardly be possible, for today even more than before the 1953 election the C.D.U. is the party of Dr Adenauer. Chancellor, foreign minister, and president of the party, his control is absolute, and his colleagues are subordinates whom he may consult but who never know all that is in his mind. Thus Dr Heinrich von Brentano, the leader of the C.D.U. parliamentary group, was telling some journalists that he was sure to become foreign minister at the very moment when the Chancellor was telling some other journalists that he would continue to hold the post himself. As for Professor Hallstein, secretary of state at the foreign office, he is merely an executive. Dr Adenauer had to part with his secretary of state at the chancellery, Dr Otto Lenz, because he became a deputy and would indeed have been made minister of information—if the plans for that ministry had not leaked out and been opposed, and if the banker-deputy Pferdmenges had not been against them. Pferdmenges is perhaps the only adviser who has real influence with the Chancellor, unless the same can be said of Dr Globke, the new secretary of state at the chancellery, who is a very controversial figure, having formerly been an expositor of the Nuremberg racial laws and then head of the "Alsace-Lorraine" section of the foreign office during the war. Within the C.D.U. the Chancellor's chief role is as arbitrator in personal quarrels, and usually a word from him suffices—even in the matter of federalism, in which, as we have seen, the Bavarian C.D.U. is liable to kick over the traces. But the question whose growing importance is being more and more felt in the C.D.U. is the religious question.

The creation of the ministry for family affairs under Dr Würmeling was perhaps unavoidable for the Chancellor in view of the development of German Catholicism* and the Catholic church's increasing claim to influence in public

* See chapter v.

affairs. But Dr Würmeling's uncompromising language ever since his appointment—not even hesitating to criticise the institution of civil marriage—has provoked continual incidents in which men like Dr Ehlers have joined with the F.D.P. in protesting against the minister's attitude. Within the various ministries extreme care had to be taken to ensure approximately equal influence for Protestants and Catholics; and for the moment the Protestant leaders in the C.D.U. feel no uneasiness. Nevertheless one or two of them are beginning to perceive the danger of finding themselves hostages within a party increasingly dominated by the other faith, and the Chancellor also is aware of this danger. In May, 1954, he called his ebullient minister to order and extracted from him a promise to talk less in public. But the problem will remain so long as the churches continue to suspect one another instead of reviving their collaboration of the period 1945 to 1950.

Above all, if a successor were required for the Chancellor the religious problem might become very acute indeed. For who could succeed him as president of the C.D.U.? The Protestant Ehlers, president of the Bundestag and vice-president of the party, is stolid and vigorous but somewhat lacking in diplomacy. Heinrich von Brentano, a moderate Catholic, is a conscientious and respected leader, but rather colourless. The Bavarian Dr Schaeffer is able, but in a technical department somewhat removed from the main political problems. Another possibility is Dr Hans Ehard, Minister-President of Bavaria, whose appointment might lead to a change in the parliamentary majority. There is really no-one who is an obvious choice, and it is all too likely that in selecting a new president the C.D.U. would be swayed more by religious and political tactics than by the personal qualities of the candidate.

But even apart from the contingency of the elderly Chancellor's disappearance there are three other dangers which the C.D.U. is likely to have to meet. First, a possible economic recession, which we have already discussed. Second, the return of men and ideas which the allies and the German leaders themselves had hoped, after 1945, to eliminate for ever; and this danger, which we have mentioned several times, is one that threatens the C.D.U. both from without and from within. And thirdly, it seems—writing in the Spring of 1954—that the Chancellor's foreign policy is meeting with failure after failure. The Europe he looks for seems in no hurry to appear, and hence the growth of uneasiness, doubt, and criticism in the government coalition and within the C.D.U. itself.

There is a tendency in Germany to make France responsible for these setbacks, and foreign observers, too, are attaching more and more importance to Franco-German relations as a factor in the foreign policy and the position in international affairs of the Federal Republic. It would seem, then, that a description of the Federal Republic's development needs to be completed by a brief sketch of the various attitudes of the French towards their neighbour.

NOTES TO CHAPTER VI

[1] On the general problems of the Federal Republic see E. H. Litchfield and associates, *Governing post-war Germany* (Ithaca, 1953), and Alfred Grosser (ed.), *Administration et Politique en Allemagne occidentale* (Paris, 1954), which has a full critical bibliography on constitutional questions. The texts of the constitutions are to be found in R. W. Fuesslein, *Deutscher Verfassungen* (Berlin, 1951). For the sentences on officials see Bundesvorstand des deutschen Beamtenbundes, *Der Spruch von Karlsruhe* (1954). On the working of the Federal constitutional court see W. Geiger, *Gesetz ueber das Bundesverfassungsgericht* (Berlin, 1951).

The problem of Länder boundaries is analysed in Institut zur Foerderung der oeffentlichen Angelegenheiten, *Die Bundeslaender, Beiträge zur Neugliederung der Bundesrepublik* (Frankfurt, 1950) (with maps). Proposals for reintegration since the end of the first world war are examined in W. Muenchmeimer, *Die Neugliederung Deutschlands* (Frankfurt, 1949), with 10 maps and very useful commentaries on the present federal structure.

All the documents dealing with the prolonged dispute over the Südweststaat have been collected in Institut fuer Staatslehre und Politik, Mainz, *Der Kampf um den Südweststaat* (Munich, 1952).

Commentaries on the working of the régime may be found in Hans Luther, *Weimar und Bonn* (Munich, 1951); L. Bergstraesser, *Die Problematik des deutschen Parlamentarismus* (Munich, 1951); F. Glum, *Kulturpolitik in der Bundesrepublik* (Munich, 1952).

On the parties see Gabriel A. Almond, op. cit., Drew Middleton, op. cit., Basil Davidson, op. cit., and L. Bergstraesser, *Die Geschichte der politischen Parteien in Deutschland* (Munich, 1952), an up-to-date edition of a work that has become a classic, though the section on the present parties is fairly superficial; Wilhelm Mommsen, *Deutsche Parteiprogramme*, 2nd. ed. (Munich, 1954), a valuable collection of German party programmes over the last century; E. W. Meyer, *Political Parties in Western Germany* (Washington, 1951), the best overall survey; R. Barzel, *Die deutschen Parteien* (1952) a solid work; Toni Pippon, *Was Jeder von der Bundesregierung wissen muss* (1950), dealing with the ministers, the internal organisation of the Bundestag, and speeches by party leaders in the first legislature. Statistical information about elections is given in E. Franke, *Parteien und Parlamente in Wahlrecht und Statistik* (Bonn, n.d. [1951]). A comparison of party programmes and strengths is made in P. Grebe, *Die politischen Parteien in Vergangenheit und Gegenwart* (Wiesbaden, 1951).

Biographical information can be found in *Wer ist wer?* 11th ed. (Berlin, 1951); F. Wesemann, *Kurt Schumacher* (Frankfurt, 1952); xxx, *Der Bundeskanzler* (Frankfurt, 1953).

The Social-Democratic Party (S.P.D.), and the Christian-Democratic Party (C.D.U.) publish *Parteibücher* containing a wealth of political, administrative, and statistical information. C.D.U., *Politisches ABC* (Bonn, n.d.) is interesting for its memoranda for rank-and-file militants. On the S.P.D. see Alfred Grosser, *La Structure du Parti Social-Démocrate d'Allemagne* (1952, duplicated), an enquiry carried out by the Association française de Science politique. For 'neutralism' consult Ulrich Noack, *Die Nauheimer Protokolle* (Nauheim, 1948), and Marina Salvin, *Neutralism in France and Germany* (New York, 1951), extremely superficial. On the evolution of German liberalism see F. C. Sell, *Die Tragödie des deutschen Liberalismus* (Stuttgart, 1953), an historical account. For the views of the moderates in the Deutsche Partei see the book by one of their leaders, H. Mühlenfeld, *Politik ohne Wunschbilder. Die konservative Aufgabe unserer Zeit* (Munich, 1952).

The achievements of the Federal Government are described in *Deutschland im Wiederaufbau*, *Sechs Jahre danach*, and Hans Scholz, *Drei Jahre Bundesrepublik*.

[2] On this question see *L'Allemagne contemporaine*.
[3] Wilhelm Mommsen, op. cit., pp. 166 *et seq.*
[4] Ibid., pp. 183 *et seq.*
[5] Toni Pippon, op. cit., p. 118.
[6] The text is given in Presse und Informationsamt der Bundesregierung, *Deutschland und das Judentum* (Bonn, 1951).
[7] There are few German studies of foreign policy. See, above all, Hermann Rauschning, *Deutschland Zwischen West und Ost* (Berlin, 1950), more philosophical than political, and W. W. Schütz, *Deutschland am Rande zweier Welten* (Stuttgart, 1952), an attempt to outline an independent foreign policy. Ulrich Noack's book, *Deutschlands neue Gestalt in einer suchenden Welt* (Frankfurt, 1946) may still be read as a study of illusions now lost. Gerald von Minden, *Europa zwischen U.S.A. und U.d.S.S.R.* (Berlin, 1949) is as far as I know the most accurate German work on the first four post-war years.

On the resumption of foreign relations, and relations with the United Nations, see Heinz Krekeler, *Deutschlands Vertretung im Ausland* (Munich, 1952), and Hendrik van Bergh, *Deutschland und die Vereinten Nationen* (Munich, 1952).

Documents relating to the dispute before the Federal Tribunal at Karlsruhe over the constitutional legality of recruiting have been collected in Institut für Staatslehre und Politik, Mainz, *Der Kampf um den Wehrbeitrag* (Munich, 1952).

[8] The three speeches are given in Toni Pippon, op. cit.

CHAPTER VII

FRENCH OPINION ON GERMANY[1]

BETWEEN 1945 and 1954 French policy towards Germany has changed considerably.* Up to 1947 it was governed by the simple aim of eliminating Germany's "Prussian, centralising, and militarist" tendencies,[2] and obtaining reparation for the enormous human and material losses inflicted upon France by Hitler's war. The French government's plans envisaged a Germany divided into "a certain number of States" constituting a federation whose central authority should have a merely co-ordinating function. The Ruhr was to be completely separate, under an international statute, the Saar to be economically united to France, and the Rhineland to be permanently occupied. By "re-education" and an isolation cure, the German people was to be prepared for a new participation in international life at some distant date. This policy, with its aim of preventing any revival of German aggressiveness, presupposed that the victorious powers would continue to have no other purpose than the control and transformation of a Germany which they regarded as a danger rather than a political asset; but the discord between the great powers, and the Atlantic pact policy, and the growth of the European idea combined to make the French policy inapplicable.

M. Robert Schuman, when he became minister of foreign affairs on 27 July, 1948, had a different idea of the way to prevent a nationalist revival in Germany. He desired to integrate her into a Europe united in such a way as to make any renewal of German aggressiveness a political and psychological impossibility. To achieve this it was necessary to place a reasonable confidence in Germany's democratically elected post-war leaders and at the same time convince the Germans of France's sincere intention to hasten the day when the two countries would work together in partnership. This policy did not necessarily compromise the reparations question; nor did it

* See chapters I, II, and III.

involve a hasty restoration of Germany's full freedom of action before she had had time to find her feet as a democracy. It did, however, imply a definite choice—between treating Germany as an enemy to be kept in bonds or as a future partner whose recovery was to be encouraged, though without relaxing due and proper caution. To apply both policies at once would be to stultify the first while failing to create the atmosphere of confidence necessary for the second.

And this is what in fact happened, for between 1948 and 1950 France's policy favoured the European idea and yet remained completely negative in Germany. Its sole aim seemed to be to withhold for the time being something which everybody knew would have to be granted later on. In time, many concessions were made, under pressure from the Americans as well as the Germans (who were thus encouraged to exert even more pressure); but fewer concessions, granted earlier and for the sake of a constructive policy, would have earned gratitude and confidence. The affair of the Thyssen factories in 1949 was typical. The factories were scheduled for dismantling, but the Germans secretly asked the French government to consider a compromise which would have saved 12,000 workers from unemployment while giving the ownership of the factories to France as an item of reparations. Nothing was done, however. Yet a few weeks later, at Washington, France agreed that the dismantling should cease—so the end of the affair brought her neither material nor moral benefit.

After 9 May, 1950, French policy consisted in giving and withholding simultaneously. On that day M. Schuman made his proposal for a European coal and steel community, which was perfectly in line with the policy of curing Germany by integration within a super-national organisation. But M. Schuman went on to say that his plan would not interfere with the international authority in the Ruhr, although it was quite obvious that the discriminatory nature of this authority was fundamentally incompatible with the whole idea of the Schuman plan. In 1952, when the coal and steel treaty came into force, the Ruhr authority did in fact come to an end; so the Germans and especially the socialist opposition, were able to regard its disappearance as a concession extorted from France, although in fact it was a necessary consequence of the united Europe policy. Again, during the laborious negotiation of the contractual agreements French policy showed the same lack of consistency.

Perhaps the discussions about E.D.C., which was an additional French preoccupation from May, 1950, onwards, would have been less confused if the pre-E.D.C. policy had been a more definite one. But to what extent can a man in M. Schuman's position be blamed for an incoherent policy? From the beginning, as we see it, he always favoured a policy of partnership, but he either could not or dared not plainly tell public or parliament what modifications of the French attitude towards Germany the effective pursuit of such a policy must necessarily involve. It was the uncertainty of deputies and public alike that was most often responsible for the government's hesitations. It is necessary, therefore, to enquire what the principal currents of opinion in France concerning Germany have been since 1945.

* * *

The great majority of Frenchmen in 1945 held the German people as a whole responsible for the atrocities committed in their name, but there was nothing like unanimity concerning the reasons for German aggressiveness and barbarity. In some quarters racial explanations were offered. Thus, a claim that the population of Cologne disapproved of the excesses of the nazis was explained by saying that the population of Cologne was "immune from these shames on account of its Celtic heredity". But on the other hand—"In the regions roughly corresponding to the ancient Hercynian forest it was chimerical to hope to extirpate racialism and anti-semitism by the methods so far proposed, that is to say, by eliminating nazi officials, or reforming education . . . or by prohibiting performances of Wagner's *Ring*. Such measures will prove illusory because it is impossible within the space of a few years to modify psychic forms which are rooted in pre-history".[3] Racial theories of this kind were sometimes advanced by self-styled enemies of racialism who as recently as 1940 were acclaiming the triumph of force. Thus one of Charles Maurras' disciples wrote: "The mistake today as yesterday—the political mistake, we mean—is that people persist in treating the Germans as though they were in every respect the same as other men".[4] Some people were anti-German in the way that others were anti-semitic; and Léon Daudet's venomous book on Germany was republished and advertised as a study of "German-Jewish espionage in France since the Dreyfus affair".[5] We shall say no more about this type of extreme opinion.

Most Frenchmen desired neither revenge nor any sort of permanent outlawing of all Germans. They wished Germany to be rendered powerless for a long period, strictly controlled, and thoroughly "re-educated". The policy of General de Gaulle and M. Bidault expressed, we believe, the wishes of the majority of the electorate and of its parliamentary representatives. It was understandable and inevitable that German aggression and brutality should produce a reaction of terror and repulsion towards Germany; but unfortunately, in judging her as a sort of metaphysical being, her economic, social and political situation as a country in a state of utter collapse was forgotten, which meant that the opportunity to influence her development was ignored.

It was also forgotten that the German problem was only a part of the world problem, and from 1947 onwards a great many Frenchmen found themselves trying to reconcile two incompatible aversions; to be at the same time anti-communist, or anti-capitalist, *and* anti-German. The communists, however, soon succeeded in distinguishing between a good and a bad Germany, separated from one another by the Elbe. On the east bank there lived a hard-working people, rapidly repairing the effects of the great sacrifices it had made—greater than those of any other people, except the Russians. Its healthy and confident younger generation would soon be accomplishing, in alliance with Soviet youth, great deeds of world importance;[6] while to the west there lurked a very different Germany, still nazi and planning for revenge. It was more difficult for anti-communists to find a clear position, but they did their best. The east Germans were Germans, so it was not surprising that they should be turning into communist-nazis; but at the same time they were martyred victims of Soviet oppression. West Germans, on the other hand, might prove solid allies in the struggle against communism, but they were still Germans—and therefore enemies of France. The fear of bolshevism, however, finally so prevailed over the anti-German sentiments of some Frenchmen that their praise of everything German began to be as undiscriminating as their condemnation just after the war had been wholesale and categorical. They even accused of Germanophobia the very men whom they formerly criticised for entering into relations with Germany after her defeat—men who are in fact merely refusing today, as in 1945, to indulge in mistaken and disastrous generalisations.

For ever since the end of the war there have been Frenchmen who believed that the future could not be built upon aversion and fear. Most of them came from the Resistance, and many from German prisons and concentration camps; and they did not believe in collective guilt. They understood that the majority of Germans were weak and undecided and profoundly shaken by the total ruin of their country, and that these people were going to be exposed to the conflicting influence of two minorities. One of these minorities was composed of all those who, inspired by nationalism and hatred of the conqueror, looked back with regret to Germany's recent greatness. The other consisted of those who sincerely desired to help in creating a new world in which nationalism would have no place. To refuse to assist the latter amounted to increasing the influence of the former, and it should be remembered that the Germany we would have to deal with in the future would be "the Germany we have deserved".[7] We should so act as to support the courage of the young, and the faithful, both Protestant and Catholic, and the trade unions, and the anti-nazi intellectuals, who wanted to rebuild their country. They were asking for help. To refuse it because they were Germans would be a betrayal of the ideals of the Resistance.

The first meetings between French and German youth were arranged in 1945, thanks mainly to the efforts of certain officials of the French occupation*—whose "Youth and Sport" section alone made it possible for the contacts which we shall describe in this chapter to be so numerous. This department not only encouraged contacts between French and German youth but

* See chapter II.

also made them materially possible, while at the same time permitting private initiatives and stimulating the interest of the French authorities in the work. Although only a few dozen young people of the two countries met one another in Germany in 1945, the number increased to 1,000 in 1946, 1,200 in 1947, 2,000 in 1948, and 5,000 in 1949—in which year the French frontier was at last opened to young Germans, who had hitherto been blamed for knowing nothing about France and at the same time prevented from learning anything. The establishment of contacts between "adults" was necessarily slower but here also a beginning was made immediately after the war.

These organised meetings and contacts, which were supplemented by independent groups and individuals, were not at all on the same lines as the attempts at Franco-German *rapprochement* before 1933. The participants were not interested in sentimental effusions and their purpose was not merely the development of superficial friendships between individuals. They wished to prepare a common future, based on a correct reading of the lessons of the past. There were endless discussions on collective responsibility, on French policy after the first world war, on the occupation, on the Saar, on German nationalism. . . . It must be admitted that much the same arguments were used year after year and that agreement was by no means always reached. But agreement was not the main purpose of the meetings. What was desired was that the youth of each country should learn what the past had meant for the other, and then—while his knowledge was still fresh—be ready to put it at the disposal of the people at home.

Talk about the past is sterile if both sides merely dwell upon their own grievances, but fruitful if it leads them to counteract this tendency in their respective countries. Thus, if the French, on returning home, described the Germans' experience under the bombings and if the Germans described the French sufferings under the occupation, then the discussion had served its purpose. It was for the Germans to make known to their compatriots the full horror of the massacre at Oradour, for example, and for the French to protest in France against the law of September, 1948.*

* See chapter II.

But discussion of the past was only the first stage of Franco-German contacts, and it was always a surprise to the participants when they went on to discover how similar their present problems are. The French discovered that they had much more to offer than their historic literary and artistic values, for the Germans were also interested in the many and fruitful new experiments in France since 1945. The performances by the Théatre National Populaire had an almost incredible success with the public of Frankfurt and Berlin, because they were the revelation of a new form of theatrical art. But the contemporary French culture which can be of value to Germany is not only literary and theatrical; it includes research work like that of 'Economie et Humanisme', the new kinds of youth activities, the geographical and sociological studies of the electorate by political parties, and the educational experiment of the 'new classes'.

But if these international contacts are rightly managed, their principal advantage is to reveal the realities of each country to the other. To know a country's wines, or even its music, is not to know the country, for we also need to know what are the economic and social and political problems which confront it.[8] It is good that since 1945 Brahms is more often heard in France and Ravel in Germany, but mutual ignorance and mistrust are not dispelled in that way. A French article on the German refugee problem does more to promote understanding than the translation of ten volumes of Goethe.

Various methods have been adopted to enable individuals of different types to appreciate the realities of the neighbour country. For example, specialised discussions on a particular subject, such as reconstruction problems in France and Germany, and meetings between members of the same profession or people with similar intellectual interests. In discussions between teachers or engineers, trade unionists or countrymen, Catholics or socialists, there is a common background of experience or thought independent of nationality, which makes it easier for them to tackle their national differences or disagreements. There has been an increasing number of visits by groups organised for study, both French groups in Germany and German groups in France; and although such visits require preparation and careful arrangements for hospitality, they are far more useful than tourist visits, whose disadvantages sometimes greatly outweigh their advantages.

Several organisations have been created with the specific purpose of fostering Franco-German relations, and two of them in particular have been increasingly active. The International Bureau of Liaison and Documentation was instituted in 1945 at Offenburg in Baden, and is run by Catholics, both clerical and lay, which gives its work coherence though without imposing any narrowly denominational bias. It publishes two reviews: *Dokumente*, which provides Germans with information about France, and *Documents*, which is by far the best French publication devoted to Germany. Apart from the organisation of contacts and exchanges, this bureau is principally concerned with the refugee problem.

Each year parties of French youth go to spend several weeks with the refugees who are still living in camps, to help them resist despair and hatred; and the International Bureau, assisted by the Red Cross and the Secours Catholique, arranges for some refugee children to spend two months in the year with French families or in French summer vacation colonies. Four hundred children were accommodated in this way in 1951, 900 in 1952, and 1,400 in 1953, and 1954. It would be difficult to exaggerate the value of such an action, which does more than any amount of talk to teach the children what human solidarity means and to show the French who receive them what Germany's real problems are. It is unfortunately not surprising that the homes where the children have been welcomed, with all the trouble and expense involved, have nearly always been among the poorest.

The Comité français d'Echanges avec l'Allemagne nouvelle was created in 1948 by the philosopher and author Emmanuel Mounier. It is directed by a committee of journalists, writers, politicians and university men, all of whom—though their religious and political convictions are as varied as they could be—derive their inspiration from the spirit of the Resistance and are in agreement about the value of the kind of Franco-German contacts we have described. Since 1949 the committee has issued an information bulletin, *Allemagne*; it organises public Franco-German debates on such subjects as the press, the political parties, or the problems of youth in both countries; it selects individuals and groups in France for study and contacts in Germany, and it welcomes to France a large and varied assortment of groups of Germans.

The attitude of suspicion towards everything German is certainly an obstacle to these activities, but probably there are today many in France who are not so much hostile as indifferent. Either attitude, however, is open to the charge of pharisaism, for it is unjust to blame the Germans for their prejudice against France unless one is prepared to help to remove it when they ask for such help. If nationalism should raise its head again in Germany, Frenchmen who have done nothing to help those Germans who tried to resist it will have no right to say: "We told you so. *They* will never change".

But in reality, although we believe the Frenchmen who have understood the necessity of getting to know Germany better are still a minority, it is an extremely important minority because it is continually increased by the addition of members of what might be called "France militant"—that is to say, the movements and groups of individuals who in every sphere are seeking to meet old problems with new solutions. There is little doubt that as a result of this, and of the penetration everywhere of a new sort of European internationalism, the great majority of Frenchmen would before long have been willing to take a dispassionate view of Germany's problems. And this would have led them to perceive that the lines of cleavage of opinion are very much the same in both countries, and to understand clearly a truth which today is only glimpsed—namely, that on fundamental questions men are no longer separated by frontiers but by their conceptions of social justice or of the right methods for safeguarding liberty and peace. On such questions there are some Frenchmen who see almost eye to eye with some Germans as opposed to other Frenchmen who also have their German counterparts. But unfortunately a new factor has appeared, which revives all the nationalistic apprehensions which were beginning to die down—the factor of German rearmament.

* * *

But before this there were already several currents of French opinion hostile to the united Europe policy as expressed in the Schuman plan. It was objected that to incorporate the Federal Republic into a supra-national unit was to make permanent the division of Europe, and consequently of the world; and also that it was dangerous to create a European community without including Britain; and further that if markets were pooled the French industry could not hold its own against the German. But none of these arguments was conclusive, for it could be replied that chaos and stagnation in Europe was too high a price to pay for resisting the division of the world; and that to wait for British participation before taking any steps towards European union was to surrender to inaction; and as for the danger of German competition, was it not equally great if the barriers between nations remained? This last danger, in any case, appears to us to be very largely due to the Malthusian policy which French industry has practised for so long. It would be a necessary, and also a desirable result of economic union that France would have to abandon the principle of using customs barriers to protect an industry producing little at great expense.

The project of a European army was a very different matter. We have seen in what circumstances it came to birth, and one might say that the French leaders in 1950 used the prestige attaching to the European idea to cover up their acceptance of German rearmament. It could be claimed, of course, that the international character of the plan made impossible the creation of a German army with any aggressive spirit; but German military power would certainly predominate in the Europe of the six powers, at least so long as there was a French expeditionary corps locked up in Indo-China. It was also claimed that a "defence community" would facilitate the propagation of the united European spirit; but in fact, to accord priority to military over political unification was to strike a very heavy blow at the European idea.

The fact that the victorious powers considered the revival of the German armed forces essential, while openly admitting their fear of them, reawoke the dormant spirit of nationalism in Germany; while in France people whose opinions were opposed on every other question were forced into unnatural alliance. It is not our business here to retrace the history of E.D.C. in France or even to summarise the rival arguments, but there is one point that must be made clear. Contrary to what was alleged by certain politicians, both German and French, the division of opinion about E.D.C. in France was not between the regular Germanophobes and those who wanted to co-operate with a democratic Germany. Among the supporters of E.D.C. were many whose only idea was to put fetters upon a feared, if not also a detested, neighbour; while among those who opposed ratification were many who had been working ever since the end of the war for a better understanding between the two countries.

It is true that both nationalists and communists spoke as if the existence of a German army implied the immediate danger of an invasion of France. But in addition to those who feared, or pretended to fear, that a rearmed Germany would attack the west tomorrow, the opponents of E.D.C. also included those who feared that she would one day involve the western nations in a world war for the recovery of her eastern territory. Those who disliked German rearmament because of the bad effect it would have in Germany found themselves compelled to join in opposing E.D.C. with those who condemned everything German categorically and indiscriminately.

Between 1952 and 1954 the debate became more heated on both sides and people who had themselves become reinfected with nationalism brought up secondary questions like the Saar in order to inflame resentment against the nationalism of the other country. It is of course true that a solution of the Saar problem will be hard to find if it has to be a satisfactory one for both France and Germany; but it would serve no purpose here to describe in detail the French policy since 1945 nor the present state of the controversy—for that would be to attribute to the Saar problem an importance which it does not possess. Whereas it ought to be a test of genuine European feeling, both in France and Germany, it has become the platform for exhibitions of nationalism.

It would be wrong, however, to conclude that the crisis of E.D.C. has wiped out all the progress made since 1945. One might say, on the contrary, that it provides a touchstone for men of good will in France and Germany alike. It calls on them to show courage and tenacity and to demonstrate that their desire for mutual understanding was not mere opportunism. With the rejection of E.D.C. the moment has come for every defender of the treaty in France to prove that his desire was to work with Germany and not to keep her under supervision, and for every opponent to prove that he was actuated by a higher motive than mere aversion for everything German. There seems good reason to hope that the policy initiated by M. Mendès-France of "basing the construction of Europe upon Franco-German reconciliation" will command wide approval—though the problem of German rearmament, which has done so much harm in the past, is still with us and is still, alas, a poison for Franco-German relations.

NOTES TO CHAPTER VII

[1] For recent French books on Germany see the bibliography in *Allemagne*, Oct.-Nov. 1952, and Jacques Angel, Robert Minder, Edmond Vermeil, *L'Allemagne contemporaine*, André Drijard, Michel Virally, Henri Menahem, *La Zone française d'occupation*, Albert Wyler, Edgar Morin, *Les Allemands parlent d'Allemagne*, Georges Soria, Jean Guignebert, Robert d'Harcourt, Maxime Mourin, Marcel Merle, Donnedieu de Vabres, *L'accusation française*, Raymond de la Pradelle, Jean Sigmann, Marcel Martin, *L'éducation de l'Allemagne occupée*, André Piettre, Louis E. Davin, *Contrôle de l'Allemagne, Le rôle de l'Allemagne dans l'économie européenne*, L. F. Otto, *Les Églises en Allemagne*, Alfred Grosser, all previously cited. For contemporary political history, add André François-Poncet, *De Versailles à Potsdam* (Paris, 1948), a remarkably clear analysis of a very complex development, Jean de Pange, *L'Allemagne depuis la revolution française* (Paris, 1947), very well informed, Catholic in tone; Maxime Mourin, *Histoire de l'Allemagne* (Paris, 1951), a solid work; Pierre Lafue, *Histoire de l'Allemagne* (Paris, 1950), very superficial.

Two very suggestive books on the personal relations of enlightened Frenchmen with Germany and the Germans are Alexandre Arnoux, *Contacts allemands* (Paris, 1950), with illuminating comments on the contraction of the international horizon by the obsession with the German problem, and Aurélien Sauvageot, *Rencontre de l'Allemagne* (Paris, 1947).

Plans and proposals for the political and psychological treatment to which Germany should be subjected are to be found in Pierre Benaerts, *Partage de l'Allemagne* (Paris, 1945) Vladimir d'Ormesson, *L'éternel problème allemand* (Paris, 1945); Pierre Grappin, *Que faire de l'Allemagne?* (Paris, 1945); Georges Weill, *Le problème allemand* (Algiers, 1944); Ariel, *Reéduquer les Allemands* (Paris, 1945); Gabriel-Louis Jaray, *Prusse et Allemagne* (Paris, 1946); Paul Olagnier, *Les trois Allemagnes* (1946). See also Robert Redslob, *De l'esprit politique des Allemands* (Paris, 1946); above all, two fine books which put the Franco-German problem as, in my opinion, it should be put, before and after liberation. Albert Camus, *Lettres à un ami allemand* (Paris, 1948), written between 1942 and 1944, and Albert Béguin, *Faiblesse de l'Allemagne* (1945), written before 1940. The introduction, written in 1945, is indispensable.

The first special issue of a review devoted to Germany was *Fontaine: La 'question' allemande* (Nov. 1945). The most important which have appeared subsequently are *Esprit: Les Allemands parlent de l'Allemagne* (June, 1947); *L'Âge nouveau: L'Allemagne vue par Allemands* (June, 1949); *Les Temps Modernes* (Aug.–Sept. 1949); and *La Nef* (Nov. 1952).

German studies include: E. E. Noth, *Ponts sur le Rhin*; Paul Distelbarth, *Franzosen und Deutsche, Bauern und Krieger* (1947), an interesting book, the analysis often very subtle; and Otto Abetz, *D'une Prison*; the author appears genuinely to have believed that a *rapprochement* was possible between any kind of Germany and any kind of France.

To these should be added, for the post-war years, René Lauret, *Faites travailler l'Allemagne* (Paris, 1948), a penetrating study; Henri Berr, *Allemagne. Le contre et le pour* (Paris, 1950), well documented; and also Comité Franco-Britannique 'Alliance', *Après la défaite. L'Allemagne cette inconnue* (1946); Henri Temerson, *L'Allemagne de 1945 à 1950* (Paris, 1950), a collection of quotations, often unverifiable, designed to combat the Schuman plan from the most narrowly nationalist point of view.

[2] Official texts and documents in *Documents français relatifs à l'Allemagne*.

[3] Paul Olagnier, op. cit., pp. 91, 101–2.

[4] Henri Massis, *Allemagne d'hier et d'après-demain* (1949), p. 10.

[5] Léon Daudet, *Connaissance de l'Allemagne* (1947).

[6] Letter from Stalin to Wilhelm Pieck, 13 October, 1949.

[7] The phrase is taken from Joseph Rovan, and was used as the title of a series of articles in *Esprit* in 1945.

[8] On the preparatory work required see, for example, Centre d'Echanges internationaux, *Voir et Comprendre l'Allemagne* (1950). For the importance of meetings bringing together people of like interests or of the same religion, see for example the Protestant statement in the special number of *Foi et Vie*, *Positions allemandes et françaises* (July–August 1950).

CONCLUSION*

OUR sketch of western Germany and its development has been certainly in many ways incomplete and superficial, yet we believe it has served to bring out the influences which have determined the development, and the nature of the contending forces which are now in operation. It appears to us regrettably true that at the moment the forces of progress are in danger in every sphere of being overborne by the forces of the past; and for this we cannot blame the Germans as a whole, or even the majority of them. A renewal of Germany was possible, in spite of all the remaining traces of an abominable past and in spite of all the mistakes by the occupying powers after their victory; and still today it would be possible to avert reaction. But for this to be done it would be necessary for the other countries to remodel their policies. The Federal Republic is definitely in the western world, and what happens there depends upon the United States and its allies. We deplore the reaction now taking place in Germany, but can we honestly pretend that other countries also have not tended towards reaction since 1947–48?

It is not in any dogmatic spirit that we have continually emphasised the disastrous influence in every sphere of the crusading spirit, and of the rearmament situation. Obedience to truth made this emphasis necessary. Even before being actually carried out, rearmament is compromising Germany's renovation; and, as we have said, it is also hindering the development of Franco-German understanding. But, for all that, was not rearmament inevitable?

The answer is 'yes' if we admit that the immediate and speedy and intensive rearming of western Europe is essential. For in that case it is impossible to do without German soldiers; and since Germany is now strong enough to refuse discriminatory treatment the only remaining choice, since the rejection of E.D.C., is a choice of lesser evils—to commit Germany as heavily as possible while committing the other countries as little as possible. By one means or another it is hoped to muster

* Revised to April, 1955.

sufficient troops, if not to halt any possible invader from the east, at least to put some fifty divisions into the field to obstruct the advance of probably three times as many; and this on the assumption that the aggressor will not move until the defence forces have been raised.

In fact, of course, it is well understood that Europe's real defence—on the supposition that the Soviet government intends military aggression—is that government's certain knowledge that the crossing of the Elbe would automatically start a world war which, apparently, nobody really wants. But if Russia should attack nevertheless, there seem to be only two ways to prevent her success—that is to say, to prevent western Europe from becoming a second Korea. Either a very large American force should be stationed in Europe, as Dr Schumacher demanded, but most Europeans hardly desire this and Americans of every shade of opinion desire it much less still— or else the democracies of western Europe should assume a totalitarian character, for it is only by dictatorships that large armed forces can be raised and severe sacrifices imposed on the public in economically enfeebled countries.

But is external attack the greatest danger to which European countries are exposed? Is there not at least an equally great danger of ruin in their economic and financial difficulties, in the social misery of the German refugees in their camps and of the French and Italian slum-dwellers, and in the general air of lassitude which is increasingly perceptible? To give priority to rearmament is inevitably to sidetrack the economic and social reforms which would make the idea of Europe attractive to the young of all nations.

The emphasis upon German rearmament is only one aspect of a general choice made by the western powers—the choice of an anti-communism based upon fear and upon the defence and preservation of what exists in Europe, instead of upon a challenge, which would imply the abolition of all that makes "the west" so vulnerable, whether in France, Italy, India or South America. It is also the acceptance of the cold war atmosphere in politics and in intellectual and even spiritual life, which ends by equating non-conformity with treason. Fortunately, the gravity of such a decision has been slowly recognised in the United States, largely owing to the course of events in the Far East. At the moment when an East-West détente seems possible, a number of official declarations suggest a new emphasis on the importance of economic, social, and intellectual weapons.

How does this affect relations with Germany? In a very definite way. The United States came to insist upon German rearmament as the test of western solidarity; and, after the reluctant ratification of the Paris agreements by the French parliament, the disastrous repercussions of the measure can only be mitigated by giving military questions a secondary place. The Federal Republic must find a way to bring together those so recently opposed to one another on rearmament, and to reconcile to a State which has seemed to ignore their deepest wishes a large number of the young and of trade unionists and militant Protestants. This can only be done by emphasising constructive work. And the same is true as between France and Germany; the ill effects of the rearmament dispute will be cured if the two countries can combine on constructive tasks in Europe and Africa. This presupposes that France will find within herself the moral energy for co-operation, just as the direction taken by western policy as a whole largely depends upon an internal effort by America.

The conclusion we arrive at is paradoxical only on the surface. The internal policy of the other European countries affects *also* the future of the Federal Republic. Every national problem today has international repercussions; and all international problems affect the internal affairs of every nation. The question of the German refugees is a European question. Militarist anti-communism encourages nationalism and irredentism in Germany. Every act or failure to act by every individual, whether German or French or American, has repercussions in every other country; and each one of us, in so far as he understands his responsibilities, will seek to understand both his own country and all other countries better.

No one has the right to observe Germany as a disinterested spectator, and if she appears tomorrow under an odious aspect every Frenchman and Englishman and American will have a share of the responsibility. But it is not yet too late to prevent it.

INDEX

INDEX

Abs, H., 95
Achenbach, Dr., 221
Acheson, Dean, 48
Adenauer, K., 43, 108, 135, 142, 178, 184, 185, 187, 196, 199, 201–3, 208, 218, 224, 225
Agrarian reform, 93
Agriculture, 89
Allied Control Commission, 21, 32–3, 37
Allied policy, 7, 16–19, 20–4, 26–32, 33, 47, 64, 120
Anti-semitism, 60, 150, 206, 207–8
Army, 60
Arnold, K., 197
Atlantic Charter, 15, 23
Attlee, C., 26
Aue, L. von, 125

B.H.E. (Bund der Heimatvertriebenen und Entrechteten—Refugee Party), 125, 200, 213, 215, 218, 220
Banking, 100
Bavarian Party, 189, 198, 199, 204, 213
Berlin, 52, 110; blockade of, 41–2; elections in, 42, 192; rising in, 51, 190
Bermuda conference, 51
Bevin, E., 27, 43
Bidault, G., 36, 38, 52, 231
Bismarck, 138
Blank, T., 217
Bloom, Congressman, 13
Blücher, Vice-Chancellor, 48, 107, 198, 203, 221
Böckler, H., 131, 135, 139
Brentano, H. von, 48, 224, 225
Brüning, Dr., 199
Building, 122
Byrnes, J. F., 37

C.D.U. (Christian Democratic Union), 40, 140, 142, 189, 191, 192, 195–7, 204, 213–17, 224–6
Catholic Church, 157–9, 162–4
Centre Party, 189, 199, 213
Churches, 156–66

Churchill, W. S., 14, 15, 16, 19, 21, 2 28, 64
Cinema, 171–3, 205–6
Clay, General L., 35, 39, 72, 109
Co-determination, 95, 132, 135–8, 139, 163
Communist Party, 189–90, 214, 217
Connally, Senator, 13
Conservative Party, 189
Constitution, 43, 182–9
Constitutional tribunal, 188
Currency reform, 41, 97–8

D.R.P. (Deutsche Rechtspartei, later Deutsche Reichspartei, neo-nazi), 214
Dehler, Dr., 14, 208, 222
Democratisation, 32, 34, 39
Denazification, 7, 27, 34, 40, 71–4
Dibelius, Bishop, 162
Disarmament, 13, 17, 26, 40
Dismemberment, 19, 21, 25, 27
Doenitz, Admiral, 25
Draper, W. H., 39

E.D.C. (European Defence Community), 46–50, 186, 209, 230, 238
E.P.U. (European Payments Union), 113
East-west conflict, 13, 34, 36–7, 39, 49, 53, 127, 140
Eastern Germany, 7, 29, 40, 43, 93
Eden, A., 13, 19, 24, 27
Education, 79, 144–5, 166–8
Ehard, H., 185, 196, 225
Ehlers, H., 178, 196, 225
Eisenhower, General, 16, 25, 45, 72
Elections, 43, 59, 189–91, 211–18
Emigration, 117–18
Erhard, L., 97–101, 122, 203
European Coal and Steel Community (Schuman Plan), 43, 44, 52, 107–9, 140, 209, 229
European integration, 40, 44–5, 195, 208, 228, 237
Evangelical Church (E.K.D.), 142, 159–62

247

Fette, C., 139, 141
Föcher, M., 141
Foreign Ministers, Council of, 33, 36, 37–8, 42
Foreign policy, 44, 218
Foreign trade, 89–90, 108, 110, 111–15
France, 38, 46, 69; as occupying power, 20–1, 33–4, 77–80; relations with, 114, 226, 228–39
Free Democratic Party (F.D.P.), 197–8, 204, 221–2
Freitag, W., 139, 141, 142
Frings, Cardinal, 163
Frontiers, 19, 27–9, 124, 210

de Gaulle, General, 231
Gerard, J. W., 63
German Christian movement, 159
German Party (D.P.), 189, 199–200, 204, 220
Gerstenmaier, E., 197
Gesamtdeutsche Volkspartei (G.V.P.), 199, 217
Goebbels, J., 63
Goerdeler, C., 65
Goering, H., 60
Gollancz, V., 81
Grotewohl, O., 44, 191
Guderian, General, 65

Harlan, V., 205
Harriman, A., 23
Health, 80, 86, 117
Heinemann, Dr., 161, 197, 199, 217
Heuss, T., 43, 187, 198
Himmler, H., 62
Hindenburg, President, 59
Hitler, A., 13, 14, 25, 59–60, 61, 74, 159; opposition to, 61–6, 207
Hoover, H., 81
Hopkins, H., 14, 17, 19, 20, 25
Housing, 86, 104–5, 120
Hull, C., 15, 16, 17

I.G. Farben, 17, 87, 95
Income distribution, 10, 123
Industry, deconcentration of, 31, 39, 87, 93–7; level of, 31, 34, 87, 88, 108, 229; output of, 86, 94–5, 97, 104, 107–8; nationalisation of, 95
Intelligentsia, 168–70
Israel, payments to, 110

Jessup, P., 48
Jews, *see* Anti-semitism
Jodl, General, 65

Kaiser, J., 64, 65, 203
Kather, L., 125
Kilgore, Senator, 17
Korean war, 44, 46, 70, 99
Kraft, W., 215, 219, 220
Krebs, Mayor, 204
Krupp, A., 96–7
Krupp, G., 60

Leuschner, W., 65
Liberal Party, 189
Lilje, H., 159
Literature, 170–1
Litvinov, M., 19
Lukaschek, H., 125, 127
Lüth, Senator, 205

MacNarney, General, 76
Maier, R., 198, 216, 221, 222
Manstein, General, 65
Marshall aid, 37–8, 109
Meyer, R., 46
Middelhauve, Dr., 221, 222
Military Security Board, 42, 44, 88
Molotov, V. M., 13, 14, 15, 35, 36, 51
Morgenthau plan, 17–19, 82, 88
Mounier, E., 235
Müller, G., 185

N.A.T.O. (North Atlantic Treaty Organisation), 13, 43, 45
Naumann, W., 198, 221
Nazi atrocities, 58, 62, 190, 207–8
Neumayer, Dr., 219
Niemöller, Pastor, 158, 159, 161
Nouvelles équipes internationales, 45
Nüremberg trials, *see* War criminals

O.E.E.C. (Organisation for European Economic Co-operation), 40, 109, 114
Oberländer, T., 122, 127–8, 219, 220
Occupation costs, 90, 109
Occupation statute, 44
Oder-Neisse line, *see* Poland, frontier
Ollenhauer, E., 191, 193, 223

Parliamentary Council, 43, 182
Partition, 13, 30, 36, 44, 53, 162, 210
Patton, General, 77
Pferdmenges, R., 95, 105, 219, 224
Pfleiderer, Dr, 217, 222
Pieck, W., 44
Poland, 14, 21; frontier of, 19–20, 22–3, 28–9, 37
Pope Pius XI, 157

INDEX

Population, 57, 89, 118
Population transfers, 22, 29, 30
Potsdam conference, 7, 24, 26–32, 33, 47, 120
Press, 79, 173–80
Preusker, Dr, 105, 219
Prisoners of war, 38, 91
Protestant churches, 51, 158, 192
Publishing, 170

Radical Social Freedom Party (R.S.F.), 214
Railways, 106
Rearmament, 45, 151, 209, 211, 237–9, 241, 243
Refugee Party, see B.H.E.
Refugees, 30, 50, 57–8, 110, 118–28, 214–15
Reich Socialist Party (S.R.P.), 205
Reparations, 23–4, 30–1, 34–5, 90–2
Robertson, General, 109
Rommel, Marshal, 65
Roosevelt, F. D., 13, 14, 16, 19, 21, 24, 64
Röpke, W., 99
Ruhr, International authority for, 41, 43, 44, 88, 92, 107, 229

S.E.D. (Sozialistische Einheitspartei), 36, 42, 50, 191
Saar, 38, 91, 208, 210, 238
Schaeffer, F., 99, 106, 203, 222, 225
Schmid, C., 209, 216, 223
Schmid, Dr. R., 141
Scholl, H., 65
School system, 164–6, 194, 198
Schroeder, G., 219
Schumacher, K., 191–5, 202, 206, 208
Schuman, R., 228, 229
Schuman plan, see European Coal and Steel Community
Seebohm, Dr. 204, 221
Socialist Party (S.P.D.), 140, 189, 190–5, 215–16, 223
Sovereignty, 39, 44, 47–8, 52, 208

Soziale Marktwirtschaft, 98–9, 105–6, 197
Stalin, J. V., 14, 15, 16, 19, 21, 23, 25, 50
Stauffenberg, Count, 66
Stimson, H. L., 16, 17
Stinnes, H., 88
Strauss, F. J., 219
Students, 151–3, 206
Sudetens, 58

Taxation, 101
Trade union federation (D.G.B.), 136–7, 139–43, 194
Truman, H., 25, 27, 37

Unemployment, 92, 98, 102–3
Unification, 48, 50–1, 208
Unification of western zones, 36, 41–2
Union for Economic Reconstruction (W.A.V.), 189, 198
United Kingdom, 13, 14, 35, 76
United Nations, 49
United States, 13, 14, 25, 35, 37, 46, 76–7, 79, 110–11, 242
U.S.S.R., 14, 15, 35, 49–51

Verband Deutscher Landsmannschaften (V.D.L.), 125
Versailles treaty, 58, 60

Wages, 129–30
War criminals, 27, 34, 66–70
Weimar Republic, 60, 131, 188, 191, 194, 201
Welles, S., 17
Willkie, W., 13
Witzleban, Marshal, 65
Würmeling, Dr, 166, 219, 224–5

Yalta conference, 20–4
Youth organisations, 143–53

Zentralverband der Vertriebenen Deutschen (Z.V.D.), 125
Zuckmayer, C., 64

For Product Safety Concerns and Information please contact our EU
representative GPSR@taylorandfrancis.com
Taylor & Francis Verlag GmbH, Kaufingerstraße 24, 80331 München, Germany

www.ingramcontent.com/pod-product-compliance
Lightning Source LLC
Chambersburg PA
CBHW070601300426
44113CB00010B/1349